BEGINNING
POWER BI® FOR BUSINESS

T0094073

BEGINNING

Power BI® for Business Users

BEGINNING

Power BI® for Business Users

LEARNING TO TURN DATA INTO INSIGHTS

Paul D. Fuller

WILEY

to Carl Franklin Fuller (1946–2003)
—thank you, dad, for bringing home that
Commodore 64

ABOUT THE AUTHOR

 **Paul Fuller** is a director of consulting services for Core BTS, a full-service digital transformation consulting firm. Paul thrives off helping clients solve their most pressing challenges by delivering data-driven solutions that connect people, processes, and technology to defined business outcomes. At Core, Paul provides technical leadership and delivery oversight for complex and challenging data platform projects. Paul has over 25 years of experience in app development, business intelligence, and data warehousing. Paul specializes in complex data modeling and modern data platform development in Azure. Paul is a graduate of the University of Wisconsin—Oshkosh with a bachelor's degree in business administration.

Paul has also been a pastor for nearly 20 years. He currently is co-pastor at Edgewood Church in Danville, Illinois, where he serves alongside his longtime friend, Matt Harmless. Paul holds a Master of Divinity degree from the Southern Baptist Theological Seminary.

ABOUT THE TECHNICAL EDITOR

Zach Schultz is a solution architect at a Microsoft Gold Partner, Core BTS. He has been helping organizations across the United States build enterprise Power BI solutions for the last five years. He holds multiple certifications in Microsoft Power BI. His educational background is a master's degree in data science from the University of Wisconsin—La Crosse and a bachelor's degree in applied mathematics from Bemidji State University.

ACKNOWLEDGMENTS

There are two kinds of knowledge: *a priori* knowledge and experiential knowledge. Let me illustrate—I *knew* that writing a book is arduous and life-interrupting, but until I undertook this effort, I really had no clue! One of the most impactful things I learned in this process is that you can't do it on your own. At least not well. So, let me take a moment to give credit to whom it is due.

I owe this opportunity to Christina Wheeler, who recommended me to the Wiley team. I'm not sure whether I should thank you or not!

The Wiley team has been immensely helpful and patient with a new author. Thanks to Kenyon Brown, Magesh Elangovan, Pete Gaughan, Navin Vijayakumar, and especially David Clark and Evelyn Wellborn. You put so much into making this work look fantastic!

My managing director, Eric Vandenberg, at Core BTS has been more than supportive and encouraging. You were right; I wasn't able to write this in 15-minute blocks!

Josh Pinsonneault was very instrumental in my career in pushing me to do more than just programming. He encouraged me to develop skills I didn't know I had. Thanks, Josh!

I'm not a gambler, but I took a chance on a new guy on our Core BTS team, Zach Schultz, and that was a bet more rewarding than I imagined. As my technical editor, Zach labored to make sure that these exercises would actually work for you, the reader, and would make sense. But the big payoff for me in choosing Zach was a friendship that will last a lifetime.

My teammate for so many years, Sue Lemery, volunteered to proofread every chapter. I think Sue missed a career as a college composition professor! Thank you for giving up evenings to read this, spotting so many errors, and making so many good suggestions.

My fellow pastor, Matt Harmless, also deserves recognition for supporting me in this effort and for your own undertaking of learning Power BI for use in the educational world. Thanks for finding the missing *of*, by the way.

I have worked with many talented people at Core BTS over the years, but I want to especially acknowledge Marcus Radue, Bob Charapata, Cory Cundy, Scott Hietpas, Nick Searle, and Chris Miller. You inspire me always to be learning.

Back to that *experiential knowledge* thing. . .I knew that writing a book would be like taking on a part-time job, and it would impact my children and my wife, Audrea. But until I jumped in, I didn't realize how much time with Dad they would sacrifice. Thank you, my dear ones.

Finally, but most important of all, anything good I've produced in my life, I truly owe to the grace of my Lord and Savior, Jesus Christ. *Soli Deo Gloria!*

—PAUL D. FULLER

CONTENTS

INTRODUCTION

As a data analytics engineer, I've loved using Power BI since it was introduced many years ago. But I'm a tech nerd. And many of the experts in Power BI are also geeks like me. But here's the thing—Power BI is meant to be a tool for business users and data analysts. It's intended to be simple enough to get started and see amazing things quickly but sophisticated enough that the information technology (IT) folks can use it as well.

In my years in consulting, I have worked with many clients who are simply business users wanting to learn Power BI. They typically have been Excel gurus who live and die by their spreadsheets. And they still will need those spreadsheets at times, but they know that Power BI will take them where they couldn't go with Excel. But they were stuck.

Their IT departments would give them access to use Power BI. Some of these clients would start with Power BI quickly but get discouraged because they weren't exactly sure how to use it correctly. Some of these clients didn't know how to begin. And some of them took training or read books on Power BI but got overwhelmed by the technical aspects.

Sadly, all the introductory Power BI books that have been published to date are tailored more toward technical individuals than business users. That's where this book comes in.

This book is intended to get you started on your journey with Power BI in a way that teaches you the methods and principles that the IT professionals know but are simplified so that you don't feel like you're switching careers in learning this tool! If I had to use technical terminology in this book, I worked hard to make sure that I explained it in a way that anyone working in a business or organization could understand.

This book is intended to help guide you in the best ways to use Power BI to help you build sustainable tools for doing business analysis that, in turn, will lead to insights. That's my goal. I intentionally do not cover all the numerous bells and whistles, which continue to grow monthly. The concepts that you'll learn here have stayed the same since nearly the very beginning of Power BI. While Microsoft will continue improving this product, what you learn here will still apply for years to come.

WHAT DOES THIS BOOK COVER?

This book is divided into three parts.

Part 1 starts with an introduction to Power BI as a tool. In Chapter 2, I lay out three guiding principles that should shape how you think about *business intelligence* and *visual analytics* (terms which we'll define in that section!). One of those guiding principles is a proven method that professional data engineers use and is important to follow when using Power BI.

Part 2 provides detailed, step-by-step walk-throughs of using Power BI. In Chapter 3, we'll look at the general features of Power BI and start playing with it immediately. In Chapter 4, you will jump right into creating your first report. From there, we'll apply that proven method discussed in Chapter 2 to the content in Chapters 5 and 6. In Chapter 5, we'll talk about how to prepare data to be useful for doing analysis. In Chapter 6, you'll learn a technique to ensure that your data is arranged in a way that makes sense to business users like yourself but is also optimized for working well with Power BI.

Part 3 is about taking you deeper into Power BI features. In Chapter 7, you'll learn all about relationships in data (not dating) and how Power BI can help you slice and dice data. Chapter 8 walks through how to add more sophisticated features to your reports to make them extra engaging. In Chapter 9, we will look at how to share your Power BI content with others, how to keep your reports automatically refreshed with recent data, and package up your reports for different audiences. In Chapter 10, we'll cover the most technical content of the whole book—a formula language similar to Excel's formula language called Data Analytics Expressions (DAX). Chapter 11 concludes with resources for learning further about Power BI.

WHO SHOULD READ THIS BOOK

As the title states directly, this book is intended for business users. By "business users," I mean pretty much anyone not in IT departments. This could be an actuarial in insurance, a department head at a college, a chief financial officer of a nonprofit, a business analyst for a manufacturer, an administrative assistant in a law firm, or anyone else you can imagine. It's for those who use data every day in some way to do their job, and probably with Excel. If there is any prerequisite to using this book, it might be that you have a basic understanding of how to use spreadsheets.

Although this book is intended for business users, IT professionals can still glean something from it. In this book, I have introduced the technical principles I have learned over the years in data analytics. If you're in IT, but in a completely different field, this may be a great introduction for you to the world of business intelligence!

COMPANION DOWNLOAD FILES

The first several chapters of this book do not require any additional downloads other than installing Power BI Desktop. However, as the book progresses, there are some data files and sample Power BI files that will be helpful to you. These items are available for digital download from https://beginningpowerbi.com/resources. Look for the BPBIResources file, which contains all the materials from the book in a single zip file.

PART 1
Introduction

➤ **Chapter 1:** Introducing Power BI

➤ **Chapter 2:** From Data to Insight

1

Introducing Power BI

In the "old days," the kinds and sources of data available to us in the workplace were limited. Making data-driven decisions was a process of gathering enough reports, synthesizing that data into spreadsheets, and pivoting that data into various ways of slicing and dicing until you reached some level of clarity to proceed with a decision. Some folks were lucky enough to have data warehousing tools to assist them with that process, but more often than not, even they had to wrangle that data from the warehouse and pull it all together into multiple tables and charts side-by-side to try to make heads or tails of what was seen. And if someone had the audacity to ask, "What would happen if I changed this one variable?" or "How does this data category impact this other category?" then you'd be spending another week reloading, rearranging, and reformatting the results.

But things have changed dramatically even in the last decade. The simultaneous growth of processing power and data availability has been accompanied by applications that are designed to leverage that explosive growth. Data analysis tools now easily enable exploration of large volumes of data and provide a dynamic experience where one *can* quickly visualize, "What would happen if I change that one variable?" or "How does this data category impact this other category?" Enter Power BI: Microsoft's game-changing data analysis service.

> **NOTE** All those efforts, tools, and infrastructure to gather data from the various sources that are available in order to provide good insights for making business decisions is what the industry calls business intelligence (BI).

WHAT IS POWER BI?

Microsoft describes Power BI like this:

"Power BI is a collection of software services, apps, and connectors that work together to turn your unrelated sources of data into coherent, visually immersive, and interactive insights. Your data may be an Excel spreadsheet, or a collection of cloud-based and on-premises hybrid data warehouses. Power BI lets you easily connect to your data sources, visualize and discover what's important, and share that with anyone or everyone you want."

https://learn.microsoft.com/en-us/power-bi/fundamentals/power-bi-overview

Power BI has three primary components: a Windows desktop application, an online service, and a mobile application.

Power BI Desktop

FIGURE 1.1: Power BI Desktop

The desktop application is used to create reports and build datasets (from which reports can consume data). While Power BI reports can be created online in the Power BI Service (more to come on that in a little bit), Power BI Desktop (see Figure 1.1) allows you to take advantage of all the features available in report creation and data modeling (Chapter 6 will cover what in the world that means).

HOW DO I GET POWER BI DESKTOP ON MY COMPUTER?

There are two primary ways to install Power BI Desktop: through the Microsoft Store (https://aka.ms/pbidesktopstore) or through the Microsoft Download Center (www.microsoft.com/en-us/download/details.aspx?id=58494).

The advantage to using the Microsoft Store is that your desktop version will continue to stay updated to the latest version. Microsoft releases a new version of Power BI Desktop every month with new features or enhancements as well as bug fixes. Staying on top of the latest version ensures you have the best experience using Power BI.

The downside to staying up-to-date on the latest version would be if you are working with another person who is unable to use the Microsoft Store and has to use the Download Center; in that case, if you used a new feature that came out this month, published a report using that feature, and then asked your colleague to work on that report, they would be forced to update their installed version.

You may wonder, "Isn't that an odd situation? Shouldn't everyone just stay up-to-date on the latest version?" And you wouldn't be out of bounds to think that—it *is* a best practice to use the Microsoft Store version so that you can stay up-to-date. *However,* I have found that many of our customers work in large enterprises that have what are referred to as *managed desktops.* This means most of the users do not have the ability to install software on their Windows computers. In those situations, the central IT department manages which version of software is available. In this case, the IT department would indicate which version of Power BI Desktop they would want to be used.

You might also be wondering, "Wouldn't my colleague and I automatically have the same version then?" You wouldn't be off your rocker to think that! Again, *however*, I have run into scenarios where some individuals have elevated privileges on their Windows computers and some of their colleagues do not.

So, the first lesson to be learned is: take some time to learn within your organization what version of Power BI Desktop they would prefer you to use. And. . .ask to use the Microsoft Store version! The second lesson would be to consider whether you'll be working within a team of people who will all be creating Power BI reports and talk about how you'll plan on staying in sync and which version of Power BI Desktop you'll use as a group.

With Power BI Desktop you will import data from your different sources, arrange it in ways that make business sense, and then create reports on top of that imported data. (You won't always have to *import* data, but in this book that is the approach we will take.) Once you have a report in a state that you think is useful enough to share, then you will publish that report to the Power BI Service (see Figure 1.2).

Power BI Desktop   Power BI Service

FIGURE 1.2: Publishing to the Power BI Service

The Power BI Service is a cloud-based service (sometimes you'll hear it referred to as *software as a service*, or SaaS) that serves as a central repository for all of your reports and datasets and those others have created in your organization. The Power BI Service's main job is to serve up the reports that you published. The service enables you to share content with others. Here you'll organize your reports and datasets into workspaces. While workspaces give you the ability to organize like-for-like, more importantly, they give you a space in which to collaborate with other people developing reports with related content. Furthermore, workspaces give you the ability to say *who* and *how* others can access your reports. This is called *governance*. While it's great that you can share your insights and allow others to gain insights, you always have to think, "Who should have access to reports and data in this workspace, and what should they be able to do in this workspace?"

The third component of Power BI is the mobile application (see Figure 1.3). Unlike the Desktop version, there *is* a version for iOS as well as Android. The mobile application is similar to the online version but behaves much like you would expect a mobile application to behave and has a modern look-and-feel. When you create reports, you are able to create a separate view of the same report as it will be displayed in the mobile application. This means that it will fit well into a mobile format.

FIGURE 1.3: Power BI Mobile

There are three kinds of individuals who interact with Power BI: report creators, report consumers, and Power BI admins, as shown in Figure 1.4. We will skip talking about Power BI admins, because that is beyond the scope of this book, but just know that there is a wide array of options available to your organization to manage and control the use of Power BI.

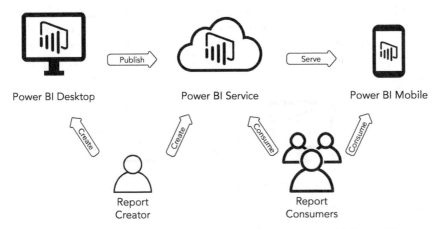

FIGURE 1.4: Report creators, report consumers, and Power BI admins interact with Power BI

Report creators are those who, well. . .create reports! Presumably that would be you. Report creators can fall into two categories: business users and IT professionals. IT professionals are sometimes referred to as *data engineers*. These are individuals who get paid to do this! Data engineers are familiar with writing sophisticated code to extract data from a plethora of sources, bringing that data into a centralized location (maybe in the cloud in a *data lake* or into a database on a server located in an on-premises data center), and then arranging that data so that it is readily consumed by business users. They often will also make very complex reports that retrieve this data and present it in a Power BI report or with some other reporting tool. On top of all this, they often are dealing with volumes of data on a scale of not just millions of rows but possibly billions of rows!

You, on other hand, may have a whole set of responsibilities that make up your job, and just one aspect is figuring out how to wrangle the data you work with into something that can help *you* or someone else make heads or tails of the data you use on a daily basis. What is interesting, though, is that the methods (and consequent skills) you will learn in this book are based on the same proven methodologies that those data engineers use day in and day out. That should give you a level of confidence as you proceed down this journey with Power BI!

That other group of individuals, *report consumers*, are your customers. They may be customers internal to your organization, like your boss! Or, they may be external customers. They are the ones for whom you are making Power BI content to consume to gain insights and make decisions. Frankly, you may be your own customer! You may be wanting to learn Power BI just so that you yourself can glean insights in better ways than you have before.

But then again, you may still be wondering, "Why would I use Power BI?" or "How do others use Power BI?"

WHY WOULD I USE POWER BI?

The ways Power BI is used by thousands of organizations around the world is innumerable. But if you're new to Power BI, it might be difficult to begin to see how you might use it. In my years of consulting with many customers, I have seen Power BI used in many creative ways. Some of these have involved sophisticated data extraction routines and leverage enterprise data warehouses and even artificial intelligence capabilities. But I'd like to describe three *common* usages. These are three real-world scenarios that involve using the same tools and methods that you will learn how to use yourself within this book.

An international gas supplier maintains a Google spreadsheet of a couple thousand contracts including the terms and lengths of the contracts. They want to be able to know when these contracts are coming close to the time they need to be renewed. They also want to know how much that customer normally purchased. That info was not stored in the spreadsheet, but in SAP. With Power BI they were able to bring both sources of data together and not only be able to visually demonstrate which contracts would need to be renegotiated within the next 90 days but were also able to prioritize those based on their sales volume.

A state-based education center exists to ensure success for all students. They collect student test data as well as training records for staff. There are more than 300 attributes that need to be tracked and correlated across multiple aspects. This center imported their collected data into Power BI and was able to identify patterns and areas of concern across the state, by school districts, or within specific schools.

An HVAC distributor has sales goals for their account reps. These goals exist at the regional level as well as for each rep. This company connected Power BI to Salesforce and was able to retrieve sales data, goals, and account information and was able to create custom dashboards that display actual sales performance against goals by day, month, quarter, and year. In addition, an account rep can quickly see which are their top customers and *only* their customers, but their regional manager can see which are the top performing account reps and the highest volume purchasers across the region. And while the regional managers are restricted to their regional data, the vice president of sales is able to see all data across the regions and is able to drill down into the lowest level of sales detail.

BUT WHY?

You may be reading this book as someone who has been using Microsoft Excel for years and have figured out all kinds of ways to push its analytics capabilities. And to be sure, Excel makes the business world go round. Powerful functions such as VLOOKUP() or INDIRECT() combined with pivot tables and macros make Excel's limitations almost seem to be nil. But there are plenty of limitations on Excel that have brought many customers to the breaking point, and they end up calling consulting groups like the one I work for and pleading with us to come up with a more robust solution. Let me give you a couple examples.

➤ An injection-molding manufacturer has several plants around the country. Each location has a financial controller responsible for gathering month-end accounting and financial data as well as other important metrics that the company wants to track. Each controller uses a template Excel spreadsheet that corporate provides and requires the controller to fill out and submit. The controller will post general ledger data for the month as well as enter the metric data. The Excel template has prebuilt pivot tables that aggregate the data by accounts. Once the controller has finished their prep work, they execute a macro stored in the template, which will further manipulate the data and copy it to a central file location. At corporate, another controller will utilize an Access database, which connects to all of the submitted Excel workbooks, extracts the data, and then lands the data in a parent Excel workbook. That parent workbook then arranges the data further for different levels of reporting needs. The workbook is quite sophisticated in its use of advanced Excel formulas, but the whole process is fraught with potential for human error. Furthermore, the company came to us asking for help because the process was grinding to a halt since the Excel workbooks were hitting size limits and experiencing significant performance issues.

➤ A health insurance company received monthly actuarial data from an outside firm and would use Excel to marry that data with their claim data. They had to upgrade to the 64-bit version of Excel to accommodate size restrictions, but they also began running into other challenging limitations. For them to prepare monthly reports for executives, they would take several days for data manipulation and to update formulas across several pivot tables that needed to be synchronized side by side. Instead of putting their efforts into analyzing the data they had at their fingertips, they paid their data analysts to spend 25 percent of their month just preparing data for analysis. This was alongside all their other job responsibilities.

Beyond the intricacies of managing complex reporting processes, there are other limitations of Excel. These limitations might not have occurred to you because you've just learned to live with them. I'm thinking about two areas: disconnected data and fixed formulas.

Disconnected Data

Imagine you have built a complex Excel workbook that has multiple related worksheets of pivot tables of data. Then on one worksheet you have multiple visuals bringing together the data from your different worksheets. And let's imagine you have a couple of charts and a handful of tables that display data from the different worksheets. If you wanted to filter out just one aspect of data that is related to each of the visuals and tables, you would have to go to each pivot table or visual and find the related data and use Excel's Hide Selected Item function (see Figure 1.5). Naturally, as you see the impact of your filtering, you'll analyze whether there is any impact by removing other data. Consequently, you'd repeat the cumbersome tasks of filtering throughout the workbook. Your worksheets of data are related to each other in a logical way in your head, but they're not connected in a technical way such that Excel "knows" they're connected.

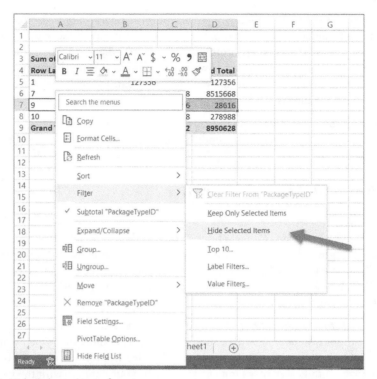

FIGURE 1.5: Excel's Hide Selected Item function

Power BI addresses this challenge with ease. First, in the previous example, the data in those worksheets are related to each other in some way, logically. In Power BI, those worksheets would be represented as tables, and those tables would have relationships defined between them. By you simply telling Power BI how those worksheets/tables relate to each other, you enable Power BI to do dynamic filtering across those related tables all from one spot. In the previous scenario, you would simply "exclude" the data as you see it on your report page, and it would automatically filter the data across all the related tables.

Fixed Formulas

A second common limitation of Excel is not as much a limitation as it is an impediment. Excel has the ability to create incredibly complex formulas using statistical calculations or aggregations that would take much manual effort to produce. However, once you create a formula to perform such calculations, you create it where you want to use it, and that formula is a fixed formula that can be used *just in that cell*. If you want to repeat using that formula in a different location in your workbook, then you must copy and paste the formula where you'd like to use it and then update the formula's cell references every time you want to reuse that formula.

Power BI addresses this encumbrance with a formula language called Data Analysis Expressions (DAX). If you're comfortable with writing Excel formulas, you will really come to love the DAX language. In the previous example, you would write the complex formula one time and use that formula wherever you need to without having to adapt it for each location. As Rob Collie has called it, they're "portable formulas."[1] Furthermore, if your formula is one of those formulas that your colleagues say, "Hey, I want to use that formula in my report!" then with Power BI you can just share your dataset with its great formulas in such a way that others can build their reports using those formulas. So not only is your formula portable within your dataset, but your dataset with all of its amazing formulas is shareable as well!

We've seen a handful of reasons why Power BI will take your report building solutions to the next level. I want to show you that Power BI will not just improve your ability to build reports but will transform your work.

Ten Reasons Why Power BI Transforms Your Work

These are the reasons:

➤ *Security, security, security*. Power BI gives you the ability to make sure that only the right individual or group has access to your reports. In addition, Power BI gives you the ability to control within a report *what* data they can see. For example, you can control whether one salesperson can see only their regional data. There simply is no way to implement this kind of security inherent in Excel.

➤ *Exponential storage capabilities*. If you've spent much time working with Excel building very large workbooks, sometimes with millions of rows, you know that when you need to make a change, sometimes you need to go get a cup of coffee while you wait for it to finish applying your change. With Power BI, as long as you design your datasets with the methodology I'll teach you in this book, you will see the file size of your Power BI reports be exponentially smaller than the size of your Excel files (or other sources of data). I recently was able to import two database tables with a combined 30 million rows that consumed 20 GB of storage. Power BI compressed that 20 GB to 45 MB: a percent change of 99.76!

➤ *Faster performance with your large datasets*. Not only will you see incredibly smaller storage size on your files, but when you follow the methods I'll teach you in this book, you'll also see insanely fast performance compared to that very large Excel workbook. This small storage size and fast performance is a result of the way Power BI is designed to store and operate on data.

➤ *Data sources just keep coming*. If you have used Excel's Get Data feature (see Figure 1.6), you know that the list of sources from which you can retrieve data is quite extensive.

But with Power BI, the list of sources available continues to grow monthly, far surpassing what Excel and many other reporting tools provide. Just check out this page from Microsoft, and you will see that the list is very impressive: `https://learn.microsoft.com/en-us/power-bi/connect-data/power-bi-data-sources`.

➤ *Collaboration*. With Excel, if you want to share your files, you can place them into a network-accessible location or use something like Dropbox or SharePoint, but collaborating on a spreadsheet is not simple. Power BI excels at collaboration allowing you to organize your files into workspaces and determine who can work in that workspace with you and how they can use that workspace.

---

[1] Rob Collie and Avichal Singh, *Power Pivot and Power BI: The Excel User's Guide to DAX, Power Query, Power BI & Power Pivot in Excel 2010-2016 Second edition* (Holy Macro! Books, 2021).

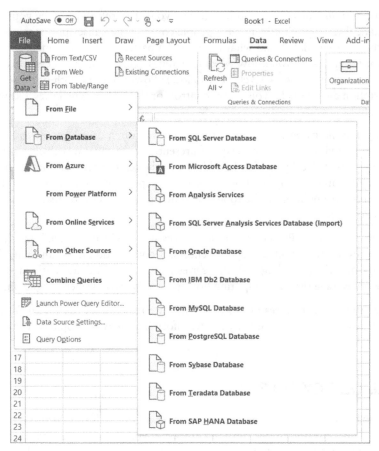

FIGURE 1.6: Excel's Get Data feature

➤ *Your Excel files don't have to go away.* It's quite likely that you have several Excel workbooks that drive your day-to-day business. Those workbooks can be the basis of source data for your Power BI reports. So all that effort you have fine-tuned into a science to prepare for month-end reports does not have to go away. You can connect Power BI to that month-end Excel report and use it to give your users a whole new level of analytical insights.

➤ *Refresh your datasets while you're away.* Once you publish your Power BI Reports to the Power BI Service, you'll have the ability to schedule that report to refresh its data automatically. That means your report will contain data that you import from some source. That source may be a file, a database, a web service, or something like that. If you schedule your report to be refreshed automatically, this means your report will be able to go out to the original source(s) of data and automatically retrieve and import your data. If you're used to working in Excel, this is like you opening your monthly report and copy-and-pasting new monthly data into your report from other sources—except now it's automatically done for you.

➤ *Subscriptions and alerts*. Beyond just getting your data refreshed, once your data is refreshed automatically, wouldn't it be great if people could set up subscriptions to receive your report with the refreshed data? And what if you had a particular business metric that you want to monitor to make sure you know when it changes below or above a certain level (like making sure you know when stock levels get too low)? Power BI does both of those things for you! Subscription and alerts let your users control for themselves when they receive automatic notifications about your data.

➤ *Visually appealing analytics*. One of the things that often drives people to Power BI is the wide array of visually stunning ways of presenting data to your users, ways that far surpass the abilities that Excel provides. In addition to the built-in visuals (such as interactive charts, tables, and graphics), Power BI provides a marketplace where you can find third-party visuals that others have built using the tools that Microsoft provides to create custom visuals within Power BI.

➤ *Basic AI capabilities*. Power BI also introduces some built-in artificial intelligence (AI) capabilities. Features such as key influencers, decomposition trees, anomaly detection, natural language querying, trending and time-series forecasting, and automatic insights give you the ability to leverage serious computing horsepower to drive deeper insights into your data.

We won't cover all of these features in this book since we're all about *beginning Power BI* here, but know that these features of Power BI truly are transforming the way people work with data in their day-to-day.

WILL I STILL USE EXCEL?

You may be wondering at this point whether you'd ever need Excel again or maybe that I'm arguing that Excel should go away, but that is not the impression you should have. Excel will likely continue for many years to be the de facto standard for businesses as *the* spreadsheet tool. I want to briefly show you four ways you'll still continue to use Excel.

➤ While Power BI can most certainly handle complex math formulas in its DAX language, you will find that Excel is conducive to quickly building complex mathematical calculations in stepwise fashion and seeing those results immediately as you work on your formulas. In fact, you may use Excel as a scratchpad to determine how you want to build your DAX formulas in Power BI.

➤ Excel is still the tool of choice if you're needing to do manual data editing of simple file data (like comma-delimited files or text files, often called *flat files*) or of Excel files that you use as the data source for your Power BI reporting. Once data is imported into a Power BI dataset, you are not able to directly edit that data. So, if your data comes from something like flat files and you have a need to update that data before it gets imported, then Excel is an excellent choice.

➤ Once you've published a Power BI Report to the Power BI Service, if you have a Power BI Pro subscription (more on what that means in just a few pages), you can connect to your Power BI datasets from Excel and explore the data that "lives" there. This has a couple of caveats, but in general if you have a paid subscription and have the right permissions to the report dataset, then you can use Excel to connect to the underlying data. (You can read about the other exceptions here, but understanding what those mean may be difficult until you work through this book: `https://learn.microsoft.com/en-us/power-bi/collaborate-share/service-connect-power-bi-datasets-excel#prerequisites`).

➤ While there are other good reasons to use Excel, the final reason I'd like to share is related to the previous bullet point about connecting to Power BI datasets with Excel. You'll find that with Power BI it is easy to apply as many filters and calculations against a set of data as you can imagine. Sometimes you'll want to take a filtered dataset and then do further analysis on top of that. That is difficult to do without having expert DAX programming skills. However, that's where Excel might come in handy for you. Because you *can* connect to that filtered dataset with Excel and then further explore the filtered data within Excel.

WHERE DID POWER BI COME FROM? (A LITTLE HISTORY)[1]

While we're on the topic of Excel, it may interest you to know that Power BI's roots are found in Excel.

Back in the mid-1990s, Amir Netz, who started Panorama Software, developed a novel way of analyzing massive amounts of data quickly. Microsoft acquired his company and invested in his team of developers so they could take the software to a whole new level.

In the late 2000s, the market was starting to morph toward "self-service business intelligence." The idea was to enable the business users to drive after their own analytical questions without having to rely on IT departments to prepare reports for them—not just to do the analysis on their own but to be able to do it quickly. One secret to doing it quickly, as Amir saw others were doing, was to figure out how to use the memory on computers instead of accessing the data on computer disk since that is so much slower.

But the challenge of how to work with very large datasets still presented itself. Together with Cristian Petculescu, Amir invented[2] a way to compress data in a completely different way than traditional database engines had done for decades. The extent to which they compressed the data and the speed of the queries they were able to gain was so shocking that some people, as Amir put it, "Thought we were defying physics." The strength of the underlying algorithm was such that it has only been slightly tweaked since 2008. They named this new analytical engine Vertipaq.

Besides performance, Amir realized that they needed an interactive experience like what Excel users were used to. When Excel users build complex workbooks with formulas and lookups, they know that if they change one value, it can ripple through

continues

(continued)

immediately in their workbook. Amir's team at Microsoft decided to focus on Excel users with this Vertipaq engine and create a new interactive analytical experience. Along the way, they also realized that they needed a query language to easily use this engine; this resulted in the invention of DAX.[3] Next to come along was the ability to interactively slice and dice the data model with charts. The final key element of the data analysis tools was the Power Query tool designed to help the user import data and transform the data.

Microsoft packaged up all these tools into Excel add-ins starting in 2010: PowerPivot, Power View, and Power Query. These three add-ins were packaged together and released as Power BI for Office 365 in 2013, but they were still embedded within Excel. Microsoft realized that as long as these tools were tied into the Excel worksheet experience, they would be limiting the possibilities of Power BI. In early 2015, Microsoft announced the acquisition of Datazen whose visual analytics service operated in the cloud. Datazen provided the initial base of impressive visualizations that would be able to take advantage of the Vertipaq engine. So, in July 2015, Power BI was released as an application separate from Excel with a desktop and web experience. Since then, constant refinement and new features have been applied to the Power BI suite every month!

[1] This history was summarized from an interview with Amir Netz and Kasper de Jonge: www
.kasperonbi.com/the-rise-and-history-of-power-bi-with-amir-netz/
[2] https://patents.google.com/patent/US8626725B2
[3] https://patents.google.com/patent/US20110087954A1

We're coming to the end of this introduction to Power BI, and if you are brand new to Power BI, you may be wondering how much this is going to cost and how do you get started. Let's deal with both of those in these last two sections.

HOW MUCH IS THIS GOING TO COST?

Power BI offers five levels of service offerings: free, Pro, Premium Per User, Premium, and Embedded. As you can imagine, the features that are available to you expand as you progress up those levels. And while you may think, "Free is for me!" you will quickly find that the free version will severely limit what you can do. The good news, though, is that most of what we will cover in this book will be possible to do with the free version. Please note that these service levels do not apply to the use of Power BI Desktop, but once you publish reports to the Power BI Service. Once reports are published, the service levels have different subscription pricing and accompanying feature sets, shown in Table 1.1.

TABLE 1.1: Power BI Service Levels

SUBSCRIPTION	COST	DESCRIPTION
Power BI (free)	Free	With the free version, you use Power BI Desktop to create content for yourself. While you can publish to the Power BI Service, only you can view that content online.
Power BI Pro	$10/ month	The Pro subscription allows you to take the content you've created with Power BI Desktop and share that content with others who also have a Pro subscription. With Pro, you are able to create live dashboards from your report content that can bring data together from multiple reports. This level works great for many business users, but it does have some limitations, including a data size limitation as well as a model size limitation. You can also set automatic refreshes of your data, but only eight times per day.
Power BI Premium Per User	$20/ month	Premium per User has everything that Pro provides but unlocks features such as advanced AI, handling for much bigger volumes of data, and the ability to connect to your data from other tools besides Power BI. As with Pro, only users with a Premium Per User subscription can view and use content created by someone else with a Premium Per User subscription.
Power BI Premium	Starting at $5,000/ month	Premium has the features of Premium Per User but removes the need for report users to each have their own subscription. Report creators will need a Power BI Premium Per User or Pro subscription, but report consumers do not need a subscription. It may seem like a very expensive entry point; however, if you have more than 250 report consumers, then it would be worth having a Premium implementation if you're using bigger data volumes. If you're just using Power BI Pro and have more than 500 report consumers, then this option would be worth considering.
Power BI Embedded	Starting at $736/ month	Embedded is a unique subscription that allows application developers to embed Power BI reporting directly within their application.

Adapted from https://learn.microsoft.com/en-us/power-bi/fundamentals/
service-features-license-type.

WHERE DO WE GO FROM HERE?

The goal of this book is to help you get started on the journey of using Power BI as a business user. But the bigger goal, the goal of that journey, is to help you learn how to turn data into insights. We want to use Power BI in a way that helps us see what we can't see on our own. The path to doing that with Power BI is straightforward: import data, prepare data, model data, visualize data, and analyze data. All these steps lead up to the goal of being able to *understand data* as a result of good analysis that comes from information presented well because it was organized logically. And you can't organize data well if it's a bit of a mess. And you can't clean up your data if you don't have it in hand. But before we start digging into the first step in that journey of *preparing data*, we'll start at the end of the journey to help understand our destination.

2

From Data to Insight

There are many things in life for which you should take the time to understand the *why* before you *try*.

Learning the *why* behind Power BI is one of those things. This chapter is about the *why* of using any tool that uses these two words to describe itself: *visual* and *analytics*. If you take time reading through this chapter before jumping in, you'll realize greater short- and long-term rewards.

In the short term, you'll reap greater rewards because you will have the big picture in mind for why we're going through some of the very detailed—and maybe seemingly odd—steps that we'll cover in later chapters. It will be easy to get lost in those details and forget where we're headed or, worse, give up. But if you have the roadmap in your head, you'll know there's a reason for everything you're learning.

In the long term, you'll benefit because you will be creating content that has a high degree of usefulness. How so? First, you'll create content in such a way that considers how the human brain works and processes information. Second, because you'll design for the human brain, you'll have a greater chance of achieving the goal of helping your users arrive at insight.

So, let me ask this of you: if you are too excited to wait and want to just jump right in and skip this chapter, then will you please consider coming back to this chapter after you feel comfortable building Power BI content but *before* you deliver to your users?

THREE GUIDING PRINCIPLES

If I could reduce the usefulness of Power BI to one thing, it would be its ability *to help people see*. What I mean by that is it can help you see things you couldn't normally see when simply looking at spreadsheets or files of data. If you had five minutes to look at the worksheet shown in Figure 2.1 and make observations of what is going on, you might be able to come up with a few good questions. But you would have to study it carefully. Frankly, most of us are not able to quickly observe that much detail and interpret it. It takes time to synthesize well.

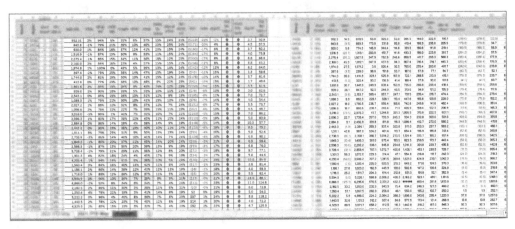

FIGURE 2.1: A sample worksheet[1]

In this chapter I will introduce three guiding principles to help make your Power BI journey a success—a success for both you and those who use your content.

➤ Distinguish between data, information, and knowledge.

➤ Follow a consistent, proven method

➤ Use visualizations well

These principles follow from one another. When you begin to distinguish between data, information, and knowledge, you'll remember where you're leading your audience. Once you know your goal, you need to have a plan to get there. Having a consistent and proven method to transform your data will give you the tools to prepare and organize your data. It will be organized in a way that is optimized toward both the platform (Power BI) we're learning and the ease of use for your report consumers. And once you have the data organized well and transformed into information, you're ready to present it in a way that will lead to understanding. Your visual content will lead to insights. If you're new to using a visual analytics tool like Power BI, it will be tempting to go hog wild with all the beautiful visualizations the tool provides. However, that's where you need to learn how to use those in a way that really does serve the human brain well.

So, let's start with the first principle.

DISTINGUISHING DATA, INFORMATION, AND KNOWLEDGE

If, as I said, the brilliance of Power BI is its ability to help people see, then we need to aim toward serving that goal of *insight* and not get distracted with fluff. Fluff gets in the way of seeing clearly. Not seeing clearly will prevent informed decision-making. That, after all, is what ultimately we're aiming for. Insights should enable decisions.

Realize first that there is a difference between data, information, and knowledge. *Data* is the raw material of this technological age. Data is simply the bare-bones descriptions of what *is*. It's replete in

---

[1]The image is intentionally blurred at the edges to mask the source of this real spreadsheet.

our world today. Over the last decade, we have generated exponentially more of it than ever before. For example, in my home, we have many devices that generate data—every second. Whether it's the Internet-connected thermostat, Internet voice assistants, smart plugs, the washing machine and dryer, or the smart thermostat switch in our chicken coop, they're all generating volumes and volumes of data every second and maybe more often than that. We haven't even talked about our phones, the TV, the game systems, or our laptops. All those devices are constantly sending information back home to whatever cloud-based service they're connecting to. Some of that is simply telemetry data (measurements that sensors record), but there is much, much more.

Think about this! If you were to look at one record of information from one event in time from one of those devices, what would that really tell you? For instance, the furnace was running when it was set at 68 degrees on the thermostat, the room temperature was 67 degrees, and the outdoor temperature was 24 degrees, at 11:33 a.m. on December 18, 2022, at 12345 Oak Street in Franklin, Tennessee, with a single-stage furnace. That is simply raw data describing the state of something. If you had a spreadsheet full of that data, each row in itself would not be very useful. But what this raw material needs is some synthesizing.

Information is about making data more useful. It's about adding descriptions to the data that help answer questions such as who, when, where, what, how much, and so on. Russell Ackoff describes information this way:

> "Information consists of processed data, the processing directed at increasing its usefulness. . . . Like data, information also represents the properties of objects and events, but it does so more compactly and usefully than data. The difference between data and information is functional, not structural."[2]

To keep with our example of thermostat data, information would be taking that data and summarizing it or aggregating it. It would be something like: the average room temperature was 68 degrees, the average external temperature was 27 degrees, and the average thermostat setting was 68 degrees on December 18, 2022, at 12345 Oak Street in Franklin, Tennessee. But maybe more useful would be the average temperatures and settings by day, by each postal code within the state of Tennessee. Let's take this one step further: maybe even more useful might be to calculate how long the furnaces had to run to achieve the desired temperature setting grouped by furnace type (single stage, dual stage, or variable stage), across the days of the year, throughout the different regions of the United States. And if you really want to up the ante, if a Wi-Fi–enabled thermostat manufacturer could incentivize their customers to provide brand *data* about their furnaces and a whole host of other interesting data such as demographics, properties of the home such as square footage and building materials, you can quickly see how that data might be transformed into something very useful that could be sold to HVAC manufacturers or retailers. Furthermore, if utility average costs by area could be connected to postal codes (likely such data could not be connected to individual addresses as this could be a privacy violation unless the customer approved it), then costs could be correlated to the thermostat and HVAC data. Such kinds of data synthesized into *information* could undoubtedly provide a competitive advantage for some companies.

---

[2]Russell Ackoff, *Ackoff's Best: His Classic Writings on Management* (New York: Wiley, 1999), 170.

Here is the point: all that data turned into information is still *not* insight. It is neither giving you knowledge *nor* understanding. They are, however, useful and essential building blocks toward achieving insight. Again, Ackoff is helpful here: "Knowledge is conveyed by instructions, answers to how-to questions. Understanding is conveyed by explanations, answers to why questions."[3] *Knowledge* in our thermostat example would be the ability to answer questions like "How can a customer reduce their utility costs in a very precise way without impacting comfort?" or "How can an HVAC manufacturer improve their equipment performance given the run times of specific equipment and environmental variables?" *Understanding* would be the ability to answer questions like, "Why do particular HVAC systems have longer run times than others during certain time periods throughout the year?" Knowledge and understanding are the intended effect of information. Being able *to know* or *to understand* is insight. Further, insight *is the goal we have for our content consumers*. But let's put the top on Ackoff's pyramid, shown in Figure 2.2.

FIGURE 2.2: From data to wisdom pyramid

To his hierarchy of data, information, and knowledge, Ackoff adds wisdom. He would say that information and understanding/knowledge contribute to learning, but learning is only assessing whether something or someone is performing well according to a predetermined standard. This is determining whether something or someone is *efficient*. Wisdom, he believes, however, is the ability to judge whether something is good, beautiful, or true. This is determining whether something or someone is *effective*.[4]

We cannot produce in our customers *insight*, much less *wisdom*, but we can certainly lead them in the right direction. By creating information that is useful we are paving the way for insight. Producing informative content that will at least not hinder insight should be a high priority for us as Power BI content creators. And once our content consumers can *see*, then they can make decisions and take action.

If you're not sure so far what the point of that previous conversation was, let me put it succinctly: simply presenting data to someone could help them make decisions, but there's no guarantee that data will give a broader or deeper view. Further, condensing the data into information will be useful but is not insight itself. The information must be synthesized in a way that *serves* insight *in a specific context*. It's much like setting a table for the right meal for the right dinner guests. Our next guiding principle is about the process of getting the meal ready.

---

[3]Ibid.
[4]Russell Ackoff, "From Data to Wisdom: Presidential Address to ISGSR, June 1988," Journal of Applied Systems Analysis 16, 1989, 5-6.

FOLLOW A CONSISTENT, PROVEN METHOD

This principle is more about a process than an idea. In many ways it's difficult to actually *not* follow this process and use Power BI, but many people find a way to avoid two steps and wonder why the last step is unsuccessful. Follow this process and you'll be well on the way to your report consumers experiencing insights.

As an aside, this process is not unique to Power BI. This is the process that data engineering professionals use to build enterprise-scale data analytics solutions. This same approach has been followed for decades. Even though technology improvements over those decades have radically expanded the technical capabilities, the process still works the same way. So, that means you'll be using a reliable, proven method without having to learn all the ins and outs of being a data engineer and yet will have the benefits that come with that method.

In the previous chapter I quickly outlined that process, but let's dive in and expand on each of the steps!

Data Sources

Sources of Data

The data you want to present in your reports and dashboards may come from Excel files that you have maintained. It might be data that you have manually entered and tracked over time. This would be data that does not originate in some other system. But 99 percent of the time you will be working with data that you do not create yourself. That data could come from a myriad of different sources, but essentially all of the data you'll import will come from primarily three different categories: files, databases, and online services. (There are a small number of other kinds of sources such as directly writing code with a programming language such as Python or R, but these are more technical topics that fall outside the scope of this book.)

Files

File data comes in two categories: stored as plain text or stored in a proprietary file format. Let's cover plain text first.

Text files may be something you've exported from software such as QuickBooks. It could be text files that you have exported from some internal system at your organization. It might be a file that you downloaded from a website. Regardless of the source, individual text-based file data is stored in such a way that you are able open the file and look at its contents without any special tools. Typically, the Notepad application on Windows is great for looking at these files, except when the file is very large.

Text-based file data is most often organized as rows of data that are separated by a return character (a line feed and/or carriage return). Each individual row will contain fields of data that are separated by a special character such as a comma, a tab, a semicolon, or a unique character code. Sometimes the fields in a row are separated by fixed widths for each column. In the case of fixed-width text files, it may help to obtain a definition from the source of what each column represents, how wide it is, and what data type is stored in each column.

Text-based file data can also be stored in industry-standard formats such as XML or JSON. These formats are fairly self-describing. Meaning, when you open the file in a text editor, the data is organized in a way that has markers that describe what you're looking at.

Proprietary file formats are files that you cannot simply open with a text editor like Notepad.

File data can be from Excel files that you've maintained by copying and pasting or manually entered. As mentioned, Excel files cannot be opened with a text editor but can obviously be viewed and edited within Excel. PDF files are another proprietary format that may contain source data you could use in your Power BI solution.

Power BI is well-suited for working with any of the text-based file types described here and has built-in connectors for Excel and PDF.

Databases

Data can also be found in databases maintained by your organization. While these could be personal databases like MS Access, I'm thinking more of large relational databases like SQL Server, Oracle, Postgres, MySQL, DB2, and SAP. All these database engines are accessible by Power BI. In addition, if there is not a direct connector from Power BI to the database you need to access, more often than not, something called an *ODBC Driver* is available to access your system, though there may be a financial cost associated with acquiring it.

Data stored in databases is an excellent source to work with because often it is easy to retrieve and is optimized for storing large amounts of data quickly. However, most of the time, these databases are not organized for you in a nice structure that is easy to understand. Sometimes the tables are named cryptically. Sometimes the data is organized into hundreds (or more!) of tables. These strange structures are optimized for applications like a customer relationship management (CRM) or enterprise resource planning (ERP) system to be able to store and edit data rapidly and by thousands of end users simultaneously. Their structure is not usually optimized for reporting and analysis of the data.[5] Many times vendors will publish documentation that will explain how the data is organized. This is sometimes called a *data dictionary* or a *database schema*. If you plan on accessing data like this for your work, you will want to find out if there is a dictionary available. But there are several other questions you'll need answering.

---

[5]In software engineering and data engineering terms, this type of database system is referred to as optimized for Online Transactional Processing (OLTP). Some databases, most often "data warehouses" are optimized for Online Analytical Processing (OLAP). Those databases would be much more readable to a business user.

Accessing databases is a tricky business. It's tricky mostly because these databases are often the life of your business. Meaning, they are used for operating the business day in and day out. Any kind of interruption to the operation of those databases could be a giant risk for your business. It is for this reason alone that most IT departments will restrict users from just accessing that backend data. You should find out whether the data you want to access is available for you to query. It may be that your organization will provide "views" of the data that are isolated from impacting the performance of the database or may even be offloaded to a separate database just for reporting purposes. *This is your number-one question: Can I get access to this data somehow?* Depending on your role in your organization, you may run into roadblocks preventing you from accessing the database. Don't fret, though, if you get blocked because there are usually multiple ways that your IT department can provide access to that data.

Online Services

The third category of data sources is online services. Online services are applications available on the Internet ("in the cloud") that provide a way to connect and retrieve the data offered by the service. For most of these services, they expose data with an interface to write code against. These services are typically applications your organization is using to run their business but are not maintaining the software on their own servers at your organization's physical location.

A well-known example of this is Salesforce. Salesforce is a cloud-based application that companies use to track customers, sales opportunities, and many other things. Salesforce provides a way for programmers to access the data via something called an *application programming interface* (API). Programmers write code to interact with that API for Salesforce and either read or write data in the system. This is often done for integrating an existing application your organization uses with Salesforce (or whatever online service you're thinking of right now) or to add additional custom functionality to the service. There are other uses for the API, but for our purposes, the APIs that an online service exposes are a data source that Power BI can take advantage of if one of two things are true. First, Power BI can access the online service if the API uses an industry standard such as OData, which is a protocol intended for sharing data in a straightforward way. Second, the organization could work with Microsoft to expose their data as a standard connector within the list of Power BI Online Service connectors. Take a minute to go investigate the list of connectors available to Power BI and you'll find that the list very likely has sources you are familiar with or have heard of: `https:// learn.microsoft.com/en-us/power-bi/connect-data/power-bi-data-sources`.

Plan Ahead

Before you begin retrieving data from these different sources, there are many questions to think about. Here are several questions about data sources that I ask my clients:

➤ *Can I get access to this data source?* I already mentioned this question, but if the answer is no, then you'll have to go back to the drawing board. It doesn't have to be a complete showstopper, but it can obviously put a damper on your plans to bring this data into Power BI.

➤ *Is the data available now?* This may sound like a strange question, but often in an organization it may be that the data exists and the system has a mechanism to provide the data, but there are efforts that need to be made to actually open up access to or expose the data you're looking for.

➤ *How much data are we talking about?* By this, I mean how many rows of data are we talking about per entity per source? Power BI can handle billions of rows, but the way you interact with a data source that contains only hundreds of thousands or millions of rows may be completely different than how you'll access billions of rows.

➤ *How large is this data?* Here I'm referring to storage size of all the data combined that you plan to access. Again, fear not that Power BI might not be able to handle the size, but if you don't follow the methods described in Chapter 6, "Modeling Data," you will likely run into volume issues importing the data as well as report performance issues. Power BI Pro allows datasets that are up to 1 GB. For some people that might sound small, but when you follow the practices promoted in this book, you'll find that millions of rows can easily be compressed into that size. If you're able to take advantage of Power BI Premium per User, the datasets can be as large as 10 GB.

➤ *How often does the data get updated?* The source of data you're using may only be a copy of data from an original source. If that is the case, then the data is likely copied to that location on a predetermined interval. Or that file is updated on a certain day and/or time. Or the data is updated live as changes occur in the source. Knowing how often the data is updated will inform you as to what limitations you may be up against.

➤ *Is there an easy way to know the data has been updated?* Depending on the answer to the previous question, you may still have to ask this question. Is there a way to look at the file or database or online service and find only data that has been changed since a specific date or time? If so, then your process of importing the data may be more efficient if you need to access only what has changed versus all of the data every time.

➤ *When can I retrieve the data?* This may be related to the previous two questions, but you may be surprised to find out that the owner of the data might allow the data to be accessed only at a certain time of day or on certain days of the month.

➤ *How often can I retrieve the data?* This question can be thought of in two senses. First, how often the data source gets updated will be directly related to this question. But also, the question may be more about how often the owner of the data says that you are able to access it. Second, if you're using Power BI Pro, you'll only be able to retrieve the data eight times in one 24-hour period if you're importing it (more on that in the next section). With Power BI Premium per User, you can refresh 48 times per 24-hour period.

➤ *How far back is the data recorded?* You may be surprised by the answer to this question. Sometimes people want to be able to analyze history several years back, but then discover that in their situation they could access the data only one year in the past. You will want to find out this answer depending on your reporting needs.

➤ *Who should have access to this data once it is made available to me?* This question is important to consider because it's possible that not everyone in your organization should be able to see the data you're working with. If you have an IT department you're working with to request access to the data, you will know they're doing their job well if they ask you who you're going to give your report to. Power BI offers great ways (as mentioned in Chapter 1, "Introducing Power BI," and will be covered later in Chapter 9, "Refreshing, Sharing, and Collaborating") to protect and secure the data.

➤ *Can I use the live production data, or do I need to access a copy of the source?* This question is usually relevant only if your data source is a database system. If it is a database system, you will need to find out if you are only accessing copied data or live data. If you are given access to live data, you should also ask, "Is there any risk in me using the live data?"

➤ *How much will it cost?* This question is usually relevant only to online sources. If you are accessing a cloud-based service, then there is a good chance that your organization will be required to purchase access to the data by either subscription, license, or per-use model. Sometimes even on-premises systems will charge a fee to access the data.

We have spent a lot of time on what probably seemed like a subject that there wouldn't be much to talk about. Ironically, the next steps in the consistent, proven method will not take as long to discuss because we will be devoting chapters to these topics.

Import Data

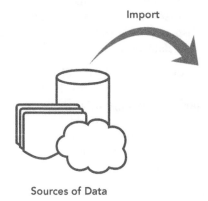

Import

Sources of Data

After identifying the data sources you need for building your reports and dashboards, your next step is to answer these two questions:

➤ Should I import this data?

➤ If I am importing this data, how will I do that?

You may think it's odd to ask whether to import the data given the fact that this step of the method is to *import the data*! But it's a valid question because for many of the database-related Power BI connectors, it is possible to directly query the data without importing it. Take another look at the list of connectors available and observe the column titled "Direct Query/Live Connection." As you'll see, there are many connectors that allow you to have a direct connection to the data source while your report consumers use your reports. In some cases, that might be helpful, but most of the time, it will be preferable to actually import the data. Here are a couple of reason reasons why you might *not* want to import your data:

➤ *I need more real-time reporting capabilities.* Power BI Pro allows only eight refreshes per day. Premium allows only 48 refreshes per day. If my users need to see what the data looks like right now when they open the report, then a direct query approach will be needed.

➤ *I have too much data to import it all.* In rare cases, there may be too much data to import. However, in this case, you're not going to create reports that display all that data. Instead, you'll likely import the data in an aggregated ("rolled up") way and then allow your users to "drill down" into the details, which might be a specific set of records such as invoice line items.

If you've decided that you are going to import, then you need to decide how you'll import that data. You may have only one option, but in some cases, there *might* be different ways to approach this.

Your first question to answer is whether Power BI offers a connector specifically for your data source. If it does, that is probably your best choice since it is optimized toward communicating with that platform. However, there are some situations where even though the connector is available, your organization may not allow connections to the system. In that case, you'll have to investigate whether there are other alternatives.

Two alternatives come to my mind in the case where either your company will not allow queries against the production system *or* Power BI does not offer a connector. First, you could find out whether your organization has a data warehouse available. A data warehouse is a centralized location where data is gathered from multiple sources in a company and organized in a way that makes reporting more efficient. If this exists at your business, you may want to inquire if the data you're interested in is already located in the data warehouse.

A second alternative may be a scheduled export. Some software vendors provide a way to export prebuilt reports within the system or even specific tables. If you're unsure of where this option might be in your system, it would be good to contact your IT department or the group that provides support for the system. Having the data exported would result in a text-based file that Power BI would be able to interact with. In this alternative, be sure to consider having the exported file placed in an area where others could get to this file if you decide to move onto another position. In other words, don't save the exported file on your laptop!

A third alternative exists that is unpreferred but might be a last resort. If the data source you're working with has an API (remember, this is an interface for software developers to program against) exposed, custom code could be written to extract the data. But following this alternative has many negative consequences. Most significantly, this will introduce the need to constantly maintain code and identify who would do that maintenance.

All that being said, there's a good chance that your data source already provides a simple way to connect directly from Power BI.

Prepare Data

Preparing data is the first step that I have seen many people avoid, and I encourage you not to skip this. Power BI, as you will see, provides a tool called Power Query that will enable you to prepare your data for reporting. This step and the next go together. For example, you will want to prepare your data in light of how you need to model the data. And in some regard, you'll want to model your data in light of the analytical needs of your report consumers. So many people try to jump right from importing data into making reports without taking the time to think through how their data is formatted, how well their data is entered in the source, how the data will be used from a calculation perspective, or how to bring together related data into single tables of data.

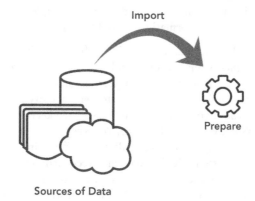

Import

Prepare

Sources of Data

The point of this step is to provide reliable and consistent reporting. This will help build the confidence of your report consumers. The benefit you'll experience is that the data you've imported will easily convert into information. Remember, we need to serve the information in a way that will promote insight. There are four areas of data preparation that you should consider: cleaning, transforming, conforming, and arranging.

Cleaning data is about making sure that the quality of the data coming in from your source is consistent and adheres to business rules. For example, you may require that every customer has a complete and valid address. When you import that data, maybe you'll want to inspect each row to ensure that each address has all the components provided (such as street, city, state, postal code). You might want to make sure that every street type value is consistent: "St." or "Street"? "Blvd." or "Boulevard"? Making sure that each postal code is a valid postal code is also a cleaning task many people undertake. Another example of data cleaning is that you may require every invoice line to have a quantity value specified. You'll need to inspect each row to verify that a quantity value exists. For rows that have a missing quantity value, you may decide to flag those rows as invalid or even move those rows to a different area so that they can be inspected by someone.

Transforming data is about making the data *ready* to convert into information. Often this task is about making sure that values are in the correct data type such as converting alphanumeric values into just numeric values. Another transforming task that is common is the need to split apart textual values into separate columns. With the address cleaning example, maybe you receive the address in one long value ("12334 East Town Road, Franklin, TN 45290") and need to split that into separate columns for each part. As you may see already, *cleaning* and *transforming* go hand in hand. Cleaning is about ensuring *correct* values, and transforming is about ensuring *usable* values.

Aggregating values into single values might also be something you do in transforming data, but I caution you to avoid aggregating data unless you are dealing with "big data" (billions of rows). The reason that aggregating is often not a good idea in preparing your data is that once you've aggregated the data, there's no going back in your report. For example, if you've collapsed multiple values (such as sales totals per day merged into a sales total for the month), your report consumers will never be able to explore deeper than at the month level. Furthermore, I'm not sure about you, but I can't predict the future or read people's minds. What I mean is, you may know today what aggregate is wanted by your users, but you don't know what new thing they'll ask for in the future. Leaving the data in an unaggregated format allows innumerable options for the future. Transforming data may also be about adding other information into your data. For example, you may inspect each row and may look up a corresponding bit of information related to that row and add it into your record.

Conforming data is about making sure data you bring in from multiple sources makes sense together, that it is connected to each other when appropriate. Let's imagine you're working for a small business and you want to tie together data from purchase orders, invoices, accounts receivable, and sales opportunity data. You want a single view of your customers' activity from end to end. But the challenge is the data comes from two systems. Your salespeople keep track of opportunities and potential customers in HubSpot, your CRM service. You keep track of all that other important stuff in your QuickBooks software. *Conforming* data will be about making sure that Customer X coming in from HubSpot is the *same* Customer X that you have recorded in your QuickBooks software. It's also about combining the two customer lists so that new customers originating in HubSpot but without sales (yet) still show up in your data. Conforming efforts are about pulling together the customer list from QuickBooks and HubSpot and making sure that they match where they should and that all customers are included even when they don't match but are valid.

Arranging data is about preparing the data to be modeled based on how your business processes flow and how you think about the various parts of your business. We'll get into modeling data a little in the next section, and all of Chapter 6, "Modeling Data," is about just that, but before modeling, you need to prepare your data so that it can be modeled well. Arranging the data may seem like restructuring the data, and that would be a right way to think about it. Arranging the data is about making sure that the same kinds of data are in the same tables and that multiple kinds of data do not exist in the same table. For example, maybe you receive a file on a regular basis that has product sales and inventory data combined. Each row, for some reason unknown to you, has both the product sold on a certain day and has a quantity on hand and quantity on order value in the same row of data. Busting that row apart into two tables is what I mean by arranging the data. If you wanted to plan for the future and also make sure that the data in one table is about one business process or business entity, then you'll want to break it up into separate tables. Another situation I see often is that the sales data has all of the customer data buried in the sales data. You'll want to pull apart the customer from the sales but still keep it linked together in some way. As we walk through Chapter 5, "Preparing Data," I'll show you how to do that.

The point of data preparation, again, is to make sure your data is *prepared* to be modeled and consequently converted into amazing reports and dashboards. Power BI's Power Query tool easily enables you to do all of this *preparing data* task, and we'll learn all about it in Chapter 5.

Model Data

Often the data you receive from data sources isn't organized in the way you think about your business. Maybe you get bits and pieces of the data, or maybe it all comes in one big file. That won't do. This next step of the method has two primary steps.

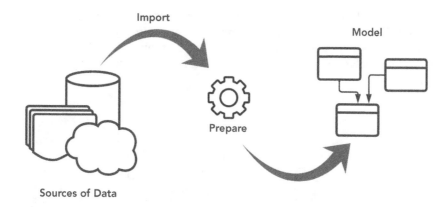

Import

Model

Prepare

Sources of Data

First, you need to *arrange the data into tables* (rows and columns of data) that either reflect the business process you want to report upon or describe that business process. There should be tables like Sales, Inventory, Shipping, Hiring, and Payroll. These are tables that describe what you *do* as a business. These should be a reflection of your business processes. Then, there should be tables like Customer, Vendor, Product, Policy, and Location. These are tables that describe your business process. For example, the Customer table describes the Sales process because it tells us *who* bought something from you and maybe what that customer is like with all of their different attributes. The Product table describes the Sales process because it tells you *what* product was sold and all the different ways to describe what the product is like.

Second, data modeling is about *relating the tables to each other*. We want to tell Power BI that every sale has a related customer, a related product, and maybe a related location. Relating tables means creating a connection between the tables that define what that relationship entails. For example, there should be only one record in your Customer table for one customer. But, ideally, there are many records in your Sales table for each time that customer bought something from you. The relationship between those tables is called a one-to-many relationship because there is one record in one table that relates to at least one but ideally many more in the Sales table. But your Customer table may also be related to your Accounts Receivable table and maybe many other business process-related tables. When you have one Customer table relating to multiple business process tables (which later we'll call *fact tables*), then you'll be able to unlock some amazing capabilities such as comparing sales volumes to outstanding account receivable balances at the same time.

Power BI allows you to create the tables you'll use in your data model and then relate them to each other and it does this in a very easy to learn way. We'll cover all those details in Chapter 6, "Modeling Data."

Report Data

Reporting data is the step that everyone wants to jump to after they've imported the data instead of getting ready to do this well. But the key thing to remember is—just because you can doesn't mean you should. And that applies too in the process of building the reports and dashboards themselves.

You will see all kinds of beautiful and interesting visualizations available to you. But many of those are not going to help you and, worse, may even hinder what you're trying to accomplish. In fact, I think this step is so important that I'm going to spend the last third of this chapter on this topic alone. Until then, remember the goal in presenting information in a report or dashboard is to make *insight* possible.

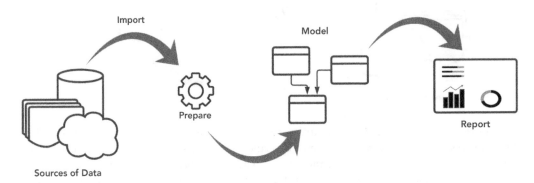

Analyze Data

I know it's strange, but in one sense, you need to jump to this step of analysis first before you do any of the other steps. By that I mean, you need to ask your report consumers (or yourself if you're the consumer!) what their needs are. What are the questions they need to answer? What are their pain points in information? What information do they lack in making decisions? What do they need to understand about their business process that they struggle to understand today? Eliciting responses to these questions will help you understand *how* they will analyze the information you'll provide. As the old phrase goes, "You'll never hit the target if you don't know what it is."

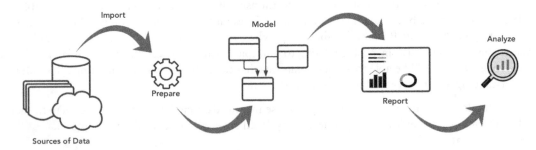

Starting with this step, determining what the end goal is will help you work backward from here to the reporting/dashboarding step because it will clarify for you what is and what is not needed to present to your users. And when you have an idea of how you need to present the information, then you'll be informed as to what the data model might look like. (But don't lock in your data model just based on these needs alone. Your best bet will be to build your data model to reflect how most people in your organization think about your business.)

But let's move on to the third guiding principle.

USE VISUALIZATIONS WELL

I cannot speak to this topic as if I am an expert. Everything I know about this topic comes from one of the top experts in the world: Stephen Few. He has contributed so much to the world of visual analytics.

I did have a sense that how I had been building user interfaces in the 1990s and early 2000s was off somehow, but I couldn't tell you why. When I was creating software for manufacturing environments, I had tools that would allow me to display gauges like the one shown in Figure 2.3 for reports. If this was for showing the current state of a machine, that would be a whole different matter. But I would use these for business reporting because they looked cool, and the software vendors were promoting it.

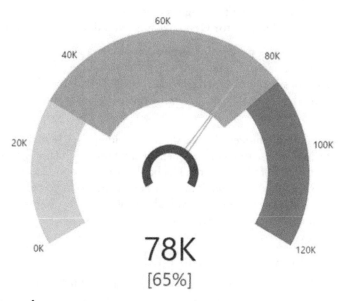

FIGURE 2.3: Using a gauge for a report

But what does this really tell me? Obviously without context, it means nothing to you. But imagine if it reflected stock levels of a product. For example, the center of the gauge (the values between 30,000 and maybe 83,000?) reflects the target levels. In other words, we don't want to let the levels drop below 30,000 and if we go above 83,000, apparently that would be a bad thing because it's in the red. Does this mean anything in between is OK? What do we need to do if it goes over 83,000? I'm sure there are other questions we could ask, but think about this: how much space on the page do you have to work with, and do you really want to consume that much space when you could probably convey that information in another more condensed and possibly more useful way?

Even though there are several issues still remaining with this reimagined visualization shown in Figure 2.4 (such as lack of labels and captions to give context being a significant issue), this take at least reduces the real estate needed on your page.

Item X

FIGURE 2.4: A more compact visual representation of the data

Using visualizations well requires practice over time to learn what works and what doesn't. In the next two sections, I will give you some simple rules to give you a head start. We'll start with some mistakes and then move on to best practices, all insights derived from the helpful work of Stephen Few.

Three Ways to Ruin Visual Analytics

After amassing an army of Lego sets as a kid, I always loved taking the most unique pieces from different sets and assembling *what I thought* was the coolest creation anyone had ever seen. My mom never had the heart to say that mixing the knight's castle with the spaceship and pirates just made zero sense! But then again, did it need to? Of course not—you don't want to stifle that creativity!

Unfortunately, that isn't the same principle when it comes to data visualization. While it's true that, as my friend Josh Pinsonneault has said, data visualization brings value and efficiency to any organization, not taking time to consider human perception is the quick path to ruining data visualization. The effect may be worse than no return on your investment. (What if your visualizations are misleading?)

While there are many common missteps in visualization techniques, I've picked the top three I've seen most in the field. How did I come to recognize them? I can't take the credit. As I mentioned earlier, Stephen Few is *the* go-to-guru of visualization. His books (*Information Dashboard Design*, *Show Me the Numbers*, and *Now You See It* are three excellent works to pick from) and his site (perceptualedge.com) have been immensely valuable tools to me. So, here are the top three ways I've found that you can really lose the impact you're hoping for in data visualization.

Use as Many Cool Gadgets as You Can Find

It can be tempting to think that the saying "variety is the spice of life" applies to dashboards. I think we worry that having the same gauges and gizmos would be visually monotonous.

For example, the designer of the dashboard shown in Figure 2.5 from a current ERP vendor seemed to think that six types of visualizations would be better, when five of them could've easily been set in a small table with simple data indicators and a corresponding value. The amount of visual real estate you gain alone would've been worth it.

Remember, you need to pick what works best to communicate quickly and effectively. If you display five KPIs five different ways, you're requiring the human brain to switch gears five times. Don't make the human brain work harder! Figure 2.6 shows a simplified version.

Overwhelm the User with Tons of Detail

Dashboard visualizations should be very high level to give an overview, not the microscopic view shown in Figure 2.7.

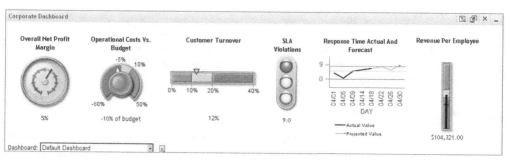

FIGURE 2.5: A dashboard with too many types of visualization

Overall Net Profit Margin	5%	
Operational Costs vs. Budget	-6.50%	
Customer Turnover	12%	
SLA Violations	9.0	
Revenue Per Employee	$104K	

FIGURE 2.6: A simplified dashboard

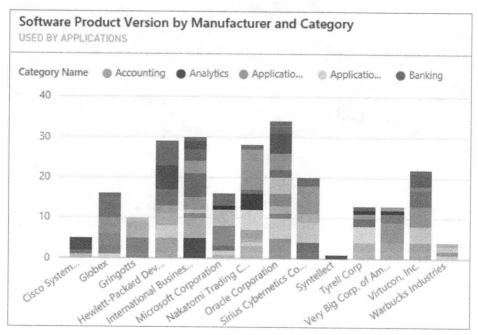

FIGURE 2.7: A dashboard visualization with too much information

Here we have too much information as opposed to too little. Can the human eye even detect the difference between the two shades of peach on that Microsoft bar? There are just way too many categories crammed into each bar for it to tell us anything meaningful. (As a side point—and a different visualization issue—what does that y-axis even represent in this chart?)

A dashboard-level visualization should highlight what needs attention, not necessarily provide the details that require action. That's where the drilldowns and links come in. As Stephen Few put it, "The dashboard does its primary job if it tells the viewer with little more than a glance that he should act. It serves him superbly if it directly opens the door to any additional information that's needed to take that action." The detail comes when you enter through that door.

Pick the Wrong Tool for the Job

I know this may sound blasphemous in today's optic-driven world, but graphs are not always the best (believe it or not). Surprisingly, sometimes a table would be better. For example, tree maps like the one shown in Figure 2.8 tell me very little, especially when you combine the previous visual mistake (too much detail) with the wrong visualization.

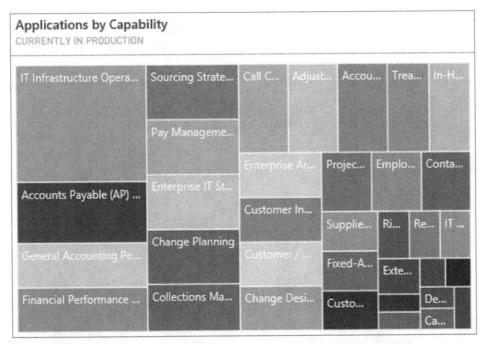

FIGURE 2.8: Wrong visualization for data

This chart could easily be replaced by a clean, lineless table with actual percentage values sorted, resulting in a more useful presentation.

Another classic example of this mistake is the abuse of the pie chart.[6] Having to move the eye back and forth between the legend and the chart is bad enough. But when you add a three-dimensional perspective, then the train really gets derailed. Consider how Apple infamously represented themselves several years ago with a chart like the one shown in Figure 2.9: notice that the 19.5 percent orange portion looks bigger than the 21.2 percent green market share.

---

[6]See Few's excellent article, "Save the Pies for Dessert" at www.perceptualedge.com/articles/visual_business_intelligence/save_the_pies_for_dessert.pdf.

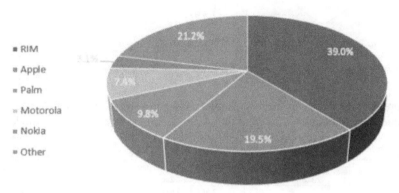

FIGURE 2.9: A visually misleading pie chart

Decision-makers need to *quickly* and *intuitively* understand their data so they can make data-driven decisions. But don't let your excitement to use bells and whistles undermine that "quickly" and "intuitively" piece that is so critical to making great insights!

But let's wrap this chapter up by thinking about some best practices that you *should* apply when building out reports or dashboards with Power BI.

Four Ways to Improve Visual Analytics

These ideas and helpful graphics are also directly from Stephen Few's *Information Dashboard Design,* and I recommend his work to you.[7] My goal in this chapter is simply to get your mind started in the direction of thinking about *how* to use the visualizations in Power BI well. Take these ideas as starters and learn from Few's directions.

The following four guidelines fall into two categories: reduce nondata pixels and enhance data pixels.

Reduce the Nondata Pixels

Nondata pixels are parts of the visualization that are not essential to displaying information. You either need to eliminate or at least reduce even the smallest bits that are not needed to convey information.

Eliminate All Unnecessary Nondata Pixels

Often, it's as simple as making sure you do not add a border to a chart, as shown in Figure 2.10. The border in the graphic on the left makes it difficult for the brain to articulate the axis values.

---

[7]Used by permission from Stephen Few.

FIGURE 2.10: Removing unnecessary borders from a graph

The same applies especially to tables. In the tables shown in Figure 2.11, notice the remarkable simplicity of the content on the right compared to the same content in the table on the left clouded by borders.

Salesperson	Jan	Feb	Mar	Salesperson	Jan	Feb	Mar
Paul Fuller	2,254	2,536	6,653	Paul Fuller	2,254	2,536	6,653
Zach Schultz	3,218	3,388	2,156	Zach Schultz	3,218	3,388	2,156
Matt Harmless	7,329	8,053	7,856	Matt Harmless	7,329	8,053	7,856
Sue Lemery	9,853	10,586	7,688	Sue Lemery	9,853	10,586	7,688
Eric Vandenberg	45,838	35,853	29,563	Eric Vandenberg	45,838	35,853	29,563
Total	$68,492	$60,416	$53,916	Total	$68,492	$60,416	$53,916

FIGURE 2.11: Removing unnecessary borders from a table

There is something remarkable about simply removing lines. Once you start building your visualizations, be sure to eliminate any unnecessary lines.

De-emphasize and Regularize the Nondata Pixels That Remain

It is not advisable to remove all lines, especially when there are multiple visuals that must be clustered
together such as in the "small multiples" visualization. When that is the case, mute the lines and make
them the same widths and styles throughout your report. In Figure 2.12 you can see that demarcation
is helpful, but simply muting the lines helps the eye focus on the content that matters most.

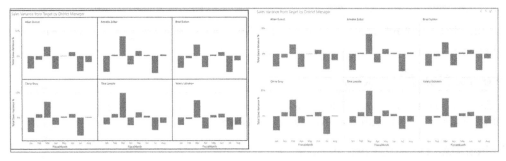

FIGURE 2.12: De-emphasizing nondata pixels that remain

Enhance the Data Pixels

The next two principles fall under the same category: maximize the focus on the content that is
necessary to retain.

Eliminate All Unnecessary Data Pixels

This principle probably seems identical to the first one; however, the first was qualified by the adverb *non*. Here we need to remove all data-related pixels that are unnecessary. While the first category was about how the visualization's surroundings are presented, this area focuses on the pixels in the midst of the data itself.

In Figure 2.13, we are looking at a table that has so many rows. Lines of some kind are needed to assist with reading across the rows. In this case, the rows aren't hard lines but are shaded. This helps, but we can achieve more by simply muting the shading so that the eye can still follow across but not be distracted by the level of shading.

Employee	Jan	Feb	Mar	Apr	May	Jun
Employee 01	77,699	88,883	77,323	73,671	92,873	97,531
Employee 02	97,585	84,224	94,509	95,632	75,429	88,444
Employee 03	75,752	85,063	78,459	83,937	97,556	83,298
Employee 04	86,744	71,332	94,431	94,468	76,181	90,308
Employee 05	87,043	79,975	78,265	80,482	85,705	76,134
Employee 06	74,211	96,961	94,250	98,705	84,892	91,628
Employee 07	91,717	97,043	75,378	86,737	78,547	74,066
Employee 08	92,514	83,429	95,492	82,818	76,008	98,791
Total	$683,265	$686,910	$688,107	$696,450	$667,191	$700,200

Employee	Jan	Feb	Mar	Apr	May	Jun
Employee 01	77,699	88,883	77,323	73,671	92,873	97,531
Employee 02	97,585	84,224	94,509	95,632	75,429	88,444
Employee 03	75,752	85,063	78,459	83,937	97,556	83,298
Employee 04	86,744	71,332	94,431	94,468	76,181	90,308
Employee 05	87,043	79,975	78,265	80,482	85,705	76,134
Employee 06	74,211	96,961	94,250	98,705	84,892	91,628
Employee 07	91,717	97,043	75,378	86,737	78,547	74,066
Employee 08	92,514	83,429	95,492	82,818	76,008	98,791
Total	$683,265	$686,910	$688,107	$696,450	$667,191	$700,200

FIGURE 2.13: Muting row shading to reduce distraction

Highlight the Most Important Data Pixels That Remain

The final principle that I want to share from Few's recommendations is to highlight what is most important. There are multiple ways to do this, some very simple indeed. In the third example in Figure 2.14, a simple asterisk immediately draws the eyes to what should hold your focus. Consider simple ways to draw attention to what is most important.

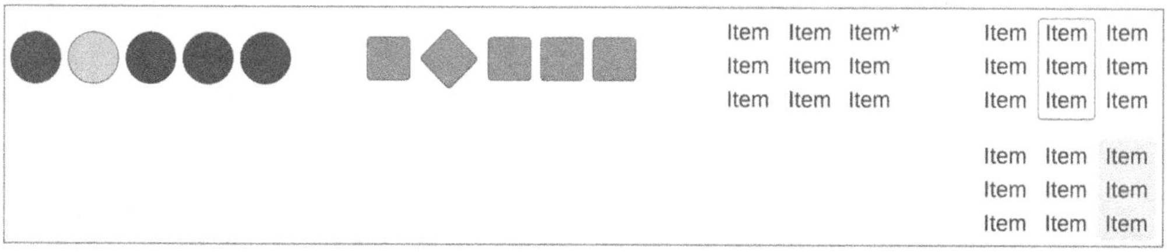

FIGURE 2.14: Highlighting the most important data

CONCLUSION

We have covered much ground in this chapter, and I'm proud of you for pushing through a chapter like this that deals with principle and theory instead of pragmatics. We've covered three guiding principles that I believe will help you develop reports and dashboards that will lead your users to valuable insights. Remember that we can serve up information and guide knowledge, but insights come only if we do this well. Remember, don't jump past the steps of preparing and modeling your data as it will serve you and your report consumers well for a long time. Finally, remember to take time to research how to format and use visualizations in such a way that runs with the grain of the human brain. When we do these things, we will be well on our way to turning data into insight.

PART 2
Power BI Guided Walk-Throughs

3

Let's Take a Flyover!

The wait is over. You've invested two whole chapters of learning without actually getting your hands dirty. I'm sure you're tired of waiting. So, let's get going, huh?

In this chapter, we're going to take a flyover of both the Power BI Service and Power BI Desktop. We'll start first with the Service side so that you can see the end result, and then we'll wrap up with an introduction to the Desktop tool.

To begin with, let's get connected to the service.

GETTING CONNECTED

Open a browser and navigate to `powerbi.com`.

If this is your first time ever logging in to `powerbi.com`, you will likely be presented with a splash screen. Enter your organizational email address and click Submit.

Once you have entered a valid organizational email address, click Submit. Once you've successfully logged in, if your organization does not already have a Power BI subscription provided for you, then you'll need to either sign up for a trial or purchase the subscription right away.

PERSONAL VERSUS ORGANIZATIONAL EMAIL

If you've entered a personal email address (such as `@yahoo.com`, `@gmail.com`, or `@hotmail.com`), you will be prompted to enter a work email address. This is because Power BI must be connected to an organization that uses Microsoft's cloud-based directory service called Azure Active Directory (AAD). That directory service is used for many things, but particularly with Power BI, AAD helps in managing licenses and giving you the ability to share, in a secure and controlled way, your content with

continues

(continued)

others. Not being able to use a personal email can be a source of frustration for some people whose organization does not use AAD. There are a couple of workarounds that you could try: sign up for a free trial of Microsoft 365 (previously called Office 365) with one of their business-level accounts (`www.microsoft.com/en-us/ microsoft-365/business/compare-all-microsoft-365-business- products`). The other option is a little more technical than we need to venture into in this book, but feel free to research how to sign up for your own Azure subscription and deploy an Azure Active Directory instance. Going through that option will create an email address (of sorts) that will allow you to sign up for a Power BI subscription.

In the upper-right corner of the window, you'll see a little gray user icon, an avatar. If you click that icon, a drop-down menu will appear that shows your login info as well as the type of license you currently have. If it shows that you currently have the free account, then that means you won't be able to share any Power BI content with anyone else. Recall from Chapter 1 that there are two primary paid subscription levels: Pro and Premium. If you see "Free account," then you can click the Start Trial button. That will direct you to an area where you can pick the level of subscription you'd like to use. Once you have a subscription set up, when you've successfully logged in, the drop-down menu will show the license type for your subscription.

That's all it takes to get set up and logged in to Power BI. Now let's explore the Service a little bit.

A QUICK TOUR OF THE POWER BI SERVICE

Let's take an in-depth tour of the Power BI Service starting with the most frequented areas you'll go.

Frequented Hotspots of Power BI

As you look at the main page upon logging in to Power BI, you'll see a gray navigation bar on the left. In Figure 3.1, I've highlighted five of those items that will be areas you will often go to.

1. The *Home* icon at the top will always take you back to this page. Just above that icon is another icon with three horizontal lines, often referred to as a *hamburger* icon. If you click that icon, the navigation bar will collapse to remove the text but retain the icons.

2. The *Apps* icon takes you to an area that allows you to present related content in packages that your report consumers can use as a sort of one-stop shop for all things related.

3. *Workspaces* are how you organize and secure your content. In workspaces, you'll store different kinds of content, but if you're doing it right, you'll keep only related content for the same audience in each workspace.

4. *My Workspace* is like a workspace you would find in the Workspaces area, however, only you can see it. You can put any of your own content in this area for your own benefit or as a sandbox of sorts to play in. This is how we will use the My Workspace until we get to Chapter 9.

5. This area is simply demonstrating that whatever you have selected on the left-side navigation menu will be the content shown on the right. In this example, we're looking at the empty My Workspace.

FIGURE 3.1: Frequent hotspots

Adding Sample Content

Now let's click the Learn button just above the Workspaces button in the navigation bar on the left. The Learn button takes you to a built-in training center for Power BI. There is so much available here that will take you to the next level after you work through this book. For now, we're going to use some built-in reports that Microsoft has provided to help us immediately begin to see the power of Power BI.

In the Sample Reports area, there is an arrow button pointing to the right. Click that until you see the Store Sales report. Click the Store Sales button to open the Store Sales report.

Before we explore this report, let's take a look at your My Workspace area to see what happened. As you can see in Figure 3.2, by simply opening the shared report and dataset, the content becomes available in your personal workspace. Exciting, huh? The contents of any workspace will always be displayed as a table like the one you see. It will list the name of the content, the type of content, who has ownership of the content, when it was last refreshed, and if there is a refresh schedule setup, when the next refresh will occur. Someone who creates and publishes content is by default the owner of the content. However, it is possible to change the ownership of content as long as you are at least in the Contributor role in the workspace (more on roles in Chapter 9, "Refreshing, Sharing, and Collaborating.")

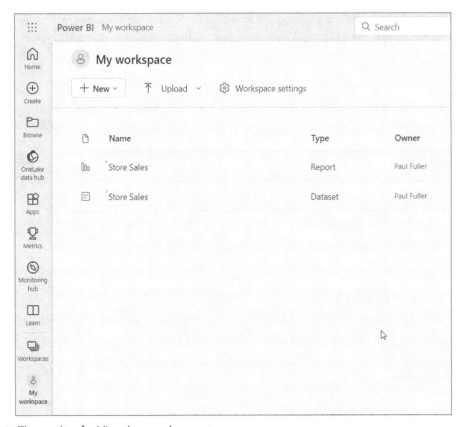

FIGURE 3.2: The results of adding the sample report

Click the Store Sales report in your workspace. These samples are provided to help newcomers see the possibilities of what can be done as well as just get acquainted with Power BI. In the past, some of the built-in samples did not follow the visualization practices that Stephen Few recommends. However, Microsoft has done a phenomenal job of improving the quality of the report design, and the sample reports provide a good start for us.

In the Store Sales report, click the Store Sales Overview page listed in the Pages lists in the upper-left corner of the report.

Understanding the Power BI Service Interface

In Figure 3.3, you're presented with visuals on opening the report: a pie chart in the upper left, a clustered column chart on the upper right, a map in the lower left, and a scatter chart in the lower right. All together this report page is trying to convey to us an overview of the retail stores sales.

There are several areas on the screen that will in general remain the same for you when looking at a Power BI report. Let's walk through those (the following numbers correspond to the numbered annotations in Figure 3.3):

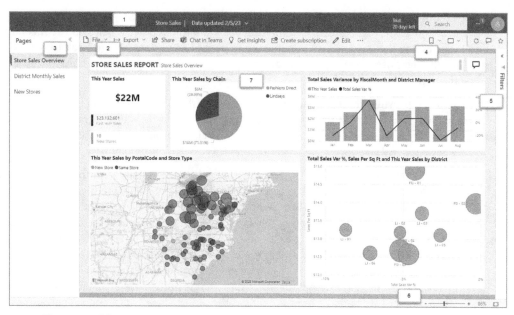

FIGURE 3.3: Elements of the Power BI report

1. The black banner across the top displays the name of the report and the date the data was last updated. If you would click the drop-down arrow, it would show the date *and time* that the report data was updated, as well as a contact to whom you could send questions in your organization.

2. The gray menu/toolbar below the black banner gives you different options depending on the permissions you have to access this report. In our case, we have Owner privileges, so we can see all the options. This is most apparent because the Edit button appears near the end of the bar on the right. I know you want to right now but hold off on clicking that Edit button.

   The first item on the left is the File menu. This menu item allows you to save a copy of the report with a different name as well as manage the settings of the report and print the report.

3. Moving to the far left of the report, you'll see a Pages section that lists the different *pages* within a report. This is a good time to explain a couple of terms that are often used inter-changeably but technically have different meanings, if we're going to be picky. A *dashboard* is not what we're looking at here. Power BI does have dashboards, but this is a *report*. We'll examine dashboards briefly in this chapter. Reports have *pages*, and here on the left you see a list of the pages within this report.

4. On the far right end of the gray menu bar, you'll see several buttons without text.

   If this button appears, it indicates that you have modified how the report was originally filtering data. This Reset Filters button will reset any filtering you have done while using the report. It is like putting the report back into the state in which it was originally published.

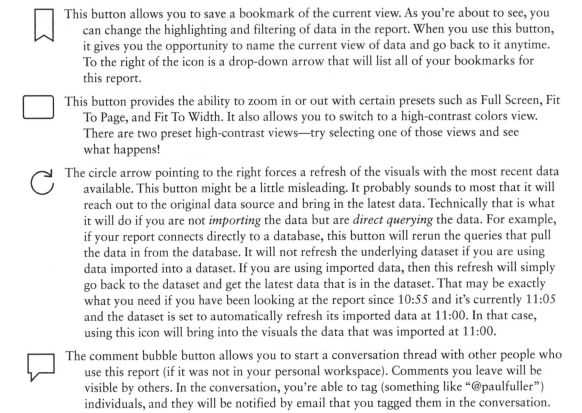

This button allows you to save a bookmark of the current view. As you're about to see, you can change the highlighting and filtering of data in the report. When you use this button, it gives you the opportunity to name the current view of data and go back to it anytime. To the right of the icon is a drop-down arrow that will list all of your bookmarks for this report.

This button provides the ability to zoom in or out with certain presets such as Full Screen, Fit To Page, and Fit To Width. It also allows you to switch to a high-contrast colors view. There are two preset high-contrast views—try selecting one of those views and see what happens!

The circle arrow pointing to the right forces a refresh of the visuals with the most recent data available. This button might be a little misleading. It probably sounds to most that it will reach out to the original data source and bring in the latest data. Technically that is what it will do if you are not *importing* the data but are *direct querying* the data. For example, if your report connects directly to a database, this button will rerun the queries that pull the data in from the database. It will not refresh the underlying dataset if you are using data imported into a dataset. If you are using imported data, then this refresh will simply go back to the dataset and get the latest data that is in the dataset. That may be exactly what you need if you have been looking at the report since 10:55 and it's currently 11:05 and the dataset is set to automatically refresh its imported data at 11:00. In that case, using this icon will bring into the visuals the data that was imported at 11:00.

The comment bubble button allows you to start a conversation thread with other people who use this report (if it was not in your personal workspace). Comments you leave will be visible by others. In the conversation, you're able to tag (something like "@paulfuller") individuals, and they will be notified by email that you tagged them in the conversation.

The star allows you to mark this report as a favorite report to use. Your favorite content is listed in the Favorites section on the home page. If you're given access to only a couple of workspaces and only a handful of reports, this feature may not seem helpful. But, if you're working with many different workspaces with many different reports, then you can imagine that not needing to hunt for a report could be *very* helpful.

5. The Filters pane shows up as a gray bar on the far right of the screen. In just a little bit we'll explore how you can filter reports with this feature.

6. In the bottom-right corner of the screen is a zoom slider that allows you to zoom in or out or, with the icon to the right of the slider, go into Fit To Page mode.

7. The center of the page is where all of the action happens. All of the report content will be displayed on the canvas in the center of all the toolbars discussed earlier.

As you move your cursor around the report and hover over aspects of the report, you'll see that Power BI displays in hovering tooltips more detailed information about what you're looking at. For example, in Figure 3.4, I have my cursor hovering over one of the dots in Tennessee on the map. You can see that the dot represents the sales for the 37919 postal code and particularly for "New Store" sales of $49,161.

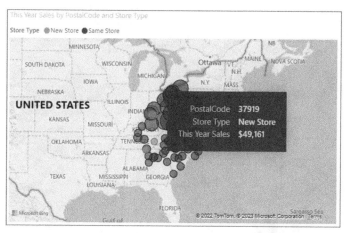

FIGURE 3.4: Example tooltip

Highlighting

In Figure 3.5 you can see that in the upper center, in the "This Year Sales by Chain" pie chart, there is a legend for the retail chains. Click the Fashions Direct chain. What happens when you do that?

FIGURE 3.5: Legend in "This Year Sales by Chain"

Clicking the chain in the legend causes the report to dynamically change in relation to what you clicked. Notice the impact in Figure 3.6.

FIGURE 3.6: Fashions Direct chain data highlighted

The visuals all adapted in some way. This action in Power BI is known as *highlighting*. The map in the lower-left corner zooms in to the Fashions Direct store locations. The "Sales Total Variance" scatter plot in the lower-right corner zooms into four dots. The visuals on the top row fade out the colors so that you can see the whole relative to the part you selected, to Fashion Direct's portion of the data. In the upper-left corner, "This Years Sales" dropped from $22 million to $16 million. This means that Fashion Direct's sales accounts for only $16 of the $22 million of total sales (about 72 percent of the overall sales, though that percentage is not displayed specifically). The upper-right corner visual retains the monthly variance data, but it's muted against Fashion Direct's variance data.

When your cursor is over the "This Year Sales by Chain" visual, you'll see that there are other icons that appear over the top-right corner of the visual. The thumbtack icon will allow you to pin this particular visual on a dashboard (more on that in a bit). The icon that looks like a stack of paper allows you to copy the visual to your clipboard so that you can paste it as an image into another program such as a document. The three horizonal lines icon will tell you how the visual is currently being filtered by filters in the filter pane and any filtering done on the report. The next icon will take you to the focus mode so that the visual is enlarged as the only visual on the screen. The ellipsis (three dots) icon pops up a menu with even more options, two of which we'll look at soon.

In the meantime, click the District Monthly Sales page on the left in the Pages area. Like the first report page, this report has four main visuals using the same data but displaying information related specifically to Districts. It's similar information, but just presented with different variables. For example, the upper-left corner now displays last year's sales against this year's sales with the Total Sales Variance numbers running across the columns.

Take some time to view each report page and click around to see how each page behaves dynamically. After you've done that, let's add another sample report by clicking the Learn button on the left side of your screen. Under Sample Reports, find the Corporate Spend report and select it. This will add the report to your My Workspace.

The Corporate Spend report digs into organizational expenditures for the year to date. The first page of the report tells the story of how the information technology (IT) spend breaks down (see Figure 3.7).

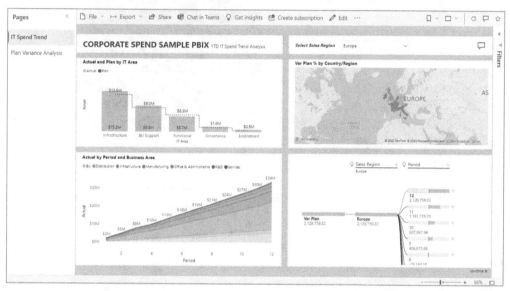

FIGURE 3.7: Corporate Spend report

This report has a few different visuals than the previous report we looked at. In the upper-right corner we have another map visual, though this time the map works by highlighting whole countries versus circles on the map. In addition, the countries are conditionally shaded so that one color indicates a negative variance to the spending plan and the other color positive. (That visual is not immediately helpful until you explore it a bit to learn that.)

In the upper-left corner, you'll see a line and column stacked chart. This visual allows you to have a separate line chart overlaid on columns. If you place your mouse over each column, you'll also notice a pop-up window that gives deeper information into that category of spending. As you move along to each column, the pop-up window adjusts to the content. This pop-up is not an automatic visualization, but after you've learned the material in this book, you'll find it very easy to create following the instructions here: https://learn.microsoft.com/en-us/power-bi/create-reports/desktop-tooltips?tabs=powerbi-desktop.

The "Actual by Period and Business Area" visual in the lower-left corner is a stacked area chart. This chart stacks from lowest to highest the spending by business area. The x-axis displays the data by financial period. As you move your mouse over the chart, a different kind of pop-up appears (see Figure 3.8). This is a built-in pop-up that helps you know what the specific details are of each point on the visual relative to your pointer.

The lower-right corner contains a very cool visual that allows your report consumers to dynamically interact with the data in a way that actually de-aggregates your data. You as a report designer will pick the way to de-aggregate the data based on how you'll model your data. But we won't be able to dive into using that visual until we cover it in Chapter 6, "Modeling Data."

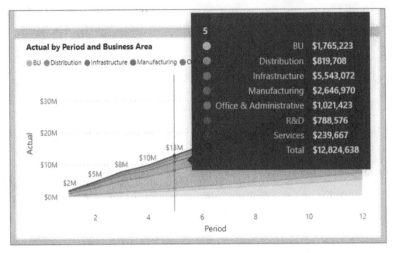

FIGURE 3.8: Built-in tooltip example

Slicers

We do have one more different kind of visual used in this report. At the top left of the screen you'll notice the text "Select Sales Region" with a drop-down field next to it. The list of sales regions is presented in a *slicer*. A slicer in Power BI is a special kind of visual. Not only does it show data visually in a list format, but it also allows the user to interact with it to actually filter the data displayed. If you have used slicers in Excel, this visual will be familiar.

> **NOTE** You saw the impacts of Power BI highlighting when we clicked Fashions Direct in the pie chart legend. Slicers are different than Power BI highlighting. Selecting an item from a slicer eliminates all data for nonselected slicer items from the visuals on the page. This differs from the Power BI highlighting, which keeps nonselected items' data on the page visuals in a transparent state.

To see how this works, you'll notice that Europe is automatically selected in the list. Instead of Europe, select USA in the Sales Region slicer.

> **TIP** You can hold down the Ctrl key and click additional regions if you want to see impacts for more than just one region.

Notice in Figure 3.9 that similar to the highlighting effect, all of the visuals change relative to the selection you make. However, as mentioned, this is actually doing something different. The slicer *filters* the content on the screen. Think about it this way: with the slicer, you are filtering the data for the entire report page to show data related only to the United States. So instead of showing how U.S. data relates to the rest of the data *when you highlight*, filtering with a Slicer shows only USA data.

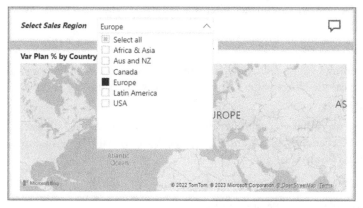

FIGURE 3.9: Using the Sales Region slicer

To remove the filter, click USA again, and the visuals will restore the view to reflect all the data. For many visuals, another way to clear a filter is to look for the small eraser icon in the upper-right corner. When this appears, you can click it to remove any currently selected items.

Explore some more to see how filtering your data with a slicer impacts the report's visuals. Remember the three horizontal lines icon? After you select some regions in the Sales Region Slicer, hover over one of those icons and it will show you specifically how the visual is filtered. For example, Figure 3.10 shows the filters applied to the Revenue percent Variance to Budget line area chart.

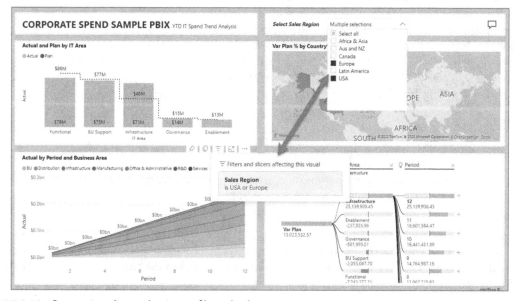

FIGURE 3.10: Comparing slicer selection to filtered values

Notice that in the slicer on the right, I have selected USA and also Europe. In the Filters And Slicers Affecting This Visual box for the "Actual by Period and Business Area" visual, you can see that the Sales Region field is filtered by those same values being applied to that visual. Click the "Actual and Plan by IT Area" visual in the upper-left corner. Then click the Filters bar on the right side of the screen, and let's see how we can further filter our report.

Filters

The Filters pane allows you to control what data is exposed. Click the Filters bar on the right side of your screen to reveal the Filters pane. There are two ways filtering can be done with the Filters pane: implicit and explicit.

Implicit filters are ways that you can filter the exact fields that are used on a selected visual. In our example, I had you click the "Actual and Plan by IT Area" visual. This visual uses four fields: Actual, Plan, IT Area, and IT Sub Area.

➤ *Actual* is the actual value of spending.

➤ *Plan* is the planned value of spending.

➤ *IT Area* is the area of the IT business.

➤ *IT Sub Area* allows the data to be categorized under each area.

As long as you have the "Actual and Plan by IT Area" visual selected on the Filters pane that opened, you can see those four fields used by that visual. Fields assigned to a visual that can be filtered will always show up in the Filters pane when you select that visual.

Explicit filters are defined when a report creator builds their report. Filters can be defined at three levels: report, page, and visual. A report user cannot create a new filter in your report (unless you have given them permission to edit the report), but they can modify for themselves what each filter is doing. (We'll see in Chapter 7, "Relationships and Filtering," that you can control which filters your users see and whether they can modify those filters.) In this case, the creator of this report did not specify any special filters to apply. We know that because when you select each visual, there are no more fields listed than what are actually used in the visuals. In addition, if you have no visuals selected, you see *no* filters listed in the Filters pane. We will create special filters as we create our first report in Chapter 4, "Building Your First Report." If special filters were defined, for each one there would be a default filter value set when the report is created and published.

> **NOTE** This is where the Reset Filters button comes into play. If your report consumers adjust any of the filters you as a report creator established and get lost in what was originally published, they can click this icon, and it will reset their view to the original filter settings with their default values.

Let's look at how you as a report consumer can modify the implicit filters that can be specified for a visual. If you've clicked elsewhere, make sure that you have clicked the "Actual and Plan by IT Area" visual. Click the Plan filter in the Filters pane.

In the Plan filter, you'll see a Show Items When The Value Is drop-down list. The drop-down allows several different options for controlling how the Plan values can be limited. Notice that those options are mathematical (such as less than, greater than, and so on). This is because Power BI knows that if a field is defined as a numeric type, then it can be filtered mathematically. There are also two options that may not seem mathematical: Is Blank and Is Not Blank. In the world of data, we think of values in a record as either being null or not null. This means that there is either a value present or not present. In Power BI filtering, the null option is referred to as Blank or Not Blank. (Once we look at filtering in more depth in Chapter 7, "Relationships and Filtering," you'll also notice options called Empty or Not Empty. This is special for textual type fields specifically. A textual field could be empty but not null. I know that probably sounds almost metaphysical, but don't worry about understanding that for now.)

Enter **14,000,000** into the Plan filter value and select Greater Than. Finally, click Apply Filter.

After you click Apply Filter, you will notice in Figure 3.11 that the "Actual and Plan by IT Area" visual changes from five columns to three because only three of the IT areas have a Plan value greater than 14,000,000.

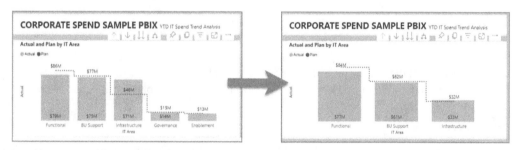

FIGURE 3.11: Impact of filtering the Plan value

The filter you created limited just the values in that visual according to what you specified. However, your filter applies to only that visual. We can demonstrate this by simply looking down at the lower-right corner where the decomposition tree is located. In that visual, you still see Governance and Enablement; the two IT areas filtered out of the "Actual and Plan by IT Area" visual are retained in the bottom visual.

In Figure 3.12 in the decomposition tree, you'll notice that every possible area is listed. You can select one or more of those areas and further filter the "Actual and Plan by IT Area" visual. Taking advantage of the Filters pane as a report creator is a smart technique versus taking up space on your report page with slicers.

What is really helpful about filters and slicers in Power BI is that the selections a report consumer makes in a filter or slicer are saved with their account. The next time they open the same report, their previous selections, whether filters or slicers, will be restored just as they had selected on the previous usage. Remember, if you ever need to go back to original filter settings, then click the Reset Filters button in the upper-right corner.

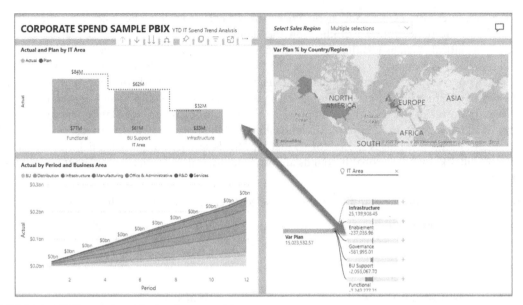

FIGURE 3.12: All IT areas listed in the decomposition tree

As I mentioned, we'll dig deeper into filters more in later chapters, but for now let's look at one more aspect of the "Actual and Plan by IT Area" visual that is not readily apparent but very useful.

Drill-Down

As your mouse hovers over the "Actual and Plan by IT Area" visual, you'll notice a set of icons with arrows, as shown in Figure 3.13.

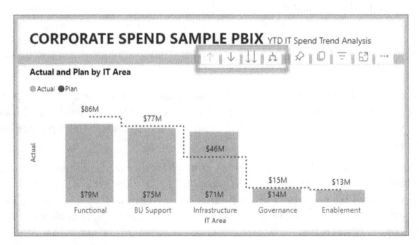

FIGURE 3.13: Drill-down arrows displayed

When fields are added to a visual that have a hierarchy to them, the visual will automatically enable you to drill up and down the levels of the hierarchy. An example of what I mean by a *hierarchy* is seen in the relationship between IT area and IT subarea. Each IT area in this example has subareas under it.

If you click the single downward arrow, it will turn on Drill-Down mode. Selecting this will change the behavior of what happens if you click one of the columns in the visual. Click the Infrastructure IT area column and observe what happens (as shown in Figure 3.14).

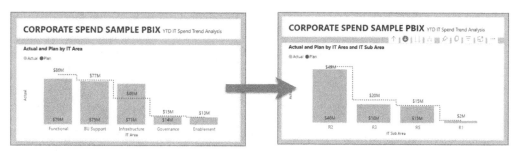

FIGURE 3.14: Drilling down into an IT subarea

To navigate back up in the hierarchy, click the upward arrow to the left of the drill-down mode arrow. The other two arrow buttons allow you to expand downward on all categories in the visual. Those two will make more sense as you start to work with visualizations that use date hierarchies and aggregate categories.

Let's explore one more type of workspace content: dashboards.

Dashboards

Once again, navigate to the "Actual and Plan by IT Area" visual, and as you hover over the visual, you'll notice the thumbtack/pushpin icon. The tooltip for that icon says "Pin visual." This button allows you to "pin" this visual to a separate kind of content called a *dashboard*.

Dashboards pull together a few visuals from multiple reports and pages in those reports. In addition, it's possible to add some insights that do not come from the reports directly but come from *insights*. These insights are calculations/aggregates that the Power BI Service discovered by looking for patterns in the data. This is what the thumbtack icon is for on each visual in a report. When you click the thumbtack, you are able to send the visual to an existing dashboard or create a new dashboard. A dashboard is different than a report in that the visuals are static, meaning you can't filter or highlight with them. They are not static in the sense of a point-in-time view of the visual; they are "live" in the sense that they query the underlying dataset. However, they don't have the interactivity that you're used to on the reports. Dashboards are intended to give you an at-a-glance impression. Stephen Few defines a dashboard as ". . . a visual display of the most important information needed to achieve one or more objectives that has been consolidated on a single computer screen so it can be monitored at a glance." That really does capture what you want your Power BI dashboards to be.

As you pin visuals from your reports to a dashboard, that pinned item is referred to as a *card*. Each card on a Power BI Dashboard is a linked item. If you click that item instead of just hovering over it, it will take you to the source of that visual—either a specific report page or an insights page. On the "Actual and Plan by IT Area" visual, click the Pin Visual icon, and let's create your first dashboard! (In Figure 3.15, I still have the Plan filter set to only show IT areas that have a Plan value greater than 14,000,000.)

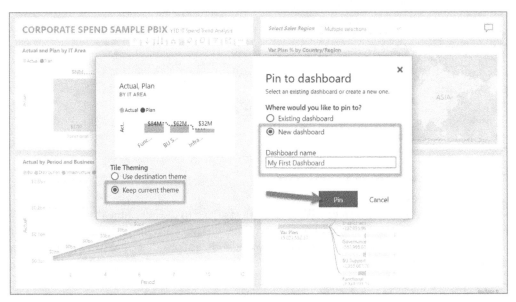

FIGURE 3.15: Pinning a visual to a dashboard

When you click the Pin Visual icon, you are presented with a screen that is asking to which dashboard you want to pin the visual. You can specify an existing dashboard or create a new one. Dashboards have a default theme of colors; however, if you want to retain the same color theme used on your report, you can Keep Current Theme. In my example, I'm keeping the current theme and creating a new dashboard called My First Dashboard. (Creative, I know!) After you click Pin, Power BI will show a confirmation window once the dashboard is created.

For now, click the X button on the Pinned To Dashboard window and let's pin a couple more visuals to our new dashboard. On the Pages pane on the left of the report, you'll see a Plan Variance Analysis page. On that page there are four cards that show single metrics: Var LE1 percent, Var LE2 percent, Var LE3 percent, and Var Plan percent. Cards are visuals that allow you to display a single metric value you're wanting to monitor. Look for the Pin Visual icon on each of these visuals and add them to My First Dashboard.

Now, navigate back to your My Workspace. Notice that you have two reports, two datasets, and a dashboard. Click the Store Sales report again, and let's add a couple more visuals to our dashboard before we reveal it!

On the Store Sales Overview report, pin the "This Year Sales" and "This Year Sales by Chain" visuals to your dashboard.

After you have pinned those visuals, you can either click the Go To Dashboard link that was displayed on the Pinned To Dashboard window or navigate back to your My Workspace and click My First Dashboard.

Your new dashboard should look something like Figure 3.16. Each of the cards on the screen can be arranged by selecting and dragging the card to where you'd like it displayed. From the dashboard, you can single-click any of the visuals, and they will direct you to the underlying report and page, where the visual is sourced.

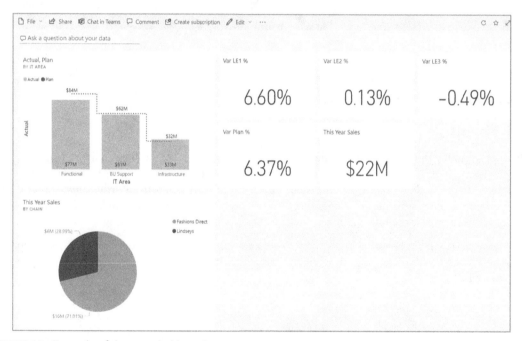

FIGURE 3.16: Example of the new dashboard

It's important to know that dashboards can contain visuals from multiple reports, but *only from reports in the same workspace.* As you can see, dashboards are simple to create, and consequently, we won't spend any more time on working with them in this book. However, if you're looking to go deeper with dashboards, you can start here: https://learn.microsoft.com/en-us/power-bi/create-reports/service-dashboards.

Let's look at just a couple more features of visuals on reports. Go back to the Store Sales report, and hover over the "This Year Sales by Postal Code and Store Type" map visual. In the upper-right corner, click the Focus Mode icon (see Figure 3.17).

Focus mode will enlarge the current visual to take up the entire report space on your screen. This is helpful for very detailed visuals. In this visual we can see that the company's sales are primarily located in the eastern United States.

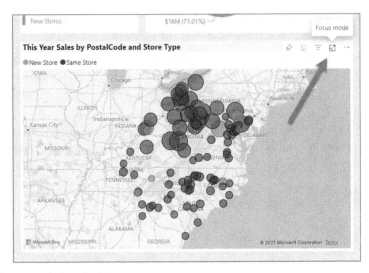

FIGURE 3.17: Focus mode icon in right corner

Drill-Through

In the tooltip for the 37919 postal code, there is a note that says "Right-click to drill through." As a report creator, you are able to create reports that enable your report consumers to navigate into more details related to a data point on your visual. This concept is different from drill-*down* in that drilling down into the data is the idea of navigating into hierarchical data. Drill-*through* is like guiding your report consumer to more information related to the data point they are looking at.

In Figure 3.18, we are hovering over a new store, and there is an accompanying New Stores report. If you right-click that bubble, you can navigate to the Drill Through menu item and the New Stores submenu item.

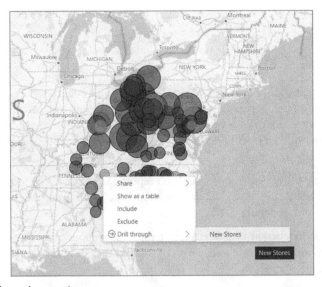

FIGURE 3.18: Drill Through menu item

Using the drill-through feature allows the New Stores report to be filtered to the new store in the 37919 postal code (assuming you were hovering over a new store and it was the same store I was hovering over in my example). By opening the Filters pane, you can confirm that the whole report page is now filtered where the postal code is 37919.

Visibility

In the Store Sales report that we drilled through to, the upper-right visual is a waterfall chart. Waterfall charts are not super intuitive if you're not familiar with them, but once you understand their purpose, they are quite powerful. A waterfall chart enables you to show a running total as something changes. In this case, the report is showing that the sales variance from the plan progressively decreased through the summer months and then flatlined until December. While that's interesting, that isn't the main thing I want you to see. Notice the two icons to the left of the waterfall chart but to the right of the gauge in the upper-left corner?

The bottom icon looks like a miniature waterfall icon, and the top icon looks like a line and column chart. Click the top icon.

When you clicked that top button, the visual on the right changed to a line and column chart. In creating reports, you may want to allow your users to have different views of the data *within the same report page*. To do that, you can create visuals, stack them on top of each other, and then configure which visual is visible first. Then, as in this report, the creator added a button that changes what is visible when each button is clicked. In Chapter 8, "Enhancing Your Report," we'll take some time to walk through how to do this yourself.

> **NOTE** *This feature is accomplished by taking advantage of bookmarks. Earlier in this chapter we briefly talked about bookmarks. In this report, you can know immediately that bookmarks are being used because the bookmark icon is*
>
>
> *colorized now.*

In the upper-right corner, there is another button that has been added by the creator with a predefined action. This time, instead of showing a bookmarked view like was done with the charts, the button will help you navigate to your previous report view. It's similar to a back button on the browser, but in this case, just navigates backward in the report journey. Click that navigation button and you should be taken back to the Store Sales report.

Show as Table

Click the ellipsis in the upper-right corner of the "This Year Sales by PostalCode and Store Type" map visual. On the drop-down menu, click Show As A Table, as shown in Figure 3.19.

The visual will be displayed in Focus mode, and a table will now appear below the visual with the raw data that is used to make up the visual. Click the Back To Report button in the upper-left corner.

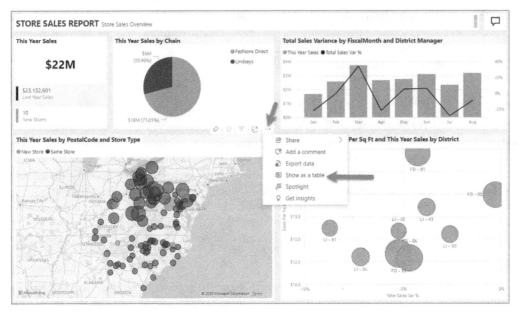

FIGURE 3.19: Using the Show As A Table feature

Sorting Visuals

The data displayed on visuals in a Power BI report can be sorted. By default, the report creator may have set a sort order, but the user can change this. This includes visuals such as tables, bar charts, and donut charts. Navigate back to the New Stores report page in our Store Sales report. The bottom half of this report uses a matrix visual, "Detailed Info." Matrices have columns and rows that each can be sorted. For example, in the column header of the "This Year Sales" visual, you can see a downward triangle. This button enables you to sort ascending or descending each time you click it.

But it's possible to change other aspects of sorting. Let's change the sort order of the first column, which is organized by ("grouped by") Chain ⇨ Store Name ⇨ Buyer. Currently it's sorted descending by highest actual sales. Click the ellipsis in the upper-right corner of the "Detailed Info" matrix visual. On the menu that pops up, click the Sort By menu item and then select Buyer. (see Figure 3.20).

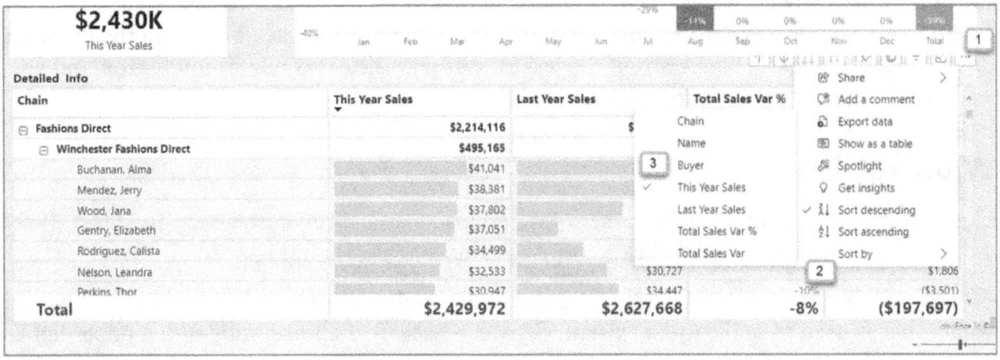

FIGURE 3.20: Steps to change sort order of visual

The first column still retains the grouping of Chain ⇨ Store ⇨ Buyer, but now the data in the columns is sorted by the last name of the buyer in descending order. On the More Options menu (the ellipsis), you can change Descending to Ascending. Changing the sort behavior for the visual in this way may be one particular way of looking for a specific person. Or, if you were looking for a certain store, you might have sorted by name (the store name). Speaking of stores, before we wrap up this section, let's look at yet one more way to create an explicit filter.

Filtering—One More Time

Let's imagine you're using this report as a report consumer and interested in looking only at the Winchester Fashions Direct store and want to quickly filter everything else out. Since the report creator did not put a Store Name slicer on your report, you can't filter that way. You could select the "Detailed Info" matrix, open the Filters pane, and manually specify a filter on the Name field. But there is one more way that is even quicker.

First, let's reset the report so that it is filtered just like the report creator intended. Do this by clicking the Reset Filters button in the upper-right corner.

Your report view should now have Winchester Fashions Direct at the top of the list since their sales were the highest. Right-click Winchester Fashions Direct and click Include (see Figure 3.21).

Now, if you scroll to the bottom of the matrix, you'll notice that there are no other chains or stores listed. This is because you just filtered that visual down to just Winchester Fashions Direct. You can confirm this by opening the Filters pane and observing that a new Included filter exists.

You might have noticed the Exclude option on the right-click menu. Reset the report and then play with the Exclude filter to see what that might do! I bet you can guess by now.

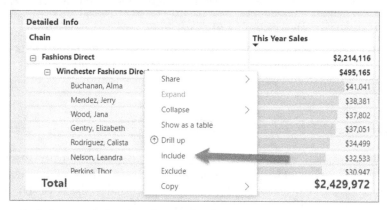

FIGURE 3.21: How to include or exclude values from a visual

POWER BI BUILDING BLOCKS

Click the My Workspace link on the lower-left corner of the page. You should now see three types of content in your workspace: dashboards, reports, and datasets. We've covered reports and dashboards briefly in this chapter, but let's summarize them and introduce the dataset content.

➤ *Dashboards*—Dashboards display tiles that are based on visuals from reports. Dashboards keep users informed about what is most important to them about their business. They are created in the Power BI Service. Each tile in a dashboard can be selected to explore the underlying report. Users can create their own dashboards allowing them to tailor their displays to their most important items.

> **NOTE** *Visuals from reports can display on multiple dashboards, but dashboards can be associated with only a single workspace.*

➤ *Reports*—Reports contain datasets and visuals that portray the data in those datasets. Reports can be developed on the Power BI Service but are usually developed in Power BI Desktop and then published to the service.

➤ *Datasets*—A dataset is a compilation of data from a specified source. Users make connections to a data source and import its data into a dataset. The dataset can then be used for reporting. Power BI can connect to the following:

  ➤ Data on-premises or in the cloud.

  ➤ Files, such as Excel, CSV, and SQL.

  ➤ Content packs from external services, such as Salesforce, obtained with an existing subscription to that application. Power BI has prebuilt dashboards and reports for such applications.

  ➤ Databases, such as Azure SQL Database, SQL Server Database, Oracle, DB2, MySQL.

  ➤ Other datasets, such as those from SQL Server Analysis Services.

Well, we have seen *a lot* on our flyover of the Power BI Service. At this point you're probably asking yourself, "How did they make those reports and datasets?" The answer is that they started with Power BI Desktop. So, let's continue our flyover but do a quick tour of Power BI Desktop!

FLYOVER OF POWER BI DESKTOP

In Chapter 1, "Introducing Power BI," I provided you with instructions on how to get Power BI Desktop installed on your computer. If you skipped over that step, you'll want to go back to Chapter 1 and walk through the install now. After you have installed the software, start Power BI Desktop by clicking the Windows Start key or by using the built-in search field on the desktop. When you open Power BI for the first time, you will be presented with a splash screen. You can sign in with your Power BI credentials associated with your Power BI subscription that we discussed at the beginning of this chapter. You can do this either by clicking the Get Started button in the center of the splash screen or by closing the splash screen and clicking the Sign In link in the upper-right corner of the window. Alternatively, if you haven't signed up for a subscription yet, you can just click the X in the upper-right corner of the splash screen.

If you do attempt to sign in, remember that the Power BI credentials are your organizational credentials and not your personal email address.

After you sign in or cancel the splash window, you will be presented with the Power BI Desktop editor. To wrap up this chapter, let's simply navigate through the interface, and in Chapter 4, we'll finally walk through how to create your first reports.

Navigating Power BI Desktop

There are nine areas I want to introduce you to here. The following numbers correspond to the numbered annotations in Figure 3.22.

> **NOTE** Since originally creating Figure 3.22, Microsoft has modified the desktop toolbar buttons to dynamically hide the captions depending upon the size of your window. At the time of writing, the icons were the same, but some of the captions have been changed or removed.

1. The Views toolbar is the gray bar on the left side of the screen with three icons. The first icon is for the Report view and is the default view. When you open Power BI Desktop, this is the view you will be taken to. The second icon is for the Data view, which provides an area to look at each table of data if you have imported it into your model. The last icon is for the Model view, where you are able to see graphically how the tables in your model relate to each other.

FIGURE 3.22: Power BI Desktop feature areas

2.   The *Menu ribbon* is structured very much like the ribbons in Microsoft Office products such as Word or Excel. Each ribbon is displayed with a tab. We will cover most of these buttons over the course of the next several chapters. We won't cover every button on these ribbons because some of them allow you to do more advanced tasks not covered in this book. Some we won't cover simply because they don't exist at the time of this writing, but because Microsoft releases an update (as mentioned in Chapter 1) every month, new buttons may be added.

3.   We talked about the *Filter pane* earlier in the chapter. It is nearly identical to the Filter pane as you used it in the Power BI Service. The difference here is that this is where you'll be able to control whether a filter is visible or invisible, locked or unlocked, and tied to a visual, page, or report.

4.   The *Visualizations pane* is your palette of options for adding visuals to your reports. There are many here that you'll find very useful and some that are for very specific needs and should be used judiciously with regard to your report consumers' experience. You can also import other visuals that you or others have created by clicking the ellipsis.

5.   The *Fields pane* shows you a list of each table in your model as well as each column and calculation (aka measures) in the tables. You will use this area to connect specific fields to the visuals you have selected to be displayed on your report.

6.   The *Values pane* is dynamic based on what visual you have selected in your report. If you have selected a bar chart visual, then the Values pane will display properties such as axis and legend properties. If you have a table visual selected, you'll be able to drop fields from the Fields pane into the columns of your table.

7.   The *report canvas* is the blank white area in the center of your screen. This is where you make all the magic happen. This is where you bring together all your hard work of importing, preparing, and modeling to then visualize your data into information in such an awesome way that your end users begin to have new insights!

8.   The bottom of the screen shows the *Pages tabs*. As you learned earlier, every report can have multiple pages. Each page gets named here on these tabs and is displayed on the left side in the Power BI Service once you publish your report.

9.   The bottom-right corner has a handy Zoom slider that allows you to quickly zoom or fit the content to your page. You can also use the mouse scroll wheel to use this Zoom slider or use two fingers on a trackpad on your laptop.

The final area that you will use all the time is not readily apparent until you have a visual dropped onto the report canvas. Once you have a visual on the canvas and the visual is selected, the Visualizations pane and Values pane will have a Format Visual button (displayed in Figure 3.23) that will take you to the *Formatting pane*.

FIGURE 3.23: Format button for every visual

The formatting pane gives you fine-grained control over every detail of how you *visualize* your information. In the example image on this page, you can see that we have complete formatting control over every area of this bar chart.

If you are somewhat familiar with using the properties of charts in Excel or images or textboxes embedded in Word documents, you will find similar formatting capabilities as well as many more here for every visual.

CONCLUSION

We have covered a ton of ground in these two flyovers. We've walked through the basics of getting started with a Power BI subscription. We introduced the concepts of importing sample data and reports. We learned the difference between a report, dashboard, and dataset. We saw Power BI reports in action with all their filtering, highlighting, and interactivity goodness. And then we started a quick introduction to using Power BI Desktop. *Now* you're ready to start building a report yourself using Power BI Desktop!

Building Your First Report

Following a consistent, proven method is the second guiding principle we talked about in Chapter 2, "From Data to Insight." In that method, the first steps were to import, prepare, and model your data. In this chapter, we're going to skip those first three steps because someone has already done that work for us! By importing those sample reports in Chapter 3, "Let's Take a Flyover!," we took advantage of two datasets that have already imported, prepared, and modeled the data. In Chapter 5, "Preparing Data," we'll dive deeper into those import and prepare steps. And in Chapter 6, "Modeling," we'll learn about a method for modeling data.

Most Power BI introduction materials I've read start individuals with using Power BI Desktop first. This leads you down a path that takes some time until you really see what is possible in the Power BI Service. It also means that when you build your first report, you're not working with a well-thought-out data model. But in Chapter 3, I wanted to flip that approach and start with the Power BI Service so that you can see where we're headed. You were able to build a report working with a typical data model that has multiple tables and measures already created. Now we're ready to use Power BI Desktop! In this chapter, we can utilize that data model in the service from Chapter 3. But enough talk. Let's get going!

CONNECTING TO A DATA SOURCE

Let's begin by opening Power BI Desktop. After the app opens, click the Get Data button on the Home ribbon bar.

The Get Data window gives you a way to see all the different options Power BI provides for connecting to data sources. Power BI provides many data sources as we saw earlier. For now, we're going to connect to a published dataset, which we indirectly published by importing the sample report in Chapter 3.

The Power Platform category of data sources allows you to connect to four different kinds of sources available in Microsoft's Power Platform: datasets, dataflows, and datamarts (all of which are created in Power BI), and the Dataverse (a way to store and manage data used by business applications like Power Apps or Dynamics 365). For now, click Power BI Datasets.

When you select Power BI Datasets, a window opens called the *Data hub*, as shown in Figure 4.1. The Power BI Data hub allows you to see datasets you have published or datasets that you have permission to see within your organization. Select the Store Sales dataset and click the Connect button in the lower-right corner.

FIGURE 4.1: The Data hub

Next time you need to create a report that uses a published dataset, you can quickly jump to the same spot another way. Two buttons to the right of the Get Data button is the Data Hub button, which bypasses the first Get Data screen and goes right to the Data hub screen.

If you're connecting to a dataset you've not used before, then you need to familiarize yourself with its *data model*. We examined a report in the previous chapter built on this data, but we really didn't dig into how the data is organized. Let's do that now!

EXAMINING THE DATA MODEL

The first thing you should notice after connecting to a Power BI dataset is the Data pane on the far right (see Figure 4.2). (In previous versions, this was labeled "Fields," so don't panic if yours says *Fields* instead of *Data*.) The Data pane shows you what tables of data are available in the data model. The term *data model* refers to how the data in your dataset is organized and how the different parts (such as tables) relate to each other. There are ways to define data models well, and we'll dig into that in Chapter 6, "Modeling." The Data pane allows you to navigate through the data model to use it while building your reports.

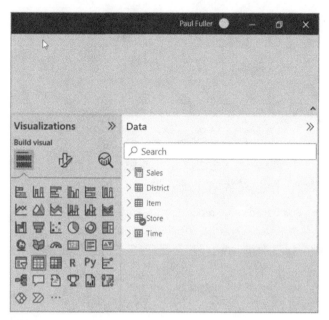

FIGURE 4.2: The Data pane

On the far left, you'll see that the Views toolbar has only two buttons. At the end of Chapter 3, when we surveyed Power BI Desktop, it had three: the Report view, Data view, and Model view. The reason that you see only two buttons now is because you are connected to a dataset that resides *outside* of your report. In Chapter 5, when we learn how to import and prepare data, we will be constructing the dataset and its accompanying data model *within* your report. We'll dig deeper into what this means for you in the bigger picture in later chapters. For now, just understand that when you are connected to an external dataset, you are not able to use the Data view where you can see the data in rows within their tables (see Figure 4.3).

After first observing the list of tables displayed in the Data pane, I then want to know how the tables are related to each other and get a big-picture view of the model. To do this, click the Model View button on the Views toolbar on the far left.

The Model view will graphically display all the tables in the data model as separate objects and how those tables relate to each other by interconnecting lines, as shown in Figure 4.4.

If your Model view opens up like mine did in Figure 4.4, the entire data model is not visible. The Data pane and the Properties pane can be collapsed by clicking the arrows in the upper-right corner of each. After you collapse those panes, you can also zoom out to see more of the data model by using the zoom controller in the lower-right corner.

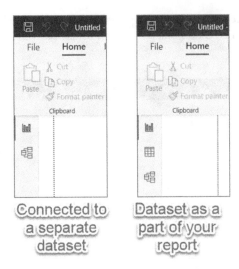

FIGURE 4.3: Datasets within and outside your report

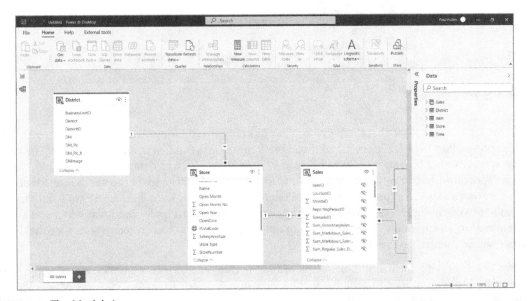

FIGURE 4.4: The Model view

In Figure 4.5 you'll see the entire data model in one glance. If your view looks different than what is shown, it may be because the tables have been positioned on the screen differently. In the Model view, you are able to reposition the tables however you'd like by clicking and dragging on the headers of each table (the top area where the table is named). You are able to control how large each table representation is by selecting the table and grabbing a side or corner and adjusting to your preference.

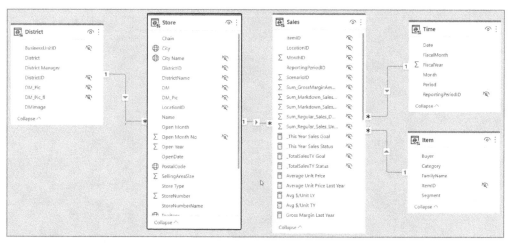

FIGURE 4.5: The entire data model in one glance

Even without having insider knowledge of where this data came from and how it is organized in the source where it came from, we can easily understand what this data model is representing: *sales* of *items* at *stores* within specific *districts* at certain points in *time*. As you can see, a well-designed data model can tell you much without that background in the business. A well-designed data model does require more than simply good naming conventions, but naming is key! Another good example of important naming is in the details of each table. In looking at this model, the columns/fields in the tables are named in a straightforward manner, not cryptically. You may have deep familiarity with the data that comes out of your own business systems. You probably have acronyms and abbreviations that are familiar to you and would make sense to you in a data model. However, you should never assume that only individuals deeply familiar with your organization who know the jargon and the naming conventions will be the ones interacting with your data model. What will Jane do in her first week on the job using your data model? She'll be confused and will be asking you many questions if your data model doesn't use good naming practices.

Let's take a look at what some of these icons mean on the tables represented in this data model shown in Figure 4.6.

1. The icon in the upper-left corner of each table tells you about where the data for this table is located. In our example, the icon shows a globe with arrows pointing up and down. This indicates that the table is not located within a dataset *imported into your report* but is using a *live connection* to a table in a dataset *outside* of your report. There are two other icons that you may run into: .

   The first icon indicates that the data is *imported* into your report and stored within the report as a dataset. The second icon indicates that the data is *not* imported into your report but is directly queried from the source *as the report is used*. In Chapter 5 we'll go into more detail about what those different modes of connecting mean.

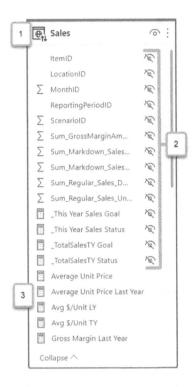

FIGURE 4.6: Meaning of icons

2. Many of the fields in the Sales table have an icon to the right of each field name that looks like an eye with a line across it. This means that the author of the dataset does not want those fields to be visible in the Data pane when building your visualizations. This feature is called controlling *visibility*.

3. Many of the fields in the Sales table have an icon to the left of each field name that looks like a calculator. This icon indicates that the field is *not* an actual field or column in the table but instead is a DAX measure. As we mentioned in an earlier chapter, DAX is the language used to create formulas for calculating. A field with a calculator icon is referred to as a *measure*. It does not represent data stored in the table.

Let's select the Store table and look at a few more details:

➤ The globe icon to the left of the PostalCode field indicates that the *category* of the data in this field is geographical. (This is different from the *type* of data. The type of data indicates how the data is stored such as text or numbers. We'll learn more about data types in Chapter 5.) When a field is marked with a category, Power BI knows how it should treat that field's values when used in a visualization. The specific categorizations that are available at the time of this writing are address, city, continent, country/region, county, latitude, longitude, place, postal code, state or province, web URL, image URL, and barcode.

➤ When a field has a sigma (Σ) next to it, then you know at least two things: its data type is numeric, and it will automatically aggregate when placed in visuals. By aggregate, I mean that if you used this field in a table visual, it would appear to automatically sum up the values in the column where it was placed. When the sigma is present, this is called an *implicit measure*. You will learn later in this book how to create your own DAX measures. Until then, you'll rely on these implicit measures to do things such as summation, averaging, minimums, and maximums.

➤ The eye icon in the upper-right corner indicates that the whole table is visible. Like the visibility icon for the fields, if you click the visibility icon for the table, it will cross out the icon telling you that this whole table will not be visible in the Data pane when creating the report.

Now let's take a look at those lines connecting the different tables. Those lines indicate *relationships* between the tables. If there is a line between two tables, it means that in some way those tables have a meaningful association to each other. There are values in one table that correspond to the same value in the other table.

Think about the sample sales data. The Sales table will have a record for every single item sold on a particular date at a particular store. It would be possible to just pull all of the information about a sale into the same record. For example, see Table 4.1.

TABLE 4.1: Sales Table with Everything

STORE NAME	STORE CITY	SALE DATE	ITEM SKU	ITEM DESC	ITEM PRICE	SALE QTY	SALE TOTAL
Store A	Kalamazoo	12/24	XYZ	XYZ Descript.	93.34	4	345.36
Store B	Chicago	12/24	XYZ	XYZ Descript.	93.34	2	186.68
Store A	Kalamazoo	12/26	ABC	ABC Descript.	21.00	1	19.99
Store B	Chicago	12/26	XYZ	XYZ Descript.	93.34	1	93.34

While this table is helpful, notice that there is much repeated data, such as the Item Desc and Store City. In a database, it is a good idea to make things more efficient by not duplicating data. What is often done is to split this data up into multiple tables such as Store, Item, and Sales. If you did that, you would want to have a field that will identify each particular record of data. That identifying field is often called a *primary key*. If we create a table called Item, it would have a unique record identifier, maybe called ItemID. That ItemID field would be referred to as the *primary key*. Sometimes that is a new field that is just a unique value, maybe a numeric value. If we did that with the data in Table 4.1 that we made up, it might look like Tables 4.2 and 4.3.

TABLE 4.2: Sales Table with Item ID

STORE NAME	STORE CITY	SALE DATE	ITEMID	ITEM PRICE	SALE QTY	SALE TOTAL
Store A	Kalamazoo	12/24	3	93.34	4	345.36
Store B	Chicago	12/24	3	93.34	2	186.68
Store A	Kalamazoo	12/26	2	21.00	1	19.99
Store B	Chicago	12/26	3	93.34	1	93.34

TABLE 4.3: Item Table

ITEMID	ITEM SKU	ITEM DESCRIPTION	ITEM PRICE
3	XYZ	XYZ Description	93.34
2	ABC	ABC Description	21.00

Notice that in the Sales table, we have an ItemID column that has values *referring* to a row in the Item table. The ItemID in the Sales table is considered a *foreign key*. We say that these tables are logically related to each other by the design of the tables and through the values that were placed in those related fields.

In Power BI, we tell our dataset that there actually is a relationship between those tables by defining the relationship with those interconnected lines. Notice in Figure 4.7 that the ItemID field is how the Sales table is related to the Item table in the dataset we've connected to. (When you click a relationship line between two tables, it will highlight the field that ties the two tables together.)

Let's look a little more at these relationship lines. In Figure 4.8, notice the three annotations.

1. Next to the Item table there is a small 1 displayed where the relationship line connects. This means on the Item side of the relationship there is only one record in the Item table for one particular ItemID value. In other words, you will *not* find two or more records that have an ItemID value of 2 in the Item table.

2. Next to the Sales table there is an asterisk where the relationship line connects. This is shorthand notation for indicating a "many" side of the relationship. That means that while there is only one record for a particular ItemID in the Item table, there can be many Sales records that refer to that Item record. Maybe this sounds confusing, but it's as simple as this: an item is defined only once in the Item table, while there can be many sales that occurred for that item.

3. The little arrow on the relationship line pointing toward the Sales table tells us something about the filtering capabilities you saw in Chapter 3. If the arrow points in only one direction, then that means that filtering will flow in only one direction, from one table to the table the arrow points to. We'll cover more about how filtering works with the relationships in Chapter 7, "Relationships and Filtering."

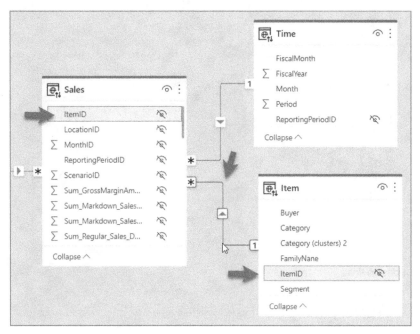

FIGURE 4.7: The relationship displayed between two tables

Let's look at one more thing in exploring the data before we start playing with the data. In Figure 4.9, the left side shows what the Sales table looks like from the Model view perspective, and the right side shows what the Sales table looks like in the Report view. Only fields and measures made visible show up in the Report view.

EXPLORING THE DATA

Now that we have explored the data model to understand how things are organized, let's take a look at the data itself so that we are well prepared for creating our report. As I mentioned, when connected with a live connection to a Power BI dataset, you are not given the Data view—only the Report and Model views. So, to explore the data that is available in the dataset, we need to use a *Table visual*. Go back to the Report view and find in the Visualizations pane a button for the Table visual. Figure 4.10 points out which is the Table visual.

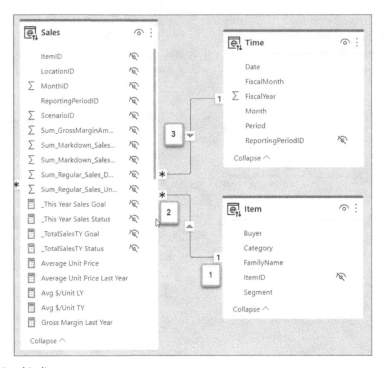

FIGURE 4.8: Relationship lines

FIGURE 4.9: Comparison of Model view and Report view

FIGURE 4.10: Selecting the Table visual

Click that Table visual button, and it will create a placeholder on the report canvas for a table, as shown in Figure 4.11.

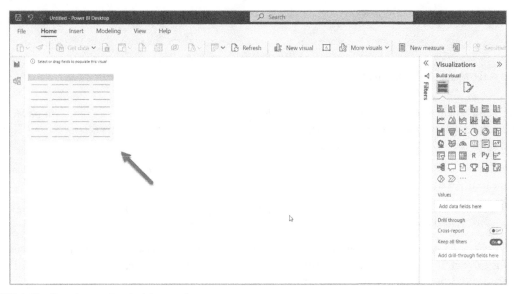

FIGURE 4.11: Creating a placeholder on the report canvas

There are three things to point out about the Table visual that was placed on your report canvas (see Figure 4.12):

1.   When a Table visual or *any* visual is selected, there are anchors on the corners and sides, which you can use to resize the visual to your needs.

2. Options available for viewing a visual will always have this ellipsis and some other icons available depending on the visual. These options may be displayed above or below the visual depending on the space surrounding the visual.

3. To add fields to the table, you can either drag the fields to the visual or select them as we'll see in a minute.

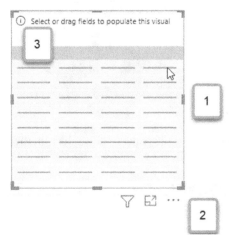

FIGURE 4.12: Manipulating the Table visual

Let's add a field from the Store table to our table. You can find the Store table in the Data pane; open it by clicking the down arrow next to the table name, and find the StoreNumberName field. Click and hold the StoreNumberName field to drag it to the Columns area under the Visualizations pane.

This is just one way of adding a field to a visual. You can also drag the field directly to the visual you want to use it on.

One more, and probably the simplest, way to add a field to a visual is to click the check box next to the field name. This method will add the field to the visual selected on the report canvas.

In Figure 4.13, several fields from the Store table have been added. Go ahead and add those same fields to your Table visual on your report canvas. (Add Chain, City, Name, Open Month, Postal Code, Story Type, StoreNumberName, and Territory.)

Take some time to familiarize yourself with the kind of data you see in this table now. Each row describes a single store. Some fields in the row appear to be just for display capabilities. For example, the first field, StoreNumberName, and the second field we added, Name, are the same but combine Name with StoreNumber. You could add StoreNumber on its own as a field, but the StoreNumberName field makes it possible to combine those values into a single field.

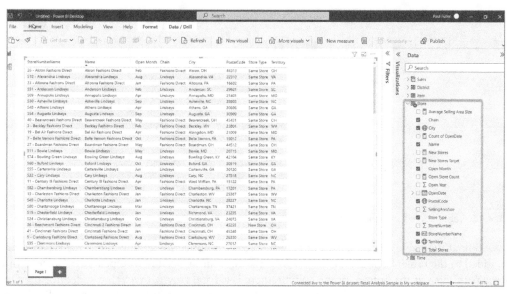

FIGURE 4.13: Fields added to the Store table

Along the top of the Table visual, you'll see the field names. When you start placing fields onto the Table visual, the data in the table will be sorted by the first field you added. However, you can change which field controls the sorting. In each column header, under the field name there is a little arrow pointing up or down *when you hover over the column*. In Figure 4.14, the table is sorted by the StoreNumberName field, but if we click the Store Type column header, you will see the data in Figure 4.15 is now sorted by that column.

StoreNumberName	Name
26 - Akron Fashions Direct	Akron Fashions Direct
518 - Alexandria Lindseys	Alexandria Lindseys
33 - Altoona Fashions Direct	Altoona Fashions Direct
551 - Anderson Lindseys	Anderson Lindseys
509 - Annapolis Lindseys	Annapolis Lindseys
530 - Asheville Lindseys	Asheville Lindseys
548 - Athens Lindseys	Athens Lindseys
554 - Augusta Lindseys	Augusta Lindseys

FIGURE 4.14: Table sorted by StoreNumberName

Let's change which fields are displayed in the table. When you look at the Store table listed in the Data pane, you see check marks beside each field used in the Table visual. Uncheck PostalCode, StoreNumberName, and Territory. Add the Open Year field.

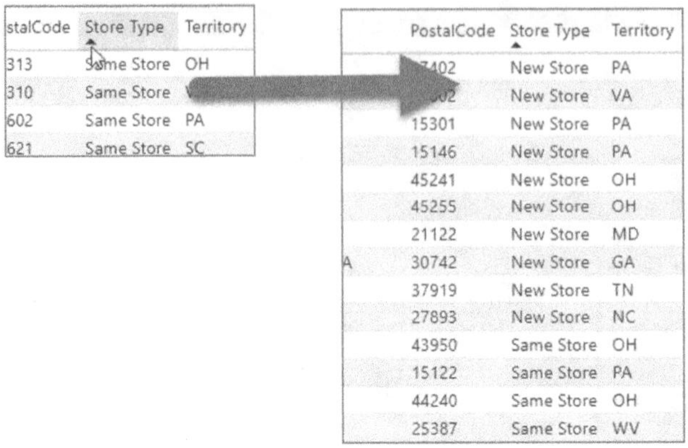

FIGURE 4.15: Table sorted by Store Type

Now look at the Table visual (shown in Figure 4.16) and notice something about the Open Year field we added to the table. For one, the header over the column says "Sum of Open Year" instead of just Open Year. Then at the bottom of the column there is a Total row with a value added for the Open Year column. This is happening because of what we referred to as *implicit measures* earlier in this chapter. Power BI assumes (unless you change the default behavior, which can be done in the Model view) that a numeric value will need to be aggregated when used on a visual. The default aggregate is to *sum* the values. This is why the column header says "Sum of Open Year." Many times, with numeric values, this is what we want to happen, but not with a year number value.

It is easy to turn off this behavior in our Table visual. Go to the Table properties underneath the Visualizations pane. Inside the Open Year field name in the Columns area, you'll see a small drop-down arrow. Click that drop-down arrow and choose Don't Summarize from the menu options. When you do that, you'll notice that the Total row disappears, and the title of the column changes to just "Open Year." Obviously, the implicit measure would be fantastic if we were dealing with a field like Sales Total.

Now, let's add the Open Date field from the Store table. This field tells us the date that the store opened. It'd be a safe presumption that the values in the Open Date field would be a *date value*, but when you add the Open Date field to the table, it adds four columns: Year, Quarter, Month, and Day (see Figure 4.17). All of those values relate to the open date itself but have broken the date value into a hierarchy of values ranging from the year to the day.

Let's say you wanted to just display the quarter in which the store was opened. To do that, navigate to the Open Date field in the Columns area and click the X next to Year, Month, and Day.

Removing those fields leaves us with a view that shows the open year and quarter in which the store opened (see Figure 4.18).

Name	Open Month	Chain	City	Store Type	Sum of Open Year
Akron Fashions Direct	Feb	Fashions Direct	Akron, OH	Same Store	2010
Alexandria Lindseys	Aug	Lindseys	Alexandria, VA	Same Store	2010
Altoona Fashions Direct	Jan	Fashions Direct	Altoona, PA	Same Store	2013
Anderson Lindseys	Feb	Lindseys	Anderson, SC	Same Store	2013
Annapolis Lindseys	Apr	Lindseys	Annapolis, MD	Same Store	2009
Asheville Lindseys	Sep	Lindseys	Asheville, NC	Same Store	2011
Athens Lindseys	Apr	Lindseys	Athens, GA	Same Store	2013
Augusta Lindseys	Sep	Lindseys	Augusta, GA	Same Store	2013
Beavercreek Fashions Direct	May	Fashions Direct	Beavercreek, OH	Same Store	2007
Beckley Fashions Direct	Feb	Fashions Direct	Beckley, WV	Same Store	2008
Bel Air Fashions Direct	Apr	Fashions Direct	Abingdon, MD	Same Store	2005
Belle Vernon Fashions Direct	Oct	Fashions Direct	Belle Vernon, PA	Same Store	2007
Boardman Fashions Direct	May	Fashions Direct	Boardman, OH	Same Store	2010
Bowie Lindseys	May	Lindseys	Bowie, MD	Same Store	2009
Bowling Green Lindseys	Aug	Lindseys	Bowling Green, KY	Same Store	2005
Buford Lindseys	Oct	Lindseys	Buford, GA	Same Store	2013
Cartersville Lindseys	Jun	Lindseys	Cartersville, GA	Same Store	2013
Cary Lindseys	Aug	Lindseys	Cary, NC	Same Store	2010
Century III Fashions Direct	Apr	Fashions Direct	West Mifflen, PA	Same Store	2011
Chambersburg Lindseys	Dec	Lindseys	Chambersburg, PA	Same Store	2008
Charleston Fashions Direct	Jan	Fashions Direct	Charleston, WV	Same Store	2013
Charlotte Lindseys	Jan	Lindseys	Charlotte, NC	Same Store	2013
Chattanooga Lindseys	Mar	Lindseys	Chattanooga, TN	Same Store	2006
Chesterfield Lindseys	Jan	Lindseys	Richmond, VA	Same Store	2009
Christiansburg Lindseys	Oct	Lindseys	Christiansburg, VA	Same Store	2010
Cincinnati 2 Fashions Direct	Jun	Fashions Direct	Cincinnati, OH	New Store	2014
Cincinnati Fashions Direct	Jan	Fashions Direct	Cincinnati, OH	Same Store	2011
Clarksburg Fashions Direct	Aug	Fashions Direct	Clarksburg, WV	Same Store	2009
Total					**209044**

FIGURE 4.16: Default aggregate is to sum the values

However, what if we really just wanted to display only the date value itself? In the Columns area, click the down arrow next to the OpenDate field. On the menu that pops up, click the OpenDate item just above the date hierarchy.

Once you change the way the date is displayed, you now see the date value you were probably expecting. However, you might not want the time value displayed. If this were a dataset we were building ourselves (as opposed to a live connection to a dataset), we could go to the Data view and change how our date field is formatted when the field is used.

Now let's add SellingAreaSize, a numeric field that will automatically aggregate as a sum. After you've added the field, click the down arrow next to the field in the Columns area and change the default aggregation to Average instead (see Figure 4.19).

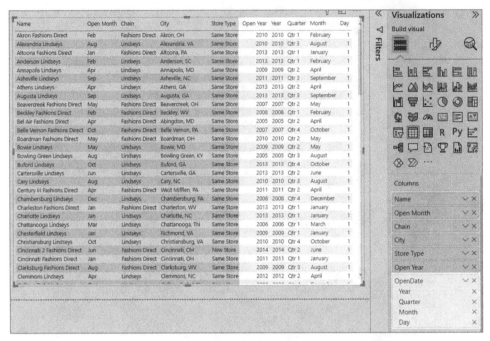

FIGURE 4.17: Four date values

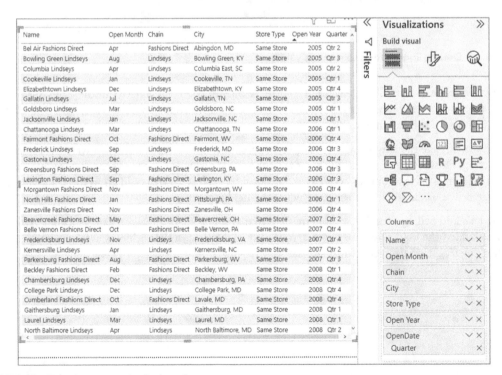

FIGURE 4.18: Only the quarter is displayed

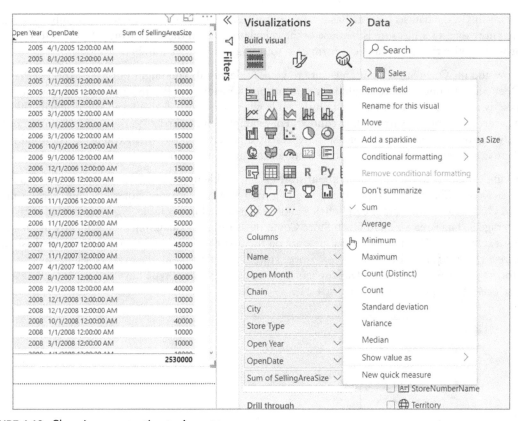

FIGURE 4.19: Changing aggregation to Average

After changing the implicit measure to average instead of sum, you will see that the Total row now shows the average value of SellingAreaSize across all the stores (see Figure 4.20).

	Average of SellingAreaSize
0:00 AM	50,000.00
0:00 AM	10,000.00
0:00 AM	10,000.00
0:00 AM	10,000.00
00:00 AM	10,000.00
0:00 AM	15,000.00
0:00 AM	10,000.00
0:00 AM	10,000.00
0:00 AM	15,000.00
00:00 AM	15,000.00
0:00 AM	10,000.00
00:00 AM	15,000.00
0:00 AM	55,000.00
	24,326.92

FIGURE 4.20: SellingAreaSize giving average value

Interestingly, the dataset already has a measure called Average Selling Area Size (remember, the reason we know that it's a measure is because of the calculator icon in the Data pane). Add that to your table as well. Notice that the measure is formatted to display as a whole number.

Now add the Open Store Count measure to your Table visual. You might not have expected that the Open Store Count measure would be a value of one for each row, but this measure is behaving exactly as it was designed. Each cell on the table where a measure is displayed will calculate the measure based on the surrounding context. For example, on the first row, the count of stores open is only one because there is only one store represented in that row. But when you get to the Total row, there is not one specific store in context, but all the stores are "visible."

To understand better what I mean about stores being visible in the Total row, remove fields from the table so that Chain, Store Type, Average Selling Area Size (the measure, not the SellingAreaSize field), and Open Store Count are the only fields and measures used in the table. Now notice that both the Average Selling Area Size and Open Store Count measures are calculating independently in each cell. For example, the Open Store Count measure on the first row is counting only stores in the Fashions Direct chain that are also of the "New Store" store type. In addition, the average selling area size of stores that are in the Fashions Direct chain and are the New Store type have an average selling area size of 45,833 square feet (see Figure 4.21).

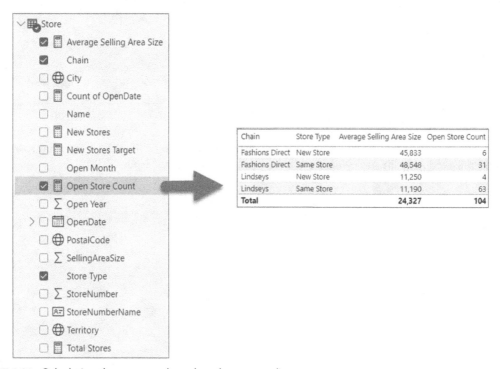

FIGURE 4.21: Calculating the measures based on the surrounding context

Now that we have taken a deeper dive into the dataset we have available and learned some cool things along the way, we're ready to build our first report.

BUILDING YOUR REPORT

In Chapter 3, you imported a sample report from Microsoft called Store Sales. During the process of writing this book, Microsoft updated that sample report to look the way you see it now. However, that sample data and report have been in place for several years, and until it was recently given a visual makeover, it was a fairly awful-looking report. Figure 4.22 is an image of that original report in all its loveliness (read sarcasm there!).

FIGURE 4.22: Earlier version of sample report

The report had some merit to it, but in general it was not a good demonstration of visual analytics. The new one is far better. And even though the new one is much better, we're going to build our own version of the report using the dataset provided.

Before we begin, make sure you've cleaned up your report canvas by deleting the Table visual we have been working with. You can delete it by selecting the visual and clicking the delete button on your keyboard. Or, you can click the ellipsis below the visual and select Remove from the menu.

You should now have a blank report canvas but still be connected to our Store Sales dataset. The way you'll know that you are still connected to the dataset is that the Data pane will still display the tables available to work with.

Let's begin by looking at some of the overall formatting options for your reports. In the Visualizations pane there are two icons visible. If you see three icons, then you still have a visual added to your report canvas, and it is selected. To access the overall report formatting options, you must have *no* visuals selected on the canvas (they can exist on the canvas; you just can't have them selected). When no controls are selected, the Format Your Report Page button appears, as demonstrated in Figure 4.23. Click that button to go to the formatting options.

FIGURE 4.23: The Format Your Report Page button

You can explore several options here. The Page Information area allows you to specify a name for the report page you're working on, control whether the whole page is used as a custom tooltip (`https://learn.microsoft.com/en-us/power-bi/create-reports/desktop-tooltips?tabs=powerbi-desktop`), and indicate whether the whole page should be considered for the Q&A (`https://learn.microsoft.com/en-us/power-bi/natural-language/q-and-a-intro`). The Canvas Settings allow you to set the report canvas ratio. Canvas Background allows you to control the look of the report canvas background. The Wallpaper allows you to control the look of the background behind the report canvas. The Filter Pane setting allows you to customize the look. Filter Cards allows you to control the look of the individual cards (each section) within the Filter pane.

To see the Wallpaper functionality in action, let's change the background color. Navigate to the Wallpaper section and select a color that you would like. I recommend the exciting, lovely White 10 percent Darker.

Next, let's put a title text in the top-left corner of the report canvas. To do this, click the Insert ribbon to the right of the Home ribbon.

On the Insert ribbon, you'll find a control with a capital letter *A* in it. This is the Text Box control. Click this control to add a text box to the report.

Inside the new text box on your report canvas, enter **Store Sales Overview,** as shown in Figure 4.24. As you can see, the Text Box control gives you the ability to control the appearance of the text similar to the capabilities you find in any text editor. Make sure that the Segoe UI Light font is selected.

Grab the anchors of the text box and resize it so that the text is in one line, as shown in Figure 4.25.

Now let's add a Card visual, as shown in Figure 4.26. A Card visual is used to display single metric values, prominently where your report consumers will see them first. It's a good practice to place these kinds of visuals across the top of your report where the eye will usually be drawn to first (see Figure 4.27).

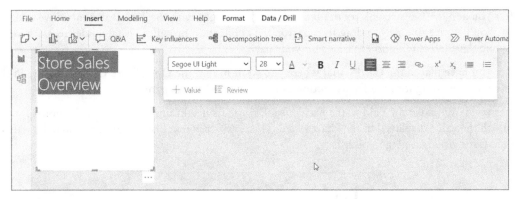

FIGURE 4.24: Adding text to a new text box

FIGURE 4.25: Resizing text in a text box

FIGURE 4.26: Selecting the Card visual

FIGURE 4.27: The Card visual in a prominent position

After you add the Card visual, try dragging it so that it aligns with the Text Box control we added first. You'll notice that as you drag the control, the application provides visual guides to assist you in aligning the control with other visuals on your page.

After you have placed the Card visual where you want it, find the Open Store Count measure in the Store table and drag it to the Fields section underneath the Visuals pane.

After you have added the field to the Card visual, resize its height until you see the caption appear beneath the value displayed in the Card visual. Then resize the text box we added to match the height of the Card visual (see Figure 4.28).

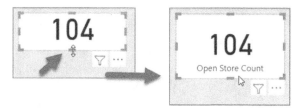

FIGURE 4.28: Resizing the text box

Once you've resized the text box, click the Format button on the Visualizations pane. For Callout Value, let's change the selected font to make sure that it uses the same font that the text box uses: Segoe UI Light (see Figure 4.29). You should always use fonts consistently across your reports.

FIGURE 4.29: Selecting the appropriate font

After you've changed the format of the actual value displayed in the Card visual, change the format of the caption displayed in the card. (Notice that you can also choose whether the caption is displayed using the toggle next to Category label.) Change the Category label so that it also uses the Segoe UI Light font (see Figure 4.30).

We're going to add a few more cards across the top. To make our lives easier, let's just copy the existing Card visual so that we can paste it. This will help ensure we are formatting each card the same way. You can copy the visual by using the ellipsis in the lower-right corner of the card. Or, when the visual is selected, there is a Copy button in the left section of the Home ribbon. The conventional Ctrl+C command works for copying as well.

FIGURE 4.30: Changing the caption font

Paste the copied visual by using the paste button in the Home ribbon or by pressing Ctrl+V. Now with the second card selected, drag the New Stores measure to the control right over the top of the Open Store Count field (see Figure 4.31).

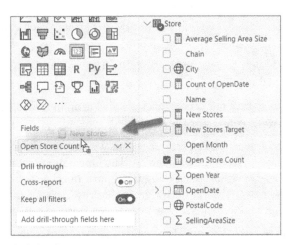

FIGURE 4.31: Pasting the copied visual

Now your report should look pretty similar to Figure 4.32.

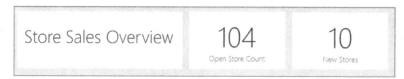

FIGURE 4.32: Report with the New Stores visual added

Now, repeat the same process of copying and pasting the card and add the New Stores Target measure to the third Card visual.

Finally, repeat the process one last time, but this time add the Sales Per Sq Ft measure *from the Sales table* (that is, not from the Stores table).

With your text box and four cards added, use your mouse to drag a selection box around all five visuals on the canvas (see Figure 4.33).

FIGURE 4.33: Selecting all five visuals

When all five controls are selected, you will see the anchors around each control displayed. Click the Format tab.

Click the Align menu and select Distribute Horizontally. This will make sure that the spacing in between each visual is equal.

Now is a great time for us to save our report (click the disk icon in the upper-left corner), because you'd really hate to lose work you've already completed!

Let's talk for a second about what you've created so far. We put four visuals on the screen that will display four different measures from the data model. The Open Store Count measure tells us the number of open stores that are visible when using the report. In other words, if you add a filter to the report, that will cause some stores to not be visible. In that case, this Open Store Count measure should respond to the filter and recalculate how many open stores are currently visible to Power BI.

The New Stores measure we added counts the number of stores within the visible set of stores that are also new stores, which also behaves dynamically. The New Stores Target measure tells you how many stores the organization wants to open this year. And the Sales Per Sq Ft measure calculates the average sales per square foot based on the set of stores visible.

But let's keep moving!

If you're like me, the font size on the text box bugs me because it's not proportionated to the text in the cards. I adjusted the font in my report to be point size 44 and took off the "Overview" text.

The original Store Sales sample report also had a pie chart on the main page, but it was less helpful as it did not convey the percentages of the distribution. At least in our current visual, those are displayed. However, in the current sample, you have to read a legend to the right of the chart to know what is being displayed. Stephen Few has a classic article on why he thinks pies are best left for dessert. We would all do well to learn from it (`www.perceptualedge.com/articles/visual_business_intelligence/save_the_pies_for_dessert.pdf`). Figure 4.34 is an example of how the previous chart used to appear. Notice that you can only guess about the percentage of the sales between the two. It might be almost 30 percent, but who knows? This may mean a world of difference if Lindsey's was shooting to hit 30 percent of the overall revenue this year. Did it make it or not?

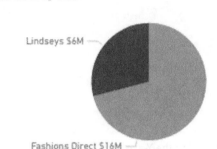

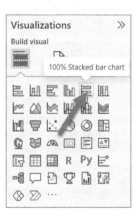

FIGURE 4.34: Original pie chart showing Lindsey's with an $ amount but not a percentage value.

Let's take an approach that will help the human brain more quickly digest the information and, in fact, be able to tell us information more precisely. Begin by adding a 100 percent Stacked bar chart to your report page, as shown in Figure 4.35.

FIGURE 4.35: Selecting a 100% Stacked bar chart

Next, while the visual is selected, notice that the properties of the visual under the Visualizations pane are completely different from the properties you saw when working with the Card visual. Now we have Y-axis, X-axis, Legend, Small multiples, and Tooltips properties. Every type of visual you work with in Power BI will have its own set of properties. There will be similarities and differences.

Open the Store table in the Data pane and add the Chain field to the Y-axis property of the visual, as shown in Figure 4.36.

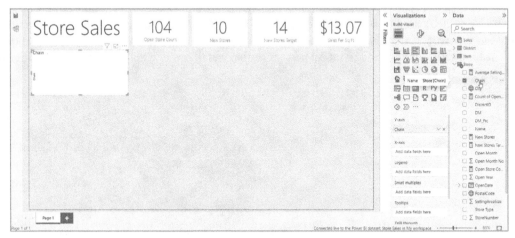

FIGURE 4.36: Adding the Chain field to the Y-axis property of the visual

As you might have noticed, all visuals have a set of properties related to the fields used from your data model and a set of properties related to formatting the appearance and behavior of the visual.

Make sure your new chart is selected and then click the Format visual icon underneath the Visualizations pane, as shown in Figure 4.37. Once you're viewing the formatting properties, you'll see that there are usually two groups of formatting properties: Visual and General. You'll find that the General properties available are similar across all visuals.

In our case, let's click in the General formatting properties and set the visual size and width to 304 and 618 pixels. Now, let's add a value from the "This Year Sales" KPI in the Sales table.

> **NOTE**
>
> The This Year Sales field in the Sales table appears different from any other field you've interacted with so far in Power BI. The icon appears as a line graph and under the field name are three subfields: Value, Goal, and Status. This conglomeration represents KPI functionality that is not available to create within a report using the Power BI Professional subscription level. This functionality is a feature built into Microsoft's Analysis Services platform and Power BI Premium. The reason we see it here is because the backend data source of this sample dataset came from an Analysis Services database. In the future, you might see the ability to create KPIs in your data model like you see here with just a Pro subscription. For more information on KPIs, see `https://learn.microsoft` `.com/en-us/analysis-services/tabular-models/kpis-ssas-` `tabular?view=asallproducts-allversions`.

FIGURE 4.37: Formatting the visual

Open the "This Year Sales" KPI and drag the Value field into the x-axis, as shown in Figure 4.38.

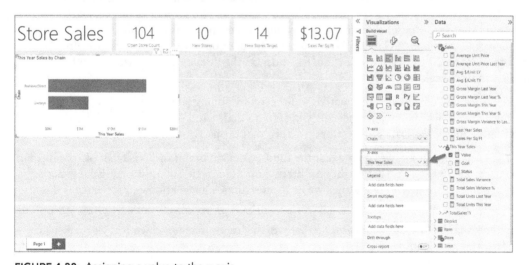

FIGURE 4.38: Assigning a value to the x-axis

By default, when you apply the field to the x-axis, it will display the value as calculated in the model. However, we want to show the value as a percentage of the overall total. To do that, click the down-arrow in the This Year Sales field inside the X-axis property. Select Show Value As and then select Percent Of Grand Total.

Now let's reduce the height of the control to 212 pixels. (You may wonder how I came up with that number! It was simply the size that I adjusted my visual to in order to proportionally fit all the visuals onto the screen. You technically don't need to set it to that value yourself, but make your report look almost identical to what we're building here in the book, I offer you this suggested height property.)

After you've set the height, find the Title property in the General area. Conveniently, Power BI builds titles for you based on the fields you've assigned to the properties. However, sometimes you'd like to have a different title. Set the title to **Percentage of Total Revenue This Year (by Chain)**, set the font size to 16, and change the font to Segoe UI Light to keep our font usage consistent.

Now your chart visual should look similar to Figure 4.39.

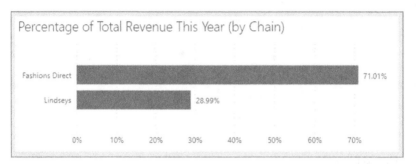

FIGURE 4.39: The titled visual

Now navigate to the field properties of the visual where you see Y-axis and X-axis. Each of those two properties have their own subset of properties. Notice that both axes have titles on them. Stephen Few points out that you want to eliminate as many unnecessary pixels as possible. In this case, putting the word *Chain* and *%GT This Year Sales* is redundant on our visual because we already identified the data in the title of the visual. So, let's turn off the title in each axis (the radio button next to Title should display "Off").

Let's make the visual immediately informative and precise by adding labels to the end of each bar so that we don't have to leave our consumers guessing. To do that, scroll to the bottom of the Visual properties until you see the Data Labels property. Turn that property on.

Now that you have done that, we can see that the Lindsey's chain is almost 30 percent of revenue, but not quite. It's at 28.99 percent. That might be a pretty important fact. And now our visual is both appealing and informative. With one glance we have more than a guess at how the revenue is distributed across the two chains.

Let's copy the visual like we did with cards so that we can create an almost identical visual to place side by side with our current visual.

Paste the copied visual and place it immediately to the right of the first bar chart, as shown in Figure 4.40.

Now rename the title of the visual to **Total Revenue This Year (by Chain)**. Remember, this Title property can be found under the Format Visual properties in the General group.

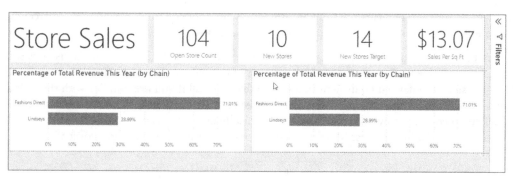

FIGURE 4.40: Pasting the copied visual

We *actually* want to use the *same* field we used before from the "This Year Sales" KPI, but instead of displaying the value as a percentage of the whole, we want to display the actual currency value. To do that, change the Show Value As setting back to No Calculation." (Remember to do this on the *new pasted visual*!)

Now let's proceed to looking at one of my favorite worst-visual-of-all-time examples! In the original Microsoft sample report, the visual displayed in Figure 4.41 was not just unpleasant to look at, but was very difficult to read and understand.

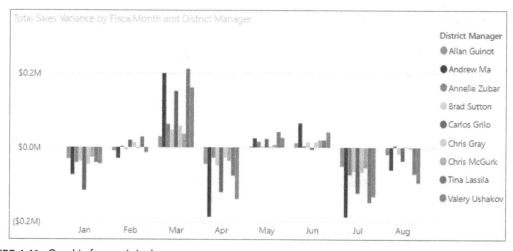

FIGURE 4.41: Graphic from original report

I stared at that visual for so long, and I still couldn't really determine what was going on. The only thing I could start to ascertain was that it seems like the sales totals are completely opposite from each other from month to month. After studying it more deeply, I discovered that this is in fact the pattern. I also realized that these values were showing dollar figures compared to the expected sales (maybe sales goals?) for each month. And with the legend, your brain is quite busy trying to determine what is what. You definitely would have to move your mouse around and explore the tooltips on this visual to determine *who* is having a good month and who is not!

So, I set out to try to replicate the same information with only one small variation: use percentages to indicate the size of the variance from the sales monthly plans.

To begin, I used a *Matrix* visual instead of a bar chart (see Figure 4.42). The Matrix visual is somewhat like the Table visual we used at the beginning of this chapter but is much more powerful. The Matrix visual is somewhat equivalent to a pivot table in Excel if you are familiar with those. It allows you to specify row values, column values, and measurements in the center. Then depending upon the values specified in the rows and columns, it dynamically grows to accommodate the data provided. So, go ahead and add your first Matrix visual to your report to the lower-right corner.

FIGURE 4.42: Selecting a Matrix visual

Your report is really starting to take shape! It should look similar to Figure 4.43.

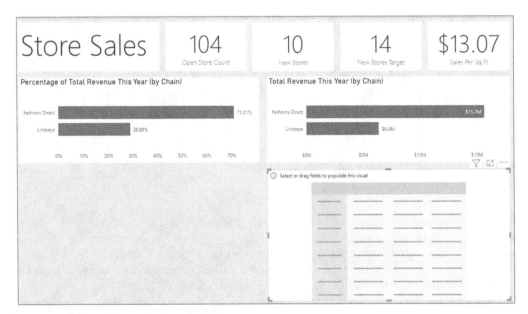

FIGURE 4.43: Adding a Matrix visual to the report

Just like on an Excel pivot table, you have to specify rows, columns, and values. Let's first add FiscalMonth from the Time table to the Columns property.

Next, add the DM field from the District table. The DM field stands for "district manager." Sometimes the fields in the dataset you're working with will not be named well, or at least named in a way that you want to present to the consumers. When a field needs to be renamed on a visual, you can click the down arrow to the right of the field name and select Rename For This Visual. Do that now and rename DM to **District Manager**.

Now let's add the Total Sales Variance percent measure from the Sales table to the Values property.

At this point, we now have a grid of the same content that the crazy rainbow visual earlier had except with percentages. However, at this point, our visual is also pretty useless because someone would have to comb through this data to determine what information is important. So, let's make it better.

You may want to show the subtotals across the bottom of the Matrix visual, but in case you don't, it is simple to remove them by simply toggling the On/Off buttons in the Column subtotals and Row subtotal options area.

To help our users make heads or tails of this data, let's add some conditional formatting to show a scale of red to blue, with very red being very negative and very blue being very positive, all relative to the whole set. Click the down arrow next to Total Sales Variance and go to the Conditional Formatting and Background Color settings (see Figure 4.44).

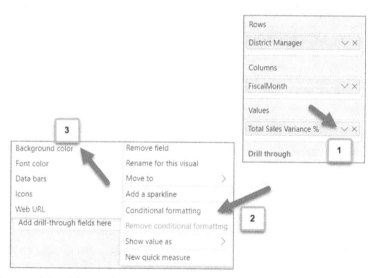

FIGURE 4.44: Adding conditional formatting

As you may notice in Figure 4.45, you have lots of options available when it comes to the behavior of conditionally formatting the background of the cells in the matrix. Configure the screen according to how it is presented in Figure 4.45. (If you're interested in knowing the exact colors I used, here are the details: #118DFF is the blue value, and #D64550 is the red value.)

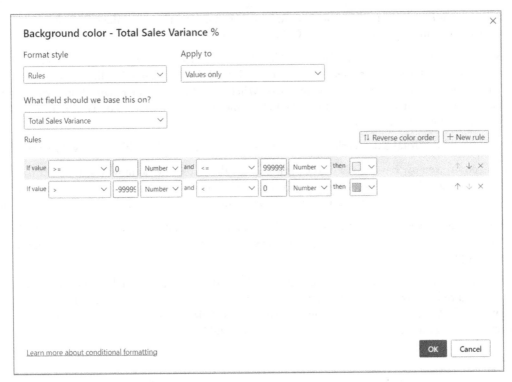

FIGURE 4.45: Conditional formatting for this example

Now let's add our last visual to our report: the Scatter chart (see Figure 4.46).

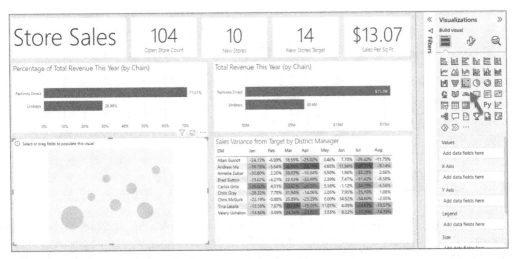

FIGURE 4.46: Scatter chart

The Scatter chart allows us to see a measure relative to x- and y-axes but also sized relative to other points on the chart. With the Scatter chart added to your report canvas, set the title (under the General formatting properties of the visual) to **District Sales Variance by Sales per Sq Ft**. Be sure to set the font size to 16 and use the Segoe UI Light font. After that, add the District field from the District table to the Values of the Visual properties. Then add the fields as displayed below in Figure 4.47.

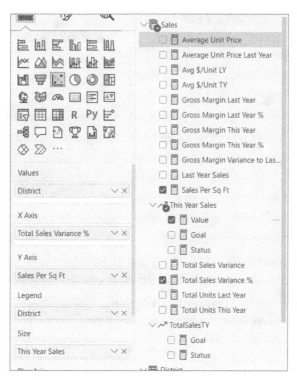

FIGURE 4.47: Scatter Plot fields added

Turn off the legend so that the visual is not cluttered.

Next, since we removed the legend, turn on the Category label so that users know exactly which bubble represents which district.

The Scatter chart represents the district sales variances for all stores, but we'd like to ignore the new stores for this report since we don't have the same concern for the new stores as we do on the existing stores. To do that, let's add a custom filter to the Scatter visual. With the visual selected, add Store Type from the Store table to Filters On This Visual.

Once you've added the Store Type filter, make sure that the Same Store value is the only one selected.

With that done, you have created your very first full-fledged report! Well done! If you've gotten stuck along the way, be sure to download the book resources file and look for the `c04report01.pbix` file (see the preface for details on how to download resources). This will have a working copy of the report as you see it displayed in Figure 4.48.

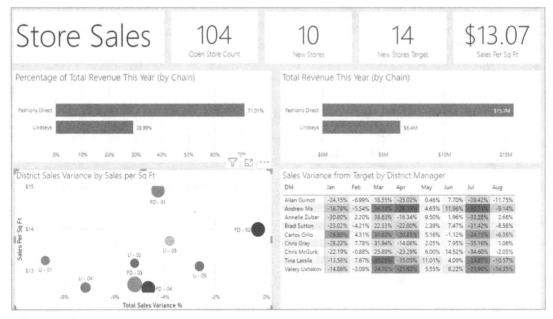

FIGURE 4.48: Completed report

After doing all that, we need to take the next big step of publishing your report to the Power BI Service! On the Home ribbon, click the Publish tab at far-right end of the ribbon.

The Publish To Power BI window that pops up asks you to pick a particular workspace to publish your report. If you have never created a workspace and if you're not a part of an organization that uses Power BI (or hasn't granted you access to any workspaces yet), you might just see the default My Workspace. That's OK! Let's publish to My Workspace.

After Power BI Desktop successfully publishes your report, you'll receive a confirmation message like that shown in Figure 4.49.

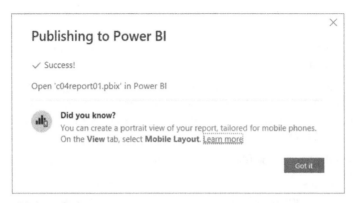

FIGURE 4.49: Report publish confirmation

If you'd like to explore your report in the Power BI Service, feel free to click the Open link that is in the success message that appeared. Once you're done exploring there, come back here, and we'll explore one more area: configuring your report to work with mobile devices.

DESIGNING FOR MOBILE DEVICES

Power BI allows you to take your existing report and create a separate view using the same visuals you created but arranged in a way that will display well on a mobile device. To begin, click the Mobile Layout button on the View tab.

The window that opens now has a report canvas but is configured for a vertical narrow layout as you would expect on a mobile device. On the right side of the window, you'll see the Page Visuals pane. This pane lists all the visuals you created when you built your report. You are free to use any or all the visuals, but you're not required to put them all onto the mobile layout. It's important to think about how a particular visual might be conducive to use on a mobile device before just dropping all the visuals onto the mobile layout.

In Figure 4.50, I dragged the report title Text Box onto the canvas and was able to modify the value. Changes you make to the mobile layout *do not* affect your report layout. You may even be given an informative message stating as much, like the one shown in Figure 4.51.

FIGURE 4.50: Modifying the canvas for mobile layout

Continue to pick which visuals you want on your mobile layout and add any formatting changes you'd like in order to make a presentation that appears to work well for a mobile device.

After you're done modifying the mobile layout, click the Mobile Layout button on the View tab to go back to the normal report view. Republish your report so that the mobile layout settings are applied to the Power BI published version. After you've republished, take some time to look in your Apple or Android app store on your mobile device to install Power BI as an app. Once you've installed the app, when you first open the app, you'll be able to log in. Log in with the same credentials you've been using when working with the Power BI Service. Once you are successfully logged in, you will be able to see the new report you've published, and it will be displayed automatically in your mobile layout version because Power BI will detect that you are working with a mobile device.

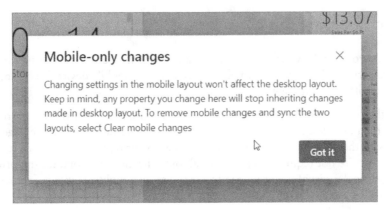

FIGURE 4.51: Note that mobile layout does not affect report layout.

CONCLUSION

I started this chapter talking about how we were able to jump over the *prepare data* and *model data* steps in our method because we would build the reports using a prebuilt Power BI Dataset. In fact, in some organizations, and possibly for some of the readers of this book, you will always be working with a prebuilt Power BI Dataset instead of preparing data and modeling data. That is often a situation I see with my clients and will possibly be your situation as a business user.[1] That means this chapter and the previous one should really launch you quickly into doing what you hoped you could get out of this book. If that describes you (that is, at your organization you'll be creating reports using a published dataset), then you may want to skip Chapters 5 and 6. You don't have to, but if you're hungry, feel free!

If, however, you're excited about learning all that you can about Power BI, then let's jump into learning how Power Query within Power BI helps us with preparing data.

---

[1] In Chapter 11, I discuss what is called *delivery strategy* and how that relates to whether you can prep and model data yourself as a business user or just use datasets prepared for you already.

5

Preparing Data

In Chapter 4, "Building Your First Report," you built a report using a prebuilt dataset. That helped us ramp up your Power BI skills quickly! However, as I mentioned in that chapter, the first step in our proven method is to prepare your data. In this chapter, we're going to dive into a tool built into Power BI Desktop that will help you prepare your data for your data model. *Power Query* is the go-to tool for you if the data you are bringing into your data model is not ready for analysis.

What do I mean by "not ready?" Oftentimes the data available to you either is organized in a way that isn't conducive to analysis or is messy. By messy, it may have all kinds of inconsistencies, especially if the data has been manually entered. There's an old phrase you might be familiar with: "garbage in, garbage out." That is what the *preparing* of data is all about. It's about making sure that what you're sending into your data model is clean, consistent, and clearly understood. By doing that you'll have a much better chance of turning your data into real insights.

In this chapter, we'll look at two different sources of real data that need some help before they can be useful to us in Power BI. (Frankly, they'd need some help even if you were going to use them in a tool like Excel.)

GDP DATA

The first source of data we'll look at is gross domestic product (GDP) data from the Bureau of Economic Analysis at the U.S. Department of Commerce. This data is updated on a monthly basis and is published on their website for public consumption (`https://bea.gov`). The GDP data is available at `https://tinyurl.com/gdp-22`. At that site, there is a Download button that will let you download the data into an Excel file. The benefit of using this page directly is that you can get up-to-date stats accumulated since the writing of this book. However, in my examples here, we will use this direct path: `https://tinyurl.com/gdp-22-xls`.

The GDP report is an interesting example for us to consider because it is just that—it's a report. In other words, it's not raw data that needs to be organized into a presentable format. In fact, it's aggregated by category, and this can present a problem.

In this report, data is summarized by categories, but then the categories are rolled up to parent categories (see Figure 5.1). This is great for presenting a summarized view instantly, but if we want to be able to just pick two of the categories and a specific set of years, you'd have to cut and paste the various pieces into a separate table.

This is the first kind of task we want to use Power Query for—to disassemble prebuilt reports to allow our report consumers to dynamically interact with the data.[1] This preparation task is about arranging data.

Line		2018	2019	2020	2021	2022
Line						
1	Gross domestic product	20,533,058	21,380,976	21,060,474	23,315,081	25,464,463
2	Personal consumption expenditures	13,904,979	14,392,721	14,116,166	15,902,575	17,360,373
3	Goods	4,355,177	4,473,510	4,670,135	5,496,516	5,939,558
4	Durable goods	1,470,687	1,510,543	1,646,793	2,060,246	2,184,666
5	Nondurable goods	2,884,490	2,962,967	3,023,342	3,436,270	3,754,892
6	Services	9,549,802	9,919,211	9,446,031	10,406,059	11,420,815
7	Gross private domestic investment	3,642,385	3,807,142	3,642,925	4,113,502	4,630,963
8	Fixed investment	3,583,297	3,734,353	3,698,748	4,132,592	4,471,993
9	Nonresidential	2,784,732	2,921,129	2,797,919	3,025,011	3,345,078
10	Structures	633,628	674,702	614,379	598,223	648,226
11	Equipment	1,193,238	1,209,842	1,077,831	1,194,044	1,322,508
12	Intellectual property products	957,866	1,036,586	1,105,709	1,232,744	1,374,344
13	Residential	798,565	813,224	900,829	1,107,582	1,126,915
14	Change in private inventories	59,088	72,789	-55,822	-19,091	158,970

FIGURE 5.1: GDP data summarized by categories

Let's begin by using the Get Data feature to connect to the Excel spreadsheet. Either use the Get Data button or go directly to the Excel Workbook button and enter this file location: `https://tinyurl.com/gdp-22-xls`.

After you've selected the Excel workbook you've downloaded, the Navigator window will open (see Figure 5.2). Select Table listed on the left. After you've selected Table, click the Transform Data button.

Upon clicking Transform Data, the Power Query tool will open. Let's get a quick overview of the Power Query interface.

---

[1]If you're excited about digging deeper into this economic data, all of the underlying detail *is* available such that you could build an entirely dynamic economic interactive data model: `https://apps.bea.gov/iTable/?isuri=1&reqid=19&step=4&categories=flatfiles&nipa_table_list=1`

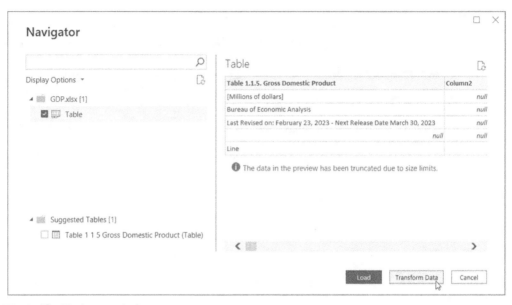

FIGURE 5.2: The Navigator window

Power Query Overview

In Figure 5.3, there are three areas I want to draw your attention to, aside from the center grid, which displays the data of the present query you are working on. *Queries* are individual units of code designed to perform a set of tasks against a set of data. What is amazing about Power Query is that you don't know that while you are using the tool, you actually *are writing code*! Every task that you'll add to a query creates a line of code behind the scenes. After you learn how to use Power Query as a tool, you might be interested in going deeper to learn how to work at the code layer where you can do even more than what you're able to do with the user interface. You are unlikely to run into many limitations with the user interface, however. If you're interested in seeing what the code looks like, at any time in the steps we walk through in this chapter, you can click the Advanced Editor button on the Home ribbon. The code that is being generated there is called M query language.

1. The left pane lists the queries that have been created in this file. Queries can be used just for getting data ready for other queries to use or can be used as the basis for the tables you'll use in your data model.

2. The ribbons along the top are categorized like this:

   ➤ The Home ribbon has tasks that will help you reduce or expand in different ways the number of rows in the currently selected query.

   ➤ The Transform ribbon has tasks for shaping and cleaning the data within the rows in the currently selected query.

   ➤ The Add Column ribbon has tasks for helping you add content to your query as new columns.

3. The Applied Steps pane lists the steps you've taken to prepare your data. Every action you take on the data is recorded here.

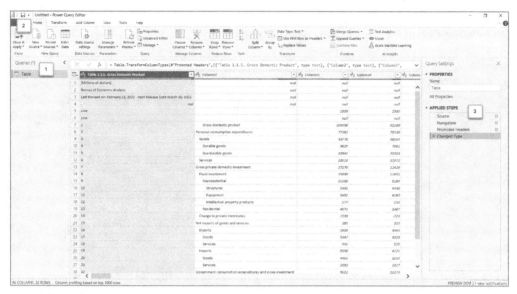

FIGURE 5.3: The Power Query tool

The magic of this tool can be illustrated if you have ever had to prepare a report from Excel data on a regular basis. To prepare the report, you probably have several steps of arranging, cleaning up, moving, and formatting data. You repeat those same steps every period, but just with different content. The thought might have even entered your mind at some time, "I wish I could just automate those tasks!" Well, that is exactly what Power Query will do for you. Think of the Applied Steps area as recording every step you do to transform or manipulate your data into the shape you want it to be for your analysis.

Data Arrangement Steps

The following steps will transform the GDP fixed report into four categories that can be independently sliced.

Rename Query

Queries each have their own name. In the Query Settings pane on the right, enter **GDP** in the Name field under Properties to change the rename the query from the default Table to GDP.

Remove Rows

If you know that you need to always remove a certain number of rows, you can click Remove Rows on the Home ribbon. As you can see, the Remove Rows button gives you several options for removing certain rows from a query. Remove Top Rows removes a specified number from the top. Remove Bottom Rows removes *x* number of rows from the bottom. Remove Alternate Rows asks for a first row number to remove, then the number of rows to remove, and finally the number of subsequent rows to keep. That pattern is repeated all the way through the query. Remove Duplicates will look for duplicate rows in the set and remove them. Remove Blank Rows will remove rows where every cell in the row is empty. Finally, Remove Errors will remove rows where error messages are displayed.

For our example, click Remove Top Rows, and let's remove the top four rows, since those are just information about the report.

Remove Columns

Sometimes the data you're working with has columns that are not useful, and you need to remove them. Sometimes there are lots of columns that you need to remove. Power Query gives you the ability to do this easily. Click the Remove Columns button on the Home ribbon.

There are two options under Remove Columns: Remove Columns and Remove Other Columns. The first will remove only the columns that you currently have selected. The second will remove all other columns that you have not selected. The latter is helpful for when you have many columns in your data that you want to remove but don't want to select them all manually. In that case, select the columns you want to keep and then use Remove Other Columns.

For our example, select just the first column, Table 1.1.5 Gross Domestic Product, and click Remove Columns. At this point, your environment should look something like Figure 5.4.

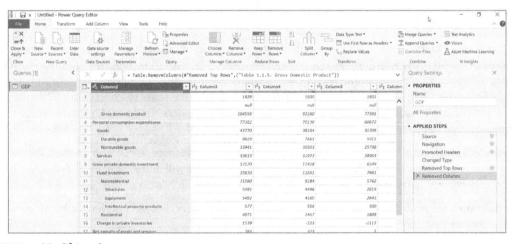

FIGURE 5.4: Modifying the query

Applied Steps So Far

Notice that in the Applied Steps pane, there are six steps already taken. You may be thinking, "I've done only two so far. Why are there six?" The first four happened automatically. The first step happens when you pick the file or source of data you want to connect to. That's why the first step is called "Source." The second step happened as we selected Table when we connected to the Excel workbook with multiple sheets and you had to pick which sheet to import. The step "Navigation" is specifying which worksheet to connect to. When you connect to other data sources that have multiple queries of content, you'll "navigate" to the one(s) you want to import. The third step happens automatically for most types of sources. Power Query assumes that the first row of the data specifies column names for each header in your query. It "promotes the header" row to be column names for your dataset. If the first row of your data *does not* have column names in it, you can always remove that step by clicking the X to the left of the Applied Step name.

And speaking of Applied Step names, a step can be renamed. Renaming the step to something less generic can be helpful when you know that there are going to be many steps involved. It will help you quickly navigate to where problems might be in your preparation steps. For our example, we won't be renaming the steps.

If you click each step in the Applied Steps pane, starting with "Source," you'll be able to watch how the data transforms through each saved step. As you click the fourth step, "Changed Type," you'll see the last automatic step that was taken when you connected to the Excel workbook. Power Query examined each column of data and attempted to identify the kind of data in each column. Before it did that, it interpreted each column as being simply a Text data type. When it looked at the data, it determined that all 96 columns except the first two columns were numeric data. So, it changed the data type from Text to Whole Number. If it detected decimal points or dates, it would have assigned the relevant type. Again, you can remove that Changed Type step if you need to. But in our example, let's leave it because it is exactly what we need: all of the columns except our first column should be whole numbers.

Promote Headers

While Power Query automatically made the first row of data in our spreadsheet be the column headers, that first row wasn't really our column headers since we had several rows of info. At this point in our data preparation, the real column headers are now our first in the query we're working with. This report has GDP values for several categories across the years starting with 1929 and going through 2022. We want those year values to be the column headers. To do that, we will repeat the same step that happened automatically when we opened the file.

Click the Transform ribbon and then click Use First Row As Headers. When you do that, Power Query will automatically try the data type detection again and will add a "Changed Type1" step. This is an unnecessary step for us, so remove that step by clicking the X next to the "Changed Type1" step.

At this point, we now have columns named for each year of data. But we also have a blank column name for our first column.

Renaming Columns

Oftentimes the column names in your data will be cryptic or technical. It is a best practice to name those columns to be very clear to your end users and useful for reporting purposes. For example, having spaces in between words is helpful.

Select the first column in our table, the one that has an empty header value, and right-click the column header. The pop-up menu has many options as you can see, but we are looking for the Rename menu item so that we can give the column a useful name. When you select Rename, the text cursor will appear in the column header and allow you to provide a value. Enter **GDP Category**.

Empty Values

At this point, our table has one row at the top that has empty values. The value in the first column is an empty value, and the values in all the other columns for the first row are *null*. It's outside the scope of this book to try to explain deeply the technical difference between *empty* (or referred to as *blank*) and *null*. When you get into that conversation, it begins to feel a little metaphysical! Alex Jankowski has a helpful blogpost that summarizes the difference.

> Two types of nuthin' in Power Query:
>
> 1. *null* is literally "no value" for any data type from text to table. In other words, the cell is completely empty.
>
> 2. A *blank* also looks like "no value", but it is equivalent to a cell formula of = " " in Excel. In other words, the cell holds a value that renders as blank.
>
> https://excelguru.ca/nuthin-aint-nuthin-in-power-query

Let's remove that first row that has both a blank cell (first column) and a bunch of nulls. To do this, go back to the Home ribbon and click Remove Blank Rows under the Remove Rows button. Note, this will remove any blank rows in the table, not just the top one you might be looking at. Our content has only one blank row, but if we had multiple blank rows in the set, they would all be removed by using the Remove Blank Rows command.

Handling Aggregated Data

Our next challenge is that this set of data has rows that are aggregated and some that are not. For example, our first row is all of the categories added together. The second row is the sum of rows 3 and 6. Row 3 is the sum of 4 and 5. If we want to slice and dice this data at different levels, we need to de-aggregate those values. That's a little more complex than we will get into in this chapter, but we will tackle that in Chapter 6, "Modeling Data." However, you should remember the following important principle:

To make our example simple for this chapter, let's reduce our data to just the topmost categories that make up gross domestic product: personal consumption expenditures, gross private domestic investment, net exports of goods and services, and government consumption expenditures and gross investment. In Chapter 6, we will include the lower levels of these categories.

> **CONCEPT** Bring the lowest, most reasonable level of detail data available into your model. Your report consumers will only be able to drill down as low as the level of detail you provide. In other words, aggregates cannot be de-aggregated unless you already provide the lower-level detail. This principle also applies to bringing in percentage values. Unless you also import a numerator or a denominator alongside the percentage value, you will be unable to aggregate those percentage values, aside from an average percentage.

Filtering Rows

To reduce our data to those four categories, we need to filter out certain content. We have already discovered that there are several options available to us when we right-click a column header. But you may also have noticed that to the right of each column header, there is a drop-down arrow (see Figure 5.5).

FIGURE 5.5: Drop-down arrows in the column header

Clicking that arrow gives you the ability to sort or filter data based on the content of that column. You can filter explicitly or dynamically using that menu. To filter explicitly, you can simply check or uncheck the values you want to retain or filter out in that column. This is one way we can reduce our current data down to the top four categories. However, let's look further at how we can dynamically filter those values out.

When you click the Text Filters menu that appears after you have clicked the drop-down arrow, you will see several dynamic filtering options available.

The Text Filters submenu provides you with the ability to filter the data to rows where the text equals a certain value or *does not* equal a certain value. Alternatively, you can filter by rows that start with a certain set of characters or that contain a certain set of characters. In our case, every row we want to get rid of starts with space values, because they indented the subcategories for the report users to know what is aggregated and what is not.

On the GDP Category column, click the drop-down arrow, and then under the Text Filters menu, click Does Not Begin With and enter a space value. Click OK. Now any row that begins with a space in that first column will be removed. Your data should now have only four rows left, as shown in Figure 5.6.

	GDP Category	1929	1930	1931
1	Personal consumption expenditures	77382	70136	60672
2	Gross private domestic investment	17170	11428	6549
3	Net exports of goods and services	383	323	1
4	Government consumption expenditures and gross investment	9622	10273	10169

FIGURE 5.6: Four remaining rows of data

Unpivoting Data

We're very close at this point to having something interesting and useful for analytical value in our Power BI reporting area. The next challenge we have is that every column in our table is just the year value. From a final report perspective, that would probably be OK, but it certainly locks us into what we can do. However, if our table had a row that had three columns, one for the category, one for the year, and one for the value itself, then we would be in a place where we could allow ad hoc analysis.

In Excel you may have faced this same situation or the opposite. You may have been trying to prepare a report and you had thousands of rows and needed those row values transformed into columns for your report users. To solve that, you would pivot the row values to be column values. It's essentially rotating the data. In our case, we want to do the opposite: we want to unpivot the data so that the columns are transformed into rows. Since this is a common task, you might imagine that Power Query would have this ability built in, and your assumption would be correct.

To unpivot the columns, you need to select the columns you want to unpivot. We have a ton of columns to select, and that would be a royal pain to do manually. To select all the columns quickly, press Ctrl+A on your keyboard. Once all the columns are selected, hold your Ctrl key and then unselect just the GDP Category column, the first column, by clicking it. While this is a fast way to select all columns quickly, with the Unpivot Columns button, you'll see that there is an even faster way to accomplish this. Select *just* the first column, the GDP Category column.

Click the Transform ribbon and click the small arrow on the Unpivot Columns button, as shown in Figure 5.7.

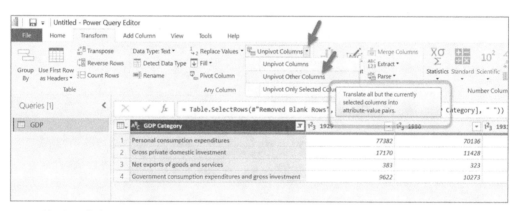

FIGURE 5.7: Unpivot Columns options

With just the first column selected, the Unpivot Columns feature allows us to unpivot *all other columns* that we do not have selected. (This is just like Remove Other Columns feature.) Notice the tooltip that appears as you hover over this option: "Translate all but the currently selected columns into attribute-value pairs." That is exactly what we want to do. We want to take each column header value (in our case, a year value) and pair that up with the value in the cell and then correlate that to the associated value on the first column that we have selected. Go ahead and click the Unpivot Other Columns menu item.

This action of unpivoting the columns resulted in creating 376 rows from our 4 rows! And this makes sense because there were 94 years of values (from 1929 to 2022) in our columns and there were 4 categories (4 × 94 =376). Now we have something very useful to work with!

Now, go ahead and rename the Attribute column to **Year**.

Change Column Data Type

We have just two more steps in preparing this data for reporting. The next step we want to take is to change the data type of the Year column to be numeric. You technically do not need to change the Year column to be numeric, but the advantage in doing so is now you can, for example, do calculations such as the number of years in between a set of years. This would be valuable when calculating change percentages between 5 years and 10 years, for example. This is something we will tackle in Chapter 12, "Introducing DAX."

To change the data type of a column, select the column (the Year column in our example), and select the Transform ribbon. On the Transform ribbon, there is a Data Type drop-down shown in Figure 5.8. Currently, the Year column is a Text data type. This will always be the case immediately after unpivoting columns. The unpivoted columns will be a Text data type.

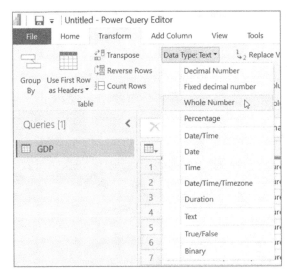

FIGURE 5.8: Selecting a data type

You'll notice in the list that the data types are categorized as numeric types, date and time types, text, true/false, and binary. Numeric types allow you to control the precision of calculations from whole numbers to specific kinds of decimal points. The date types allow you to have simple dates, date and time combinations, and even a Duration data type. A Duration data type indicates a length of time such as hours, minutes, or seconds.

In our case, we want to select Whole Number for the year value.

Changing Values in Columns

The last step we want to take in Power Query with this data is to change the GDP value itself to reflect what it actually is. The report is presenting the value in millions. In other words, if the value in the column is 1, then that actually means 1 million. To keep calculations clear for our users, we should convert that abbreviated value into the actual value. Thankfully, Power Query allows you to do any number of calculations on your data.

For example, given the specific value in each row in a column, you can perform any of the mathematical operations shown in Table 5.1.

TABLE 5.1: Mathematical Transformation Options

STANDARD	SCIENTIFIC	TRIGONOMETRY	ROUNDING	INFORMATIONAL
Add	Absolute Value	Sine	Round up	Is Even
Subtract	Square, Cube, or a specific Power	Cosine	Round down	Is Odd
Divide	Square Root	Tangent	Round to a digit	Sign
Integer-divide	Exponent	Arcsine		
Modulo (i.e., extract remainder)	Logarithms	Arccosine		
Percentage	Factorials	Arctangent		
Percentage of				

Duplicating Columns

If you want to retain the original value but duplicate the column and perform a mathematical option on that duplicated value, you can do this by selecting the column you want to duplicate. Then, select the Add Column ribbon and click the Duplicate Column. You can also quickly do this by right-clicking the column header that you want to duplicate and selecting the Duplicate Column menu item.

In addition, the Add Column ribbon repeats the same mathematical options. It will automatically duplicate the column and apply your math operations.

Multiply by a Million

In our example, select the Value column, and then on the Transform ribbon, select Standard ⇨ Multiply.

When the Multiply window opens, enter **1000000** to multiply each value in the Value column by one million.

Finally, change the data type of the Value column back to a Whole Number because when the unpivot happened, Power Query changed the data type to a decimal type.

Now, let's close Power Query and apply the changes that we created in preparing our data by selecting File ⇨ Close & Apply.

Next, we should save our work since we have yet to actually save this file! I named my file GDP.pbix, but feel free to name it whatever you would like. However, in future chapters we will be building off this example. So, if I refer in future chapters to GDP.pbix, this is the file you should use.

Your Data pane should now look like Figure 5.9 with a single table having three columns: GDP Category, Value, and Year.

FIGURE 5.9: The Data pane

Since we are not connected live to a dataset and we have our own dataset we are building, you now have a Data view in the left toolbar (in between the Report view button and Model view button). Click the Data view button because we have a couple of other data preparation steps we can perform outside of Power Query.

Removing Implicit Measures

In the Data pane, you should see a sigma (Σ) next to the Year column. As I mentioned in the previous chapter, that means this is an implicit measure. If we used the Year column on a Table visual, it will try to add up the Year values, which would be a little silly for us. So, let's make sure that we turn off that implicit measure on the Year column.

Select the Year column. With that column selected, click the drop-down in the Summarization area. Because we don't want any kind of aggregation to happen on the Year column, select Don't Summarize.

In other projects you'll work on, this step of removing the implicit measures is very important. In fact, once you learn the basics of DAX, you should remove all implicit measures, create the corresponding explicit measures you want for those columns, and finally hide the value columns themselves so that your users are exposed only to the explicit measures you create. But this will make more sense once you work with DAX in Chapter 10.

Column Formatting

If you recall, in our previous chapter there was a column that we wished we could format the value of so when it was used in any visual, it would always apply the same formatting. We couldn't do that because we did not have control over the dataset we were working with. Here, however, we have complete control. Formatting the columns is another essential step in preparing your data. It's easy to do but often overlooked.

For our example, we want the GDP values themselves to be formatted as U.S. dollar values: a currency value. Select the Value column.

Once the Value column is selected, click the dollar sign in the Formatting section of the Column Tools ribbon. You'll also notice that you can format numbers in other ways such as using percentages, setting whether to use commas, and setting the number of decimal places to display. The options you choose here control how your data will be displayed in visuals.

If the data type of the column in your table is a date type, the options in the Formatting drop-down will be options relating to date format (of which there are many!).

Calculated Columns

There is a full chapter at the end of this book on DAX. That chapter will get into the details of creating explicit measures. But before we delve into the details of DAX and measures, we're going to learn a little bit of DAX here as a way of showing another step of data preparation. In this section, I won't take the time to explain the DAX you'll be writing in detail but will simply introduce you to the concepts and what is possible, just within the data preparation.

To begin, you need to understand the primary difference between a *DAX measure* and a *calculated column*. Both things use the DAX language to perform calculations. The difference lies in *when* the calculation is performed. A DAX measure performs its calculations when the measure is used in a report. This is critical because a DAX measure responds dynamically to its surrounding context, which could be completely different depending on what filters your report consumers are utilizing and how they are slicing and dicing their data.

A calculated column performs its calculations at the time you refresh the dataset. It performs that calculation once per row, once per data refresh. The advantage to this is that the calculated value is stored in your table, and the time to perform the calculation is not seen by your report consumers since it performs the computation only when the data is refreshed. The disadvantage to this is that it is a one-time calculation that is strictly related to the row of data in the table it resides within. In other words, it is *not* dynamic like a DAX measure.

The concept of calculated columns relates to *preparing your data* because another one of the tasks you need to do is create columns of data that are needed for your users to be able to do insights more easily. With the GDP data, we could create some very useful columns. For example, if we knew what the previous year's GDP value was for a specific category, we could calculate the change value. And if we could determine the change value, we could then calculate the change as a percentage to see which direction that category is going.

To accomplish this, we need to add some columns to our table. Some of these columns will be completely useless to our users, even though they're critical to us, so we will hide those columns. The next section will walk you through creating these columns.

Add Previous Year Column

To add a column, you need to first be in the Data view. Once you're in the Data view, you need to make sure the table to which you want to add a column is selected. That's pretty easy for us since there is only one table in our model! After selecting the table, click New Column in the Table Tools ribbon.

A new column will immediately be added to your table, and a Formula bar will appear above the table, as shown in Figure 5.10. The Formula bar works like Excel. Like Excel, this is where you would write a formula to make calculations on your data. Unlike Excel, you don't place that formula on each cell because Power BI applies that same formula to every row in that column.

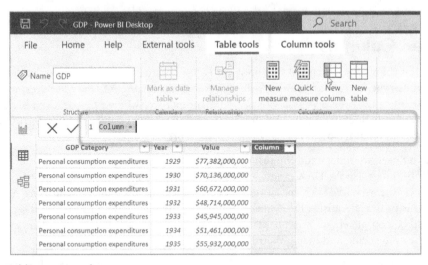

FIGURE 5.10: Adding a new column

The first column we are going to add may seem strange at first. We need a way to look up a specific value in our table. If I asked you to find a specific value in this table, you would need two pieces of information to look up the value: the GDP category and the year. To make some other calculations possible, we're going to create an *index* column that will help us identify columns uniquely. To do that, inside the Formula bar, enter the following text and hit your Enter key:

```
Index = CONCATENATE ( 'GDP'[GDP Category], 'GDP'[Year])
```

This formula creates a calculated value on each row that combines the values of the GDP Category column and Year column into one text value. It also gives a name to the column: Index. It's probably not very impressive yet, but bear with me!

Now, click the New Column button again, and we'll add a column that calculates what the previous year was. As you'll see in a minute, this is another reason why it was important for us to specify that the Year column was a Whole Number data type. Upon clicking the New Column button, enter the following DAX formula:

```
Previous Year = 'GDP'[Year] - 1
```

This formula looks at the current Year value in the row and subtracts the value 1 to identify the previous year. It then names the column Previous Year.

Now since we know the previous year and have the category available to us in each row, let's create one more apparently useless column that represents the unique index value of the previous year's row. Add a column and enter this DAX formula:

```
Previous Index = CONCATENATE ( 'GDP'[GDP Category], 'GDP'[Previous Year])
```

Our new Previous Index column represents a value that we could look up to find the previous year's GDP value for that category (see Figure 5.11).

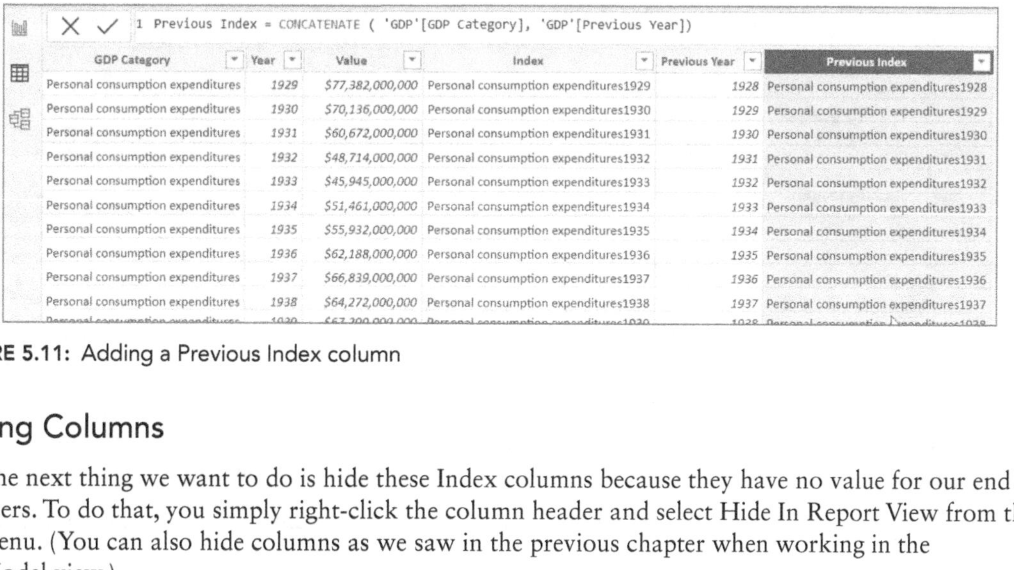

GDP Category	Year	Value	Index	Previous Year	Previous Index
Personal consumption expenditures	1929	$77,382,000,000	Personal consumption expenditures1929	1928	Personal consumption expenditures1928
Personal consumption expenditures	1930	$70,136,000,000	Personal consumption expenditures1930	1929	Personal consumption expenditures1929
Personal consumption expenditures	1931	$60,672,000,000	Personal consumption expenditures1931	1930	Personal consumption expenditures1930
Personal consumption expenditures	1932	$48,714,000,000	Personal consumption expenditures1932	1931	Personal consumption expenditures1931
Personal consumption expenditures	1933	$45,945,000,000	Personal consumption expenditures1933	1932	Personal consumption expenditures1932
Personal consumption expenditures	1934	$51,461,000,000	Personal consumption expenditures1934	1933	Personal consumption expenditures1933
Personal consumption expenditures	1935	$55,932,000,000	Personal consumption expenditures1935	1934	Personal consumption expenditures1934
Personal consumption expenditures	1936	$62,188,000,000	Personal consumption expenditures1936	1935	Personal consumption expenditures1935
Personal consumption expenditures	1937	$66,839,000,000	Personal consumption expenditures1937	1936	Personal consumption expenditures1936
Personal consumption expenditures	1938	$64,272,000,000	Personal consumption expenditures1938	1937	Personal consumption expenditures1937

FIGURE 5.11: Adding a Previous Index column

Hiding Columns

The next thing we want to do is hide these Index columns because they have no value for our end users. To do that, you simply right-click the column header and select Hide In Report View from the menu. (You can also hide columns as we saw in the previous chapter when working in the Model view.)

Hide both the Index and Previous Index columns we created. You could also hide the Previous Year column since it doesn't hold much usefulness to the users as well. Note, however, that the columns still exist along with their calculated values, and every time you refresh this dataset, it will recalculate each value. I restate this because you need to be judicious about how many calculated columns you create and how complex they become because depending upon the complexity of the calculation and the number of rows, the time it takes to refresh your dataset will increase accordingly.

LOOKUPVALUE Function

Just like Excel has a wide array of functions you can use in your formulas, DAX also has an enormous number of functions that continues to increase. See `https://dax.guide` for a great tool to give you examples and explanations of each DAX function.

In the next column you are going to add you will use a function called `LOOKUPVALUE`. This function behaves very much like the `VLOOKUP` function in Excel. Add a new column to your table and use the following formula. Observe that a DAX formula can extend across multiple lines, and doing so often makes the function more readable.

```
Previous Value = LOOKUPVALUE ( 'GDP'[Value],
                               'GDP'[Index],
                               'GDP'[Previous Index] )
```

In this formula, we look up the data in the Value column, but looking at the Index column in all the other rows (versus the one in context) and try to match it on the Previous Index value that is in the current row. This is why we needed to create both an Index column and a Previous Index column. And the reason we needed to create a Previous Year column was just so that we could create the Previous Index column. As you can see in Figure 5.12, the Previous Value for the very first row is empty. This is because there is no previous row.

```
1 Previous Value = LOOKUPVALUE ( 'GDP'[Value], 'GDP'[Index], 'GDP'[Previous Index])
```

GDP Category	Year	Value	Index	Previous Year	Previous Index	Previous Value
Personal consumption expenditures	1929	$77,382,000,000	Personal consumption expenditures1929	1928	Personal consumption expenditures1928	
Personal consumption expenditures	1930	$70,136,000,000	Personal consumption expenditures1930	1929	Personal consumption expenditures1929	77382000000
Personal consumption expenditures	1931	$60,672,000,000	Personal consumption expenditures1931	1930	Personal consumption expenditures1930	70136000000
Personal consumption expenditures	1932	$48,714,000,000	Personal consumption expenditures1932	1931	Personal consumption expenditures1931	60672000000
Personal consumption expenditures	1933	$45,945,000,000	Personal consumption expenditures1933	1932	Personal consumption expenditures1932	48714000000
Personal consumption expenditures	1934	$51,461,000,000	Personal consumption expenditures1934	1933	Personal consumption expenditures1933	45945000000
Personal consumption expenditures	1935	$55,932,000,000	Personal consumption expenditures1935	1934	Personal consumption expenditures1934	51461000000
Personal consumption expenditures	1936	$62,188,000,000	Personal consumption expenditures1936	1935	Personal consumption expenditures1935	55932000000
Personal consumption expenditures	1937	$66,839,000,000	Personal consumption expenditures1937	1936	Personal consumption expenditures1936	62188000000
Personal consumption expenditures	1938	$64,272,000,000	Personal consumption expenditures1938	1937	Personal consumption expenditures1937	66839000000
Personal consumption expenditures	1939	$67,209,000,000	Personal consumption expenditures1939	1938	Personal consumption expenditures1938	64272000000
Personal consumption expenditures	1940	$71,288,000,000	Personal consumption expenditures1940	1939	Personal consumption expenditures1939	67209000000

FIGURE 5.12: The upper-right cell shows an empty value.

Notice, also, that the currency formatting does not get applied to the newly calculated value. So, go ahead and set the formatting to show as a currency for the Previous Value column.

Now we can easily create a new column that displays the Change value. Go ahead and do that now.

```
Change =
IF (
    ISBLANK ( 'GDP'[Previous Value] ) = FALSE,
    'GDP'[Value] - 'GDP'[Previous Value]
)
```

The `IF` function works just like the `IF` function in Excel. It lets you test a condition and do one thing if the condition is true and another thing if the condition is false. In our case, we want to calculate the Change value only if the Previous Value is filled in. The `ISBLANK` function is handy because it will look at whether our Previous Value function returned a blank value. If the ISBLANK function returns false (the Previous Value is *not* blank), then it will perform the calculation.

Format the new Change column as currency. The last column we'll create is the percentage change. The formula to calculate percentage change is as follows:

$$\frac{(Current\ Value - Previous\ Value)}{Current\ Value}$$

In our case, we already have a column that calculates the numerator and a field for the denominator. So, let's implement that in a DAX calculated column!

DIVIDE Function

Before we do that, recall that zero divided by anything is zero. However, nothing can be divided by zero. In fact, in Excel if you try to divide by zero, you get the infamous #DIV/0! error. The DAX language provides a nice way to handle division by zero without generating an error. While you could just use the division operation (/), the DIVIDE function is designed to not throw an error when division by zero happens. Add a new column and use this formula to calculate our percentage change.

```
Change % = DIVIDE ( 'GDP'[Change], 'GDP'[Value] )
```

The resulting values in the new Change % column are all decimals. So, click the Column Tools ribbon and click the Percent button in the Formatting section. Now the Change % column displays the values as percentages. I left the default number of decimal places as two, but you can adjust that too if you'd like (see Figure 5.13).

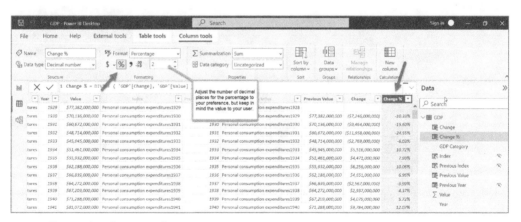

FIGURE 5.13: Formatting the new columns

Look what you did with just one value in a column! Given the context of multiple rows in the table, we were able to add three useful new columns to this table: Previous Value, Change, and Change %. There is an assumption built into this solution that made this work: we assumed that the years are contiguous, meaning there are no gaps of years in the data. If there were gaps in the years, the calculation on *just that row relative to a gap* would show an error. The calculation would remain, but every time you attempt to refresh the data, you will encounter refresh errors because the calculation would fail.

Visualize Our GDP Data

Now that we have something useful, let's create a quick report that visualizes our work. Go back to the Report view and add a line and stacked column chart to the report canvas (see Figure 5.14).

FIGURE 5.14: Adding a Line and Stacked Column chart

Enlarge the visual and align it to the right side. Add the Year column to the X-axis property, the Value column to the Column y-axis, and the GDP Category to the Column Legend property, as shown in Figure 5.15.

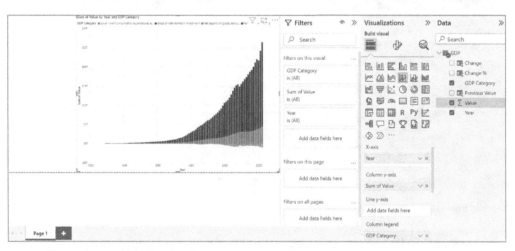

FIGURE 5.15: Formatting and labeling the chart

Now add a slicer to the left side of the report. Add the GDP Category column to the Field property of the slicer. Add another slicer below the GDP Category slicer, and add the Year column to the Field property.

Finally, add a Card visual below the Year slicer. Add the Change % column to the Field property of the Card. When you add the Change % column, it will default to a Sum aggregation. Change that to Average.

Now, at this point, you are able to select just specific GDP Categories. Try holding the Ctrl key and select the Personal Consumption Expenditures and Gross Private Domestic Investment categories. Narrow the year range from 1980 to 2022 (see Figure 5.16).

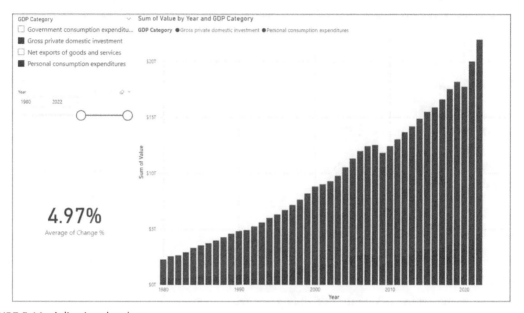

FIGURE 5.16: Adjusting the chart

Let's get crazy and add your first *second* page to a report! Along the bottom of the screen there are tabs that indicate the page names. Click the + button to add a second page. On the second page, add a line chart and two slicers. On the slicers, like before, add the GDP Category and the Year columns to the slicers. On the line chart, add the Year to the X-axis property, Value to the Y-axis property, and change to the Secondary y-axis. By adding the Change value to a secondary axis, we can see, relative to time, the movement of the relative GDP change (see Figure 5.17).

On just the Value axis (primary y-axis), you can see a dip in 2009 and slightly larger dip in 2020. However, with the secondary y-axis we can see that the change is more pronounced than it appears in the little dips. This makes complete sense since 2009 was a recession and 2020 was, well, a train wreck.

Where Are We?

So, what have we accomplished? We took a static report that covered nearly 100 years of data and arranged it so that our report consumers could slice and dice the data by categories and years. Pretty useful, but in the next chapter, after we learn how to model our data for best performance and understandability, we will take this report to another level.

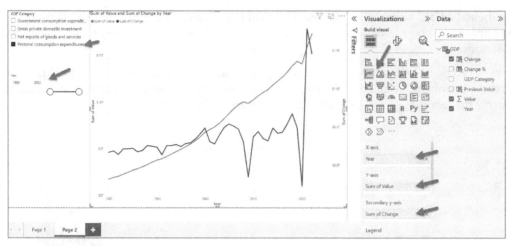

FIGURE 5.17: Viewing GDP change relative to time

But let's dive into one more topic about *data preparation*. How can you use Power Query to clean up messy data?

CLEANING MESSY DATA

To learn how we can use Power Query to handle messy data, let's work with a messy file containing movie history from IMBD.[2]

Create a new report by clicking the File ribbon and selecting New.

Once the new report is opened, click Get Data and select Text/CSV as the data source type.

When the Open File window appears, enter the following path to open the file: `https://tinyurl .com/messyimdb`.

The window that opens allows you either to take the data as is (the Load button) or to open Power Query to transform the data (the Transform Data button). As you might already be able to see from the preview window, you're going to want to hit that Transform Data button!

Once you click Transform Data, Power Query will open the movie data. Take some time to familiarize yourself with it and see what problems you might see in the data as it stands.

Here are the problems I see, but you might see more:

➤ There are empty rows.

➤ The column names have strange characters added.

➤ The Release Year column has many different date variations.

---

[2]This "messy" dataset was created by David Fuente Herraiz with publicly available data from the Internet Movie Database (IMBD) and is available with a free account at www.kaggle.com/datasets/davidfuenteherraiz/messy-imdb-dataset.

➤ The Genre column has multiple values in most of the rows.

➤ The Duration column sometimes has more than numeric values.

➤ The Country column is inconsistent and contains misspellings.

➤ The Content Rating column has different values for unrated.

➤ The Director column has multiple values in a few of the rows.

➤ Column 9 is empty.

➤ The Income column has the letter *o* in the case where a zero is needed.

➤ The Votes column uses a period instead of a comma for the placeholder.

➤ The Score column has nonnumeric values where it should only be numeric.

Sounds like we have our work cut out for us! But before we begin to clean it up, it's worth taking a minute to talk about the repetitive nature of data cleaning. This process is not a once-and-done activity, especially if the data is coming from systems where the fields are free-form or provide very little control over the user input. Because of this, in the beginning of the data cleaning phase you'll find many different issues. Over time, you'll discover new issues and add those cleanup tasks to your Power Query tasks. And just when you think you've discovered all the issues, you'll discover more.

In general, the best process is to apply all known fixes you have discovered, make a copy of the cleaned table, remove errors from the copied table, and use the newly cleaned table to import into your report. With that approach, you will have an internal table that can be used to report on new data issues you haven't discovered yet. Reza Rad has a great article that details this approach. After you work through this book, I recommend coming back to his article to learn how to apply this auditing technique: https://radacad.com/exception-reporting-in-power-bi-catch-the-error-rows-in-power-query.

What we will cover in the remaining pages of this chapter are some basic techniques for cleaning up this file. The first thing we will do is split out the columns that have multiple values (Genre and Director) into tables that will relate back to the Movies table. The second thing we will do is clean up some of the simple columns. The final area we will discuss is the very messy Release Date column.

Handle Many-to-Many Relationships

You may have noticed that nearly every movie fits into multiple genres, and a handful of the movies listed have multiple directors assigned to them. Specifically, the Genre column lists multiple genres in which a movie can be described, separated by commas. If you think for a minute about how you would try to use Power BI to filter the movies into specific genres to analyze the average revenue, it would be difficult to do this (impossible given what you have learned so far) without changing how the data is organized. Even if you could figure out a way to manage that filtering with Power BI, I guarantee it would perform very slowly, especially when you start dealing with thousands or more records.

For us to do simple analysis, we need to organize the movie data into a few different tables that relate to each other. Reorganizing or restructuring the data you are working with to effectively analyze the data is a large part of preparing data. Actually, it's very much a part of the next step we'll tackle in Chapter 6: modeling data. The process of reorganizing the data is actually modeling your data.

With this multiple genre and multiple director problem, we are introduced to a new kind of table relationship that we did not discuss in the previous chapter. Previously we mentioned a one-to-many relationship where one table defines the values (such as a Product table) and another table is related because it references, many times, a specific product. A many-to-many relationship exists when many records in one table reference many records in another table. That is exactly what we have here: one movie may fit into both the Drama genre and the Sci-Fi genre. But there are also many movies that point to the Drama genre.

Let me illustrate what I mean by a many-to-many relationship (see Figure 5.18).

FIGURE 5.18: Many-to-many relationship

As you can see, that's quite a tangled mess. And while Power BI now supports many-to-many relationships (https://learn.microsoft.com/en-us/power-bi/transform-model/desktop-many-to-many-relationships), the way our data is structured (with multiple genre values in one field separated by a comma), it would not work with the requirements Power BI has for many-to-many relationships. So, what we need is to be able to extract the genres into a table that just has genre values and then create a table that brings together the movies and the genres by which they could be described. If that sounds odd, it should be clearer with Figure 5.19.

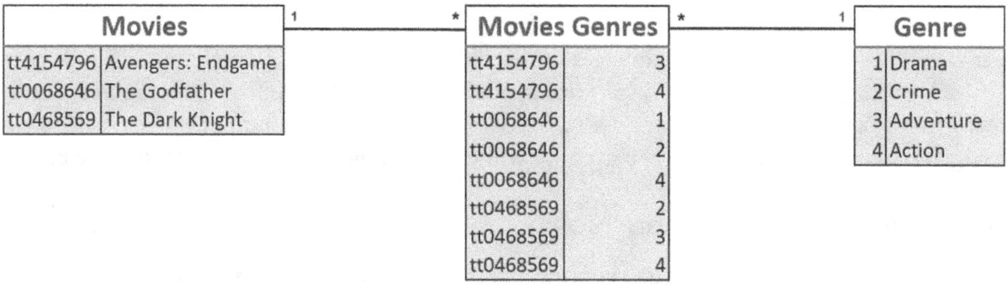

Movies		1		*	Movies Genres		*		1	Genre	
tt4154796	Avengers: Endgame				tt4154796	3				1	Drama
tt0068646	The Godfather				tt4154796	4				2	Crime
tt0468569	The Dark Knight				tt0068646	1				3	Adventure
					tt0068646	2				4	Action
					tt0068646	4					
					tt0468569	2					
					tt0468569	3					
					tt0468569	4					

FIGURE 5.19: Extract the data into multiple tables.

The challenge is to somehow strip out the genres from the Movies table, then split up the values into separate rows, assign numeric values to the genres, and finally create a table that maps the movies to the genres. While this may sound super complicated, it really is simple with Power BI and won't require any fancy coding at all. So, let's do it!

First, let's rename the query to **Movie**. Next, perform the following tasks:

1. On the Transform ribbon, click Use First Row As Headers.

2. Rename the first column, IMBD title ID, to **MovieID** by right-clicking the column header and selecting Rename.

3. Rename the second column, Original titlÊ, to **Original Title**.

4. Rename the fourth column, Genrë¨, to **Genre**.

5. Delete the ninth column, the column with no title in between Director and Income, by right-clicking on the column and selecting Remove.

Duplicate a Query

In Power Query, you can copy a table in two ways: Reference or Duplicate. Reference will copy the *results* of a query after all its steps are completed. Duplicate will copy all of the *steps* of a query to another query.

To get the genres and directors isolated into their own tables, we are going to duplicate the Movie query twice. Right-click the query name in the Queries list and select Duplicate.

After you've duplicated the table, rename it to **MoviesGenres**. Once you've renamed it, select Column1 and Column4. (You can select multiple columns by holding the Ctrl key and clicking the column header.) After you've selected those columns, right-click one of those columns and select Remove Other Columns.

Now, remove the blank rows that might be in the table by selecting Home ⇨ Remove Rows ⇨ Remove Blank Rows. Next, let's take care of those pesky comma-separated values.

Split Column

Power Query provides the ability to split apart a column in different ways. If you know that, for example, all values start with a certain number of characters or that the column is specifically divided up into a set number of character widths, you can use the Split Column function to divide a single column into multiple columns.

In our case, we know that the values we want to separate are delimited by a comma. So, let's use the By Delimiter function of the Split Column function.

The Split Column By Delimiter window will appear. Power Query recognizes, because it scanned the column values, that there are multiple commas in the cells, so it recommends splitting at Each Occurrence Of The Delimiter (see Figure 5.20).

Accept the defaults and click OK. At this point, we now have the Genre value for each movie in a separate column, as shown in Figure 5.21.

Now, we're back in a similar situation as we were with the GDP data having a column for each year. So, the solution is the same: let's unpivot the columns so that there is a row for each movie and genre combination. Select just the MovieID column and then select Transform ⇨ Unpivot Columns ⇨ Unpivot Other Columns.

The resulting table has three columns: MovieID, Attribute, and Value. We don't need the Attribute column because it means nothing to us, so go ahead and delete it. Next, rename the Value column to **Genre Name**.

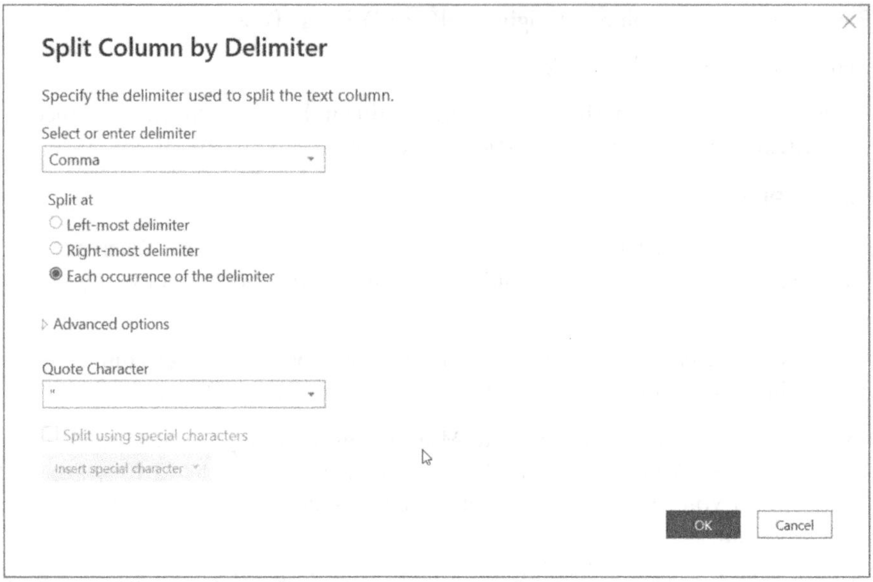

FIGURE 5.20: The Split Column By Delimiter window

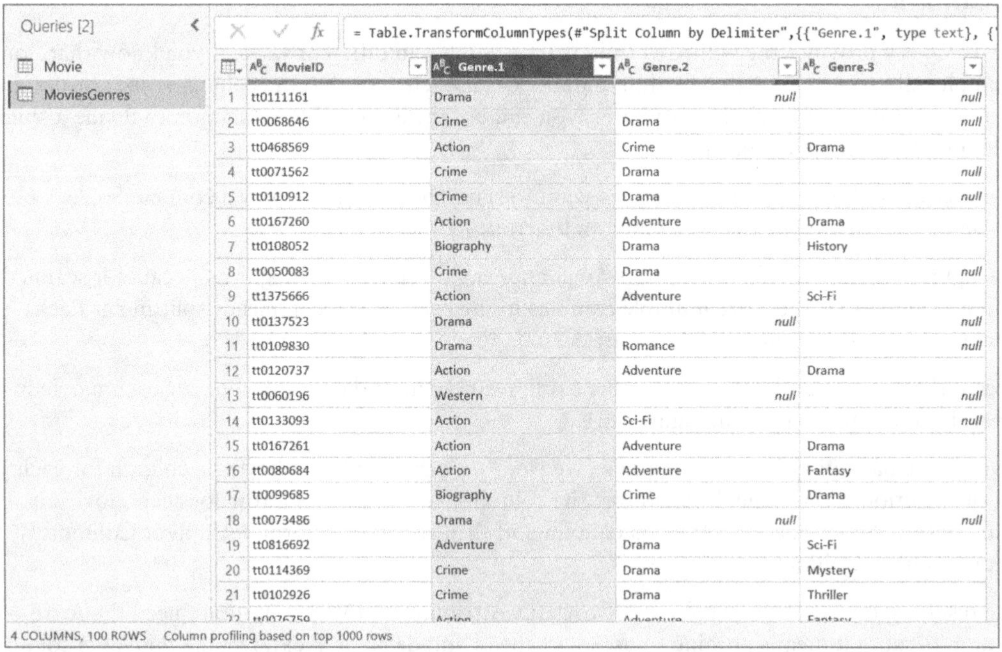

FIGURE 5.21: A Genre value displayed for each movie

Format Column

Now you might notice that several of the values in our Genre Name column have a space in front of them. Power Query provides a set of functions that let you format the text of a column. If you look at the Format button on the Transform ribbon, you'll see several options, shown in Figure 5.22.

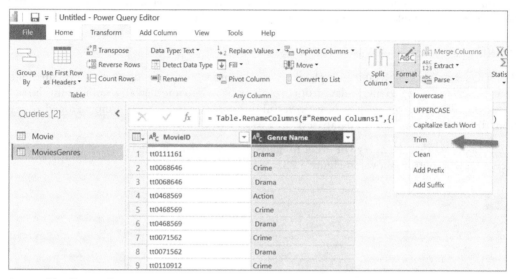

FIGURE 5.22: The Format button

The lowercase function will force all text in the column to be lower case. The opposite is true of the UPPERCASE function. And I'm sure that Capitalize Each Word is intuitive, as well.

The Trim function removes extra spaces at the beginning and end of the values in each row of the selected column. Sometimes there are nonprintable characters that can exist in your data. These characters can come in with the data for various reasons, but regardless of why, the Clean function will remove any of those characters.

Add Prefix and Add Suffix allow you to add text to the beginning of each value in the column or to the end.

For our data, let's use the Trim function to remove that extra space. We're very close now to having the many-to-many table ready. Our next step is to duplicate the results of the MoviesGenre query we just completed.

After duplicating the MoviesGenre query, rename the new query to **Genre**. Remove the MovieID column. Now we need to reduce the number of rows that we have because we have duplicate genres in our table.

Remove Duplicates

Select Remove Duplicates option under the Remove Rows button to remove duplicate values from the Genre Name column.

Index Column

Next, we need to add a unique number to each Genre value to give it an ID value. To do this, click the Index Column drop-down arrow and select From 1. This will add a new column with unique values for each row.

Rename the Index column to GenreID. Now that we have the GenreID, we want to add that back to our MoviesGenres table. To do that, we need to merge the data.

Merge Data

Power Query allows us to take multiple query results and merge them together side by side. In our example, we are going to merge data from one query back into another, all coming from the same underlying file. However, imagine how powerful this might be if you were bringing together data from different files or different databases!

First, make sure that the query you want to merge *to* is selected. On the Home ribbon, click the Merge Queries button, shown in Figure 5.23.

FIGURE 5.23: Clicking Merge Queries

The Genre query will be selected at the top automatically. However, you will need to select MoviesGenres from the queries list. Once you've selected the MoviesGenres query, select the Genre Name column in both queries. In this window, you are being asked by Power Query, "What column should I match on to merge the data?" In this case, the matching value to connect to is the Genre Name. We know that it will match perfectly because we built the Genre query itself from the MoviesGenres query. There are different ways mathematically that you could join tables together. That's what the Join Kind setting is about. If you are interested in learning more about these, this link will get you started: https://learn.microsoft.com/en-us/power-query/merge-queries-left-outer.

The result may look a little strange. While the data has been merged, at this point it is condensed into a single column called Genre. We need to expand that column by clicking the icon, as shown in Figure 5.24.

The window that opens will ask which fields from the merged query that you want to keep. It also allows you to add the name of the original query as a prefix. For our case, we need only the GenreID column, and we do not need to use the original column name as a prefix. Select GenreID and click OK.

	A^B_C MovieID	▾	A^B_C Genre Name	▾	▦ Genre	⇄
	fx		= Table.NestedJoin(#"Trimmed Text", {"Genre Name"}, Genre, {"Genre Name"}, "Genre",			
1	tt0111161		Drama		Table	
2	tt0068646		Crime		Table	
3	tt0068646		Drama		Table	
4	tt0468569		Action		Table	
5	tt0468569		Crime		Table	
6	tt0468569		Drama		Table	
7	tt0071562		Crime		Table	
8	tt0071562		Drama		Table	
9	tt0110912		Crime		Table	
10	tt0110912		Drama		Table	
11	tt0167260		Action		Table	
12	tt0167260		Adventure		Table	
13	tt0167260		Drama		Table	

FIGURE 5.24: Expanding the Genre column

The final step you can take for building the Genre to Movies many-to-many relationship, is to delete the Genre Name column from the MoviesGenres query. At this point, you should have a query that looks like what we visualized at the beginning of this section when I explained the concept of a many-to-many relationship. Great job!

Now that you have grown in your skills, take some time to repeat these same steps, but to create the tables for modeling the Director many-to-many relationship. If you're looking for a checkpoint to make sure you have done the work correctly, you can download the PBIX example files from the book resources.

Applying Changes

In the upper-left corner of the Power Query window is a Close And Apply button. There are three options here: Close And Apply, Apply, and Close. Apply will apply your Power Query changes to the underlying dataset being built without exiting the Power Query tool.

Close will not lose your Power Query changes but will not apply the changes to the dataset. If you click Close, it will close the Power Query window, and then you will be notified in the Power BI Desktop editor that there are changes that have not been applied to the dataset (see Figure 5.25).

FIGURE 5.25: Notification of pending changes not yet applied

> **NOTE** *Applying changes does not imply that the changes are saved in the file. Remember to save your file often because at this point there is not an auto-save feature.*

Applying changes is an important task because if you are working with a very large dataset, when doing your work in Power Query, the tasks are being applied only to a top set of rows retrieved by Power Query. In other words, until you click Apply Changes, you won't know if errors will occur, because your steps are applied only to a preview set of data. However, once you click Apply Changes, your steps are applied to the entire dataset.

In Power Query, the Close And Apply button will close the tool and apply the changes to the entire dataset. Go ahead and click Close And Apply in the Power Query window and navigate to the Model view, shown in Figure 5.26.

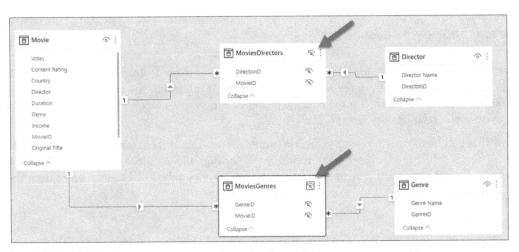

FIGURE 5.26: The Model view

As you applied the changes from your Power Query work, notice that each query is correlated to a table in your table model. Furthermore, observe that Power BI detected relationships that probably exist within the model. I say "probably" because Power BI makes assumptions based on the field names. If field names match between tables, there might be a relationship there. You should always check to see if those are accurate guesses made by Power BI. The relationships guessed here in our model are right on!

We should hide the MoviesDirectors and MoviesGenres tables since they provide little analytical value to users.

Let's do one more thing related to these new tables we created. We'll tackle why this matters in the next chapter, but for now bear with me. Double-click the relationship between Movie and MoviesGenres. This brings up the Edit Relationship window shown in Figure 5.27.

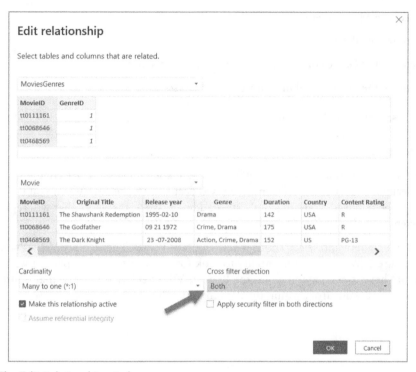

FIGURE 5.27: The Edit Relationship window

In the Edit Relationship window, change the Cross-Filter Direction property to Both. This will change the direction of the arrow icon on the relationship to point both ways. Again, we'll cover why this matters in the next chapter.

Finding the Power Query Button

Let's go back into Power Query and continue cleaning up the messy movie data. We first got into the Power Query tool by importing data and clicking the Transform Data button (see Figure 5.28). Anytime you want to get back into the Power Query tool, click the Transform Data button on the Home ribbon.

FIGURE 5.28: The Transform Data button

Simple Cleanup Tasks

Let's continue our data cleaning tasks. There are a few basic tasks to do here, and since we have already discussed how to do those tasks, I'll just list them here without images. You can do this!

1. Select the Movie query.

2. Remove blank rows.

3. Remove the Genre column since we have that in a separate table.

4. Remove the Director column (for the same reason).

Now, let's tackle replacing bad values.

Replacing Values

Take a look at the last column, Score. You'll notice that sometimes there are commas where there should be decimals, extra characters, and even two decimals in one row. When you begin to identify what needs to be removed, you can simply start adding tasks to the query that will replace or remove bad characters.

Select the Score column and select Transform ⇨ Replace Values. The Replace Values window that opens (see Figure 5.29) gives you the ability to look for one value and to replace it with something else. You don't have to put anything into the Replace With field. If you don't, that is effectively the same as removing a value from within the data in that column.

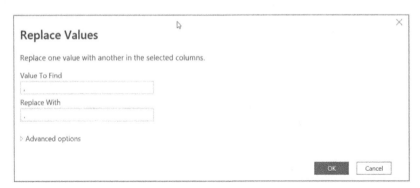

FIGURE 5.29: The Replace Values window

Enter a comma in the Value To Find field and a period in the Replace With field and click OK. This will replace all commas in the Score column with a decimal. That's great except that on the Inception movie row (row nine), there are two decimals now. So, make sure the Score column is still selected and click Replace Values again. This time, enter two periods in the Value To Find field and a single period in the Replace With field.

Repeat that Replace process multiple times with the following Find and Replace values:

Score Column Replacements

VALUE TO FIND	REPLACE WITH
F	*nothing (remove the "f" value)*
++	*nothing*

VALUE TO FIND	REPLACE WITH
e-	*nothing*
:	.

The last cleanup task for the Score column is not as simple as replacing a value. The *The Lord of the Rings: The Two Towers* movie row (row 15) has a Score that *ends* with a decimal but also has a decimal value in the correct place. You can't simply replace the decimal with nothing because that will remove the correct decimal as well. So, we have to do some fancy footwork. First, rename the Score column to **DirtyScore**.

Custom Columns

While the new DirtyScore column is selected, click Add Column ⇨ Custom Column. To address this issue of having text at the end of a field that we want to remove, we are going to create a new column that uses an `IF` formula. Our `IF` statement will look at the end of the value in a row in that column, and if it ends with the value we're looking to remove, then we'll just retain the first part of the value without the offending value. Otherwise, we'll just keep the whole value. I promise, until we get to the DAX chapter, this is as complex as we're going to get with Power Query!

In the Custom Column window that opens, enter **Score** as the new column name and then enter the formula exactly as is shown in Figure 5.30.

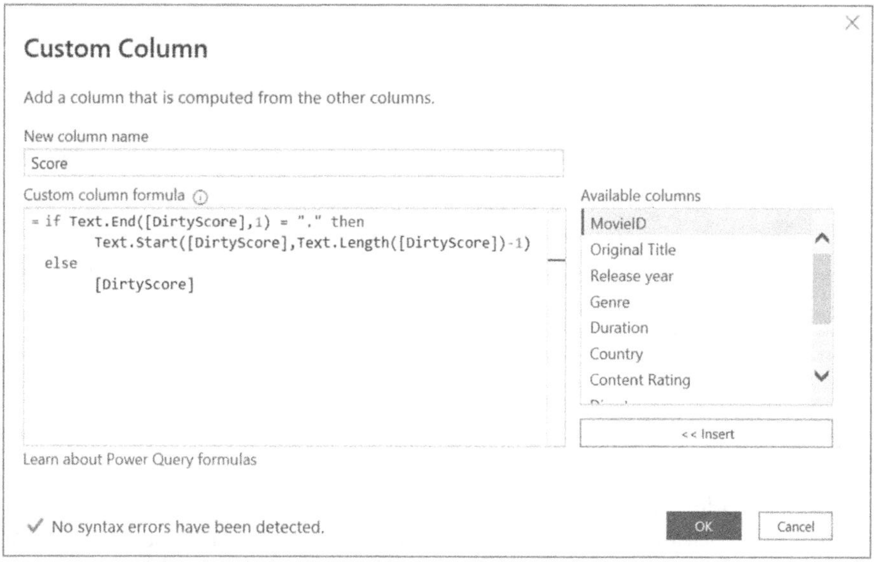

FIGURE 5.30: Creating a custom column

If you are using the digital copy of this book, it may be just as easy to copy and paste the formula here into the Formula field:

```
if Text.End([DirtyScore],1) = "." then
        Text.Start([DirtyScore],Text.Length([DirtyScore])-1)
else
        [DirtyScore]
```

Now—and this may be surprising to you—you can remove the DirtyScore column. It might seem to you that this would present a problem because our custom column references the DirtyScore column. But this isn't a problem because the *Applied Steps in the query are performed sequentially*. If you click any of your previous steps in the Applied Steps area, you will notice that the data in your query looks exactly as it did at that point in your data preparation work.

Our last step for the Score column is to change the data type. If you had tried to change the data type earlier in our process, you would've noticed multiple errors listed in the Score column, such as in Figure 5.31.

FIGURE 5.31: Data type errors

But because we have addressed every data problem in the Score column, as they exist in the data today, we now have a "clean" Score column. Select the Score column and then change the data type (on the Transform ribbon) from Any to Decimal Number. Congratulations! You have just walked through the process of cleaning the Score data. Every time the Movie dataset is refreshed, these cleaning steps will be applied exactly the same way. Remember, you may discover new data issues in the future, but that's called job security.

More Cleanup

The rest of the cleanup tasks you can do without me describing them in great detail (except for that nasty Release Year column, which we'll end with). We'll start at the end of the table since we just finished the Score column. Before you start each section shown here, make sure you have selected the column you're cleaning up:

Votes Column Cleanup

STEP	DETAIL
Replace Values	"." with *nothing*
Data Type	Whole Number

Income Column Cleanup

STEP	DETAIL
Replace Values	"o" *(that's a letter)* with "0" *(that's a zero)*
Replace Values	"$" with *nothing*
Replace Values	"," with *nothing*
Replace Values	"$" with *nothing*
Trim	Trim is found under the "Format" button
Data Type	Whole Number

Content Rating Column Cleanup

STEP	DETAIL
Replace Values	"Approved" with "Not Rated"
Replace Values	"#N/A" with "Not Rated"

Country Column Cleanup

STEP	DETAIL
Replace Values	"USA" with "United States"
Replace Values	"US" with "United States"

STEP	DETAIL
Replace Values	"UK" with "United Kingdom"
Replace Values	"New Zesland" with "New Zealand"
Replace Values	"Italy1" with "Italy"

Duration Column Cleanup

STEP	DETAIL
Replace Values	"Not applicable" with "0" *(zero)*
Replace Values	" " with "0" (replace a space value)
Replace Values	"Nan" with "0" *(zero)*
Replace Values	"Inf" with "0" *(zero)*
Replace Values	"c" with *nothing*
Replace Values	"NULL" with 0 *(zero)*, (Note: that "NULL" is not a real *null*, it is the word "NULL"--tricky, tricky!)
Replace Values	"-" with "0" *(zero)*
Data Type	Whole Number

Cleaning Date Columns

Our last column to clean up is the Release Year column. I will give you the steps in a table just like I did earlier. However, a few comments are needed.

Dates are tricky things. Sometimes there just isn't an easy way to clean them up. In this column, we have at least 10 different ways the dates were entered including Spanish for the month of March. The order in which you do your replacements really can matter in situations like this because one change may make other changes not possible. So, think through the steps. The nice thing about Power Query with the applied steps is that if you figure out you made a mistake, you can just delete the step and redo it! The ideal situation is to work with the source system to make sure data is clean to begin with! But obviously that won't always happen, especially when the data is not within your organization's control.

Release Year Column Cleanup

STEP	DETAIL
Replace Values	"The" with *nothing*
Replace Values	"," with *nothing*
Replace Values	"rd" with *nothing*
Replace Values	"th" with *nothing*
Replace Values	"of" with *nothing*
Replace Values	"year" with *nothing*
Replace Values	Double-space with a single-space
Trim	Trim is found under the "Format" button
Replace Values	" " with "-"
Replace Values	"--" with "-"
Replace Values	"marzo" with "March"
Replace Values	"/" with "-"
Data Type	Date (not Date/time, but just Date)

After you have changed the data type, you might notice that there are still five rows with errors. Those errors are happening because the value in those cells are invalid dates. A couple of them are just the month and day flip-flopped. You could address that, if you wanted to, with a custom column and write a formula to parse those apart and flip the numbers. But that's a lot of trouble for this example. In our case, and maybe sometimes in yours, you'll just need to come up with a default value to replace errors with. And then you can have a report page that lists invalid dates to address.

To fix these final date errors, click the Replace Errors button, which is visible when you click the arrow next to the Replace Values button.

Enter the value **1/1/1900** to replace all error values and click OK. Then in your report, if you needed to identify bad data, you could have a separate report page that lists the data rows filtered down to ones with that default value.

CONCLUSION

Wow! In this chapter, you learned quite a bit on the many ways to prepare your data both from an arranging perspective and from a cleaning perspective. Know that with Power Query we just skimmed the surface of what can be done. Once you hit the limits of what you can do with just the user interface, then you can go deeper by modifying the M query code in the Advanced Editor. But you are prepared now (pun intended) to prepare your own data!

We should put a bow on this work you did by at least putting one visual onto our report with this movie data. Use the Close And Apply button to close Power Query, and then save your changes.

On the Report view, add a clustered column chart (top row, fourth icon) to the canvas. On the X-axis property, add the Genre Name field (from your new Genre table!) and the Original Title field (from the Movies table). Add the Income field to the Y-axis property. (It will default to Sum Of Income, which is just fine.) You should end up with a visual that looks something like Figure 5.32 that shows that the top-earning genre is adventure movies. If you click the drill-down arrow in the upper-right corner and then click the Adventure column, you'll see that we can drill down into the different adventure movies that make up that highest-earners category (see Figure 5.32).

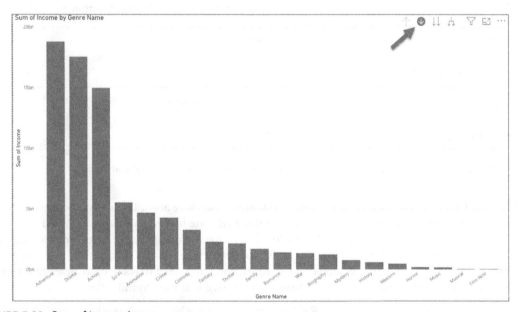

FIGURE 5.32: Sum of Income by genre name

I hope you come to the end of this chapter and say, "That was great, but how did you know that the Genre and Director columns should be organized that way?" or, "How do I know *how* I should organize my data when I'm in this preparation mode?" That's a great question, and in one sense it's a chicken-and-egg question.

Part of knowing how to prepare my data for reporting depends on knowing where I'm going with modeling. And that is exactly where we're going next in Chapter 6. Once you have a grasp on modeling your data, you will have covered those main steps: import data, prepare data, model data, and report data. And from there you'll be ready to analyze for insights!

6

Modeling Data

In earlier chapters, we've talked about tables, columns, data types, and relationships. In Chapter 5, I walked you through preparing your data to be ready for reporting. But I hope there are some lingering questions in your mind: "How do we know what data should be in which tables? Should we just bring in the data from our sources and mash it up together? Even then, how should we mash it?"

This is where data modeling enters the scene. We need to have a method to model our data that both makes sense to our report consumers and is designed to work well with Power BI. While I've used the term multiple times over the previous few chapters, it would be good to review what we mean by *modeling data.*

A data model is a way of organizing data as it corresponds to properties of real entities. For example, we could create a data model that represents real weather events. Those weather events have properties about them such as the type of weather event, the time the weather event occurred, the duration of the weather event, and the location of the weather event. A data model might represent all that data in one table or in multiple tables, depending on how the data model will be used. For example, if we are going to create a system to record weather events as they happen by gathering data from many sensors across a region, that system will need to perform very quickly. In this case, my data model must be able to handle data entry at the millisecond (or even nanosecond) level. In this scenario, we're more concerned about not losing data and capturing data as quickly as possible. Usually, data models like that do not seem, at least to a meteorologist maybe, to correspond to reality. The tables may simply be dumps of data from sensors all combined into one or two fields per row and not very useful for analysis. In fact, the data gathered might not even be stored in a table-like format. In this case, the data *model* would have a low level of correspondence to real entities.

However, once that data has been collected, I would want to create a different model that is conducive to a meteorologist's analytical needs. When they look at the model, it should correspond to how they think about weather. It might have aspects like *weather event, type of event, location, duration, etc.* So, that model would have a high level of correspondence to the real entities.

While there are different ways to model data, if you want to gain insights through analysis, then the way you model data should have a very high degree of correspondence to the real entities and processes in which you're interested.

To put this simply, if you're a business user and not a programmer, you want to look at the data model, and it should make sense to you. It should reflect the way you think about your business, its entities, and its processes.

DIMENSIONAL MODELING

The method that will work best with Power BI and will build the easiest models to understand for your report consumers is called *dimensional modeling*. It was developed by Ralph Kimball and first described in his 1996 book, *The Data Warehouse Toolkit: The Definitive Guide to Dimensional Modeling* (now in its third edition). And while you do *not* have to create data models in Power BI that follow the dimensional modeling (DM) approach, understand that Power BI was designed to operate most efficiently when you conform your data to this kind of modeling.

Now, I get that you're likely not an IT professional reading this book, probably not a data engineer. Because of that, don't expect yourself to have to fully understand DM to work with Power BI. However, if after you start diving deep into Power BI, you want to learn more about the wonderful world of data engineering and data analytics, I do recommend that you read Kimball's book, because we take only a glance here at DM.

What I want to cover here are the top-level concepts and some dos and don'ts that will help you make giant leaps ahead of those who don't take the time to learn this.

To greatly simplify DM, one could say that there are essentially two kinds of tables: one type is for *measuring* a business process, activity, or event, and the other is for *describing* a business process, activity, or event. The first type is called a *fact* table. The second type is called a *dimension* table.

A fact table is described as such because it contains *factual values* relating to a business process, activity, or event (to make things easier, I'll just refer to it as an activity). Those values are almost always numerical values that measure an aspect of the activity.

A dimension table contains related information that is used to *describe* the activities of a business or organization.

In the early days of data warehousing, databases were sometimes called *cubes*. This was because the activities being measured could be visualized as a cube with three dimensions, which is really where the notion of dimensionality might have come from. But even though it was called a cube, there were often many more than three dimensions. For the sake of learning, starting with three dimensions will help us in understanding DM.

Figure 6.1 illustrates this distinction between dimensions and facts and demonstrates it as a cube.

Think of each little box in this cube as representing one particular kind of item being sold in a retail transaction. It represents a real sale. Each little box does *not* represent the whole transaction. It represents the sale of one particular kind of product, at one particular location, at one particular point in time.

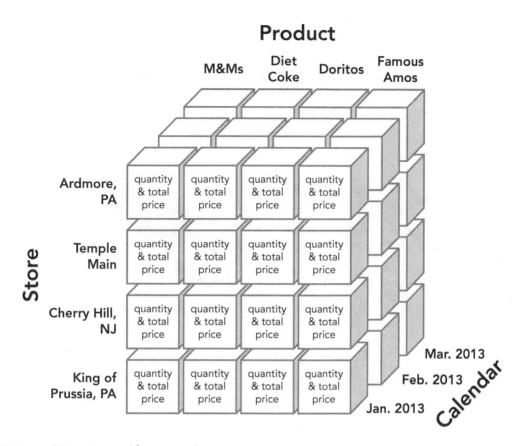

FIGURE 6.1: Dimensions and facts example

Source: Figure is based on concepts illustrated in "Strategies for Document Management" in *International Journal of Business Intelligence Research*, 1(1), 64–83, January–March 2010 and "Architecting a Dimensional Document Warehouse" in *Business Intelligence Journal*, 12(2), 34–41, June 2007.

The sale is *measured* in terms of quantity sold and total price paid. But the sale is *described* in terms of store (where), product (what), and time (when). Each way of describing the sale is one particular dimension of this cube. Think of a dimension as a group of related attributes that could describe the business process. For instance, a *product* dimension would contain attributes describing product information such as a SKU, a description, a list price, weight, and color. These are all related attributes about products. You may hear this even referred to as *dimensional attributes*. Consider the same cube with the highlighted portion shown in Figure 6.2.

The portion that is highlighted represents sales of Famous Amos cookies at Temple Main from January to March in 2013. This is what we would call *slicing* the data.

Figure 6.2 helps us now transition to how this relates to fact and dimension tables. If we take the data illustrated in Figure 6.2 and convert that to either a fact table or a dimension table, it might look something like Figure 6.3.

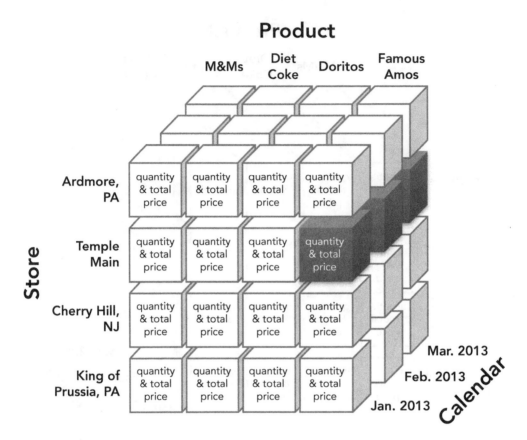

FIGURE 6.2: A dimension as a group of related attributes

Source: Figure is based on concepts illustrated in "Strategies for Document Management" in *International Journal of Business Intelligence Research*, 1(1), 64–83, January–March 2010 and "Architecting a Dimensional Document Warehouse" in *Business Intelligence Journal*, 12(2), 34–41, June 2007.

What is stored in each little box in our illustration in Figure 6.2 would be considered as one record in a fact table called Sales in Figure 6.3. The information used to *describe* the sale is not stored in the Sales table but rather is in three separate dimension tables: Store, Product, and Calendar. Each record in the Sales table has some kind of reference back to each related dimension table, but the actual data used to describe sales is stored in the dimension tables. This table relationality should look familiar to you as we have discussed table relationships in the last two chapters. The relationship between Product and Sales is one-to-many. One product is defined and described in the Product dimension, and (ideally) many times it is referenced in the Sales fact.

In our example, the tables are named according to how you would think about them from a business perspective. Now, if your organization has a data warehouse from which you are going to import data, there is a good chance that the IT data engineers have named the tables with prefixes (or possibly suffixes) that indicate what is a dimension and what is a fact. For example, they might have named these tables this way: FactSales, DimProduct, DimStore, and DimCalendar (or DimDate). This can be helpful for data engineers who may not understand the business process as deeply as you do, but just enough for them to be able to arrange the organization's data into dimensions and facts. It is my practice, and I recommend it to you as well, to remove those prefixes when bringing the tables into Power BI so that the business users who are most likely to interact with the data are not confused by the terminology.

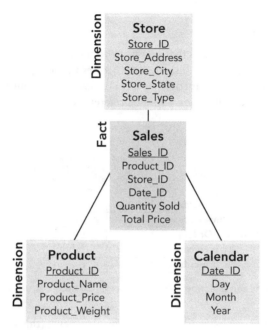

FIGURE 6.3: Fact and dimension table

If you were to create a fact table for other business processes such as inventory, shipments, invoices, or something else, they would be built the same way with just fact values in them but related back to the dimensions that describe them. That is where just one of the most valuable benefits of DM comes to the forefront.

Why Does This Matter?

By modeling your tables this way, you gain many benefits, but let me just highlight four: understandability, cross-business process analysis, flexible grouping capabilities, and significantly faster performance in Power BI.

Makes Sense to You

The simple understandability of a model like this is one of the biggest benefits. If all the data for this model were condensed into one table, it would have many columns and be difficult to work with. If, on the other hand, the data were broken out into many different tables (such as Product Category, Product SubCategory, Product SKU, Store Region, Store Chain, and Store Location), then the model would be unwieldy. That kind of data model is normal for supporting a business application because it helps the application perform quickly when entering or modifying data for thousands of records and many simultaneous users. If the tables were named cryptically such as PRD1 and LOC10, then users would have to explore deeply to understand the model.

The idea of a dimensional model is that a businessperson could look at the model and quickly understand how it relates to what they do.

Cross-Business Process Analysis

If you have multiple business processes that you want to model into fact tables, there is a strong likelihood that there are ways of describing those processes that overlap with other processes. In other words, there are dimensions that could be used to describe the business processes in the same way. For example, the Product dimension could be referenced by the Inventory, Purchase Orders, and Shipment facts (see Figure 6.4).

Dimensions	Store	Product	Calendar	Warehouse	Vendor
Sales	✓	✓	✓		
Inventory		✓	✓	✓	✓
Purchase Orders		✓	✓		✓
Invoices			✓		✓
Shipments		✓	✓	✓	✓

FIGURE 6.4: Multiple dimensions can describe Sales, Inventory, Purchase Orders, Invoices, and Shipments.

If the data stored in the fact tables can be stored at the same level (this is called *granularity*, and we'll discuss it in a little bit), particularly the date period, then you can compare side-by-side things like total sales for a date next to total inventory value on-hand. Or, you could compare for the same date quantity sold of a particular product next to the quantity on hand of a particular product.

Flexible Grouping

Dimensional modeling enables the grouping of data in as many different dimensional attributes as you have. As you begin to identify more descriptive attributes of a business process, it is simple to just add those attributes to the corresponding dimension table. This flexibility also means that you can group data in ways that might have previously been very difficult, if not impossible, to do. And given the ability to do cross-business process analysis, you could group those business measures by multiple dimensions.

Performance for Power BI

Finally, but certainly not the last word, a well-designed DM matters because Power BI is optimized under the hood to work with a DM, or, as it is also called, a *star schema*. The term *star schema* comes from what a data model diagram looks like if you have one fact related to four or five dimensions, with the fact table in the center of the diagram (see Figure 6.5).

FIGURE 6.5: A star schema

There is much you could learn about DM, but diving deeply into that topic would venture into the area of data engineering, and I'm assuming that you bought this book because you're a business user and really not looking to go into IT. If you are interested in going that deep because maybe we've piqued your interest, I do recommend reading *The Data Warehouse Toolkit*. However, we do need to cover a few details under the topic of facts and dimensions for you to be successful with DM in Power BI. So, if this feels tedious, bear with me!

FACTS

Facts are the measurements that result from a business process event and are almost always numeric. A single fact table row has a one-to-one relationship to a measurement event as described by the fact table's grain. Thus, a fact table corresponds to a physical observable event, and not to the demands of a particular report.

Ralph Kimball, The Data Warehouse Toolkit, 3rd Edition

When thinking about what data should be in a fact and what should not be, there are several things you could think through, but if you remember these points alone, you'll be doing great:

➤ If it's textual, then it probably doesn't belong in the fact table. The one exception to this might be something like an invoice ID. The way you would know if the text should be kept in the fact table is, if you were to put it into a dimension and it would be the only field in that dimension, then it could be kept on the fact.

➤ If it's numeric, then ask yourself, "Would summing up this value across rows make sense?" For example, even though a product list price is numeric, you probably wouldn't want to summarize that value across sales rows, so you would put the product list price in the Product dimension.

➤ If it's numeric, also ask yourself, "Does this value make up part of what this business process is really about?" For example, Ralph Kimball points out that ". . .In a retail sales transaction, the quantity of a product sold and its extended price are good facts, whereas the store manager's salary is disallowed."[1]

Types of Facts

There are actually different types of fact tables. For simplicity's sake, let me describe the three that are most commonly used.

➤ *Transaction.* A transaction fact records every event in a business process at the level of detail that is needed. This could be every sales transaction or component of a sales transaction. It could be every time a person is hired. It could be every click on a website. This type of fact is the most detailed and most powerful for analysis. The reason for that is because it allows the deepest level of analysis while also allowing very high-level aggregation.

➤ *Periodic snapshot.* A periodic snapshot is a point-in-time view of the data for a business process. A common example of this is inventory: a daily snapshot of the inventory of products. Each new record might be for one product for one day for one warehouse. In this kind of fact, you automatically lose the ability to track changes at a time increment less than the frequency of the snapshot. In other words, a transactional inventory fact would record each entry and removal of product. A periodic snapshot inventory fact would lose the ability to see how inventory moves in and out throughout the day.

➤ *Accumulated snapshot.* This kind of fact is used often to model a business process that goes through a defined set of steps. A common example is order fulfillment. Usually, one row in this kind of fact continues to get updated over time as the different steps occur.

Granularity

When designing your fact table, you must *always, always, always* think first about what level of detail you need to record the data for this business process. The level of detail that a single record represents is called the *grain* of the fact. For the retail sales fact, it may be at the level of product sold and specifying the quantity sold for that product. However, if the fact table needed to allow analysis at the level of barcode scanning, then the grain would need to be finer. In the example we modeled earlier, the grain of the fact is one particular product type, at one particular store, on one particular day. If needed to be at barcode scanning level, it would be one particular barcode scan, at one particular store, on one particular day.

As mentioned, what the grain is of a fact matters in order for you to compare fact data side by side with another fact. To do that, the *grain of each fact must match for each shared dimension*. In other words, if the grain of one fact is daily but the grain of the other fact is monthly, then you will not be able to compare them side by side until you aggregate the first fact to the monthly values. Both fact tables share the Date Dimension, but each fact table stores the data at a different level of detail. If you aggregated the first fact table to monthly totals, then you would be able to compare them side-by-side. This also logically means you would not be able to drill down lower than the month level in the second fact.

---

[1] Ralph Kimball and Margy Ross, *The Data Warehouse Toolkit: The Definitive Guide to Dimensional Modeling, 3rd Edition* (Indianapolis: John Wiley & Sons, Inc., 2013), Kindle Location 1781.

To explain further, let me reference a previous dataset we have worked with in this book. In our last chapter, we looked at gross domestic product (GDP) data provided by the BEA. That report that we dissected into a nice little data model was a fact table with a specific grain. Each row (in our resulting table, not the original report, because it had rows at differing levels of granularity) represented one particular category for one particular year. The BEA releases multiple datasets every month. They release datasets at the monthly level, quarterly level, and annual level. One of those datasets they provide is an accumulating snapshot with each month getting filled in as the year progresses. Most of the datasets are periodic snapshots because they give you a point-in-time view after a month ends of the GDP categories. There are differing datasets available that break down other economic indicators other than just GDP. If we downloaded the monthly US GDP report and tried to compare that data to the Annual Personal Income and Employment by State values, you would have trouble. Why? Because the granularity of those two sources is different. One is at the monthly level and rolled up to the entire country. The other is at the annual level and broken down by state. Now, if you were to download the Personal Income data at the monthly level and then, using Power Query, roll up the states to one number, then the granularity would match. Back in the days when you had to learn algebra, it was same the principle of working with like terms. You had to make sure each term was using the same units.

Relationships Between Facts (Never!)

One last point about facts. The one table relationship you should *never* do is relate one fact table to another. This is *no bueno, no muy bueno en absoluto*. The place you will be tempted to do this is where there is a parent-child (or header-detail) relationship in the business activity. The classic example is an invoice. Invoice data in a business system (as opposed to a reporting system or warehouse) is often stored like this:

Invoice Header

INVOICE DATE	INVOICE ID	CUSTOMER ID	STORE ID	SALESPERSON ID
5/2/2020	23KJD38-3	2309	34	1209
5/3/2020	30EUS23-9	6054	28	1110

Invoice Line Item Detail

INVOICE ID	INVOICE LINE NO	PRODUCT ID	PRODUCT QTY	TOTAL PRICE
23KJD38-3	1	2938	40	1250.00
23KJD38-3	2	0765	100	4750.00
30EUS23-9	1	3920	25	730.00

As tempting as it may be to make these into two fact tables with a relationship between them, you should avoid this at all costs.[2] To model parent-child/header-detail data, you "flatten" the two tables into one like so:

Invoice Combined

INVOICE DATE	INVOICE ID	CUST ID	STORE ID	SALES ID	LINE NO	PRODUCT ID	PRODUCT QTY	TOTAL PRICE
5/2/2020	23KJD38-3	2309	34	1209	1	2938	40	1250.00
5/2/2020	23KJD38-3	2309	34	1209	2	0765	100	4750.00
5/3/2020	30EUS23-9	6054	28	1110	1	3920	25	730.00

Some people may find it frustrating that data gets repeated (particularly the database administrators), but data repetition in an analytical data model is completely fine and even encouraged.

Next, let's move on to a couple of things we need to know about dimensions.

DIMENSIONS

Ralph Kimball argued that the dimensions are "the soul" of your data model.

> Dimensions provide the "who, what, where, when, why, and how" context surrounding a business process event. Dimension tables contain the descriptive attributes used by BI applications for filtering and grouping the facts. Dimension tables are sometimes called the "soul" of the data warehouse because they contain the entry points and descriptive labels that enable [a Business Intelligence] system to be leveraged for business analysis.
>
> *Ralph Kimball, The Data Warehouse Toolkit, 3rd Edition*

Remember when I quoted Kimball as saying that the store manager's allowance was not allowed in the Sales fact table? If you really felt that the store manager's salary would be useful information in your data model, there are better ways of including it other than to the Sales fact table.

You could make a Store Manager dimension that has their name, salary data, incentive data, and so on. This approach would also support the situation where someone manages multiple stores. You probably would *not* relate the Store Manager dimension to the Store dimension, but you would tie it to the Sales fact table. Then if you needed to group revenue by Store and Store Manager, you could do so.

---

[2]There is always an exception to every rule, I'm sure. But I personally haven't seen a reasonable exception for this rule. In fact, if you have the same dimension related to both the header and detail facts in Power BI, an error will occur due to a circular relationship.

However, if you wanted to analyze just Stores and Store Managers separately from the Sales data, you would need to create a one-to-many relationship between Store Manager and Store. You have to be careful with this because it can start to make the data model overly complex. Unlike the fact-to-fact relationship no-no, relationships between dimensions are not absolutely forbidden, but they are discouraged.

Using Integer Keys for Relationships

Relationships between tables, as you have seen in this book, are always tied by a unique ID that is a numeric value. In Chapter 4, "Building Your First Report," I called these values in the "many" side of the relationship *foreign keys*.[3]

If we had a Product table that had just a Product SKU, Description, and other attributes, and in our Sales table we had a Product SKU column, in Power BI, we could create the relationship between those two values. However, those kinds of columns are typically text data types. Instead of using the text data types, it is best to create an index column that is an integer data type (an integer data type is a whole number with a very high limit) and use this to relate the two tables. This is exactly what we did when we created the MoviesGenres table in the previous chapter. We could have related the Genre Name column in the MoviesGenres table to the Genres table, but instead we created a numeric index column and built the relationship with that value. Power BI performs better when relationships are built on integer keys.

Hierarchies in Dimensions

In DM, we want to do our darndest not to have a chain of tables related to each other. But data is often hierarchical. Products often have a hierarchy of categorization. For example, it's not unusual for a product to belong to a subcategory and category, as shown in Figure 6.6.

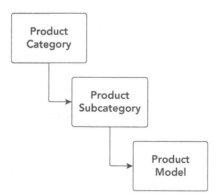

FIGURE 6.6: A hierarchy within a table

It can be tempting to create a Product Category table, Product Subcategory table, and Product table. However, with DM, we want to avoid doing that. If you did that for each dimension, your star

---

[3]In dimensional modeling terms, this is often referred to as a surrogate key. There is more behind the idea of a surrogate key in dimensional modeling than we need to delve into here.

schema would have trailing tables off each dimension. When this happens, Ralph Kimball called this *snowflaking* because your star schema starts to look more like a snowflake! Snowflaking will work, but in Power BI it will perform slowly. As I mentioned, Power BI is optimized for DM.

Instead, we want to *flatten* the hierarchy into a single table so that the hierarchy is built right into the rows. Figure 6.7 shows a clear example of a flattened product table.

ProductKey	SKU	Product	Standard Cost	Color	List Price	Model	Subcategory	Category
210	FR-R92B-58	HL Road Frame - Black, 58	$ 868.63	Black	$ 1,431.50	HL Road Frame	Road Frames	Components
211	FR-R92R-58	HL Road Frame - Red, 58	$ 868.63	Red	$ 1,431.50	HL Road Frame	Road Frames	Components
212	HL-U509-R	Sport-100 Helmet, Red	$ 12.03	Red	$ 33.64	Sport-100	Helmets	Accessories
213	HL-U509-R	Sport-100 Helmet, Red	$ 13.88	Red	$ 33.64	Sport-100	Helmets	Accessories
214	HL-U509-R	Sport-100 Helmet, Red	$ 13.09	Red	$ 34.99	Sport-100	Helmets	Accessories
215	HL-U509	Sport-100 Helmet, Black	$ 12.03	Black	$ 33.64	Sport-100	Helmets	Accessories
216	HL-U509	Sport-100 Helmet, Black	$ 13.88	Black	$ 33.64	Sport-100	Helmets	Accessories
217	HL-U509	Sport-100 Helmet, Black	$ 13.09	Black	$ 34.99	Sport-100	Helmets	Accessories
218	SO-B909-M	Mountain Bike Socks, M	$ 3.40	White	$ 9.50	Mountain Bike Socks	Socks	Clothing
219	SO-B909-L	Mountain Bike Socks, L	$ 3.40	White	$ 9.50	Mountain Bike Socks	Socks	Clothing
220	HL-U509-B	Sport-100 Helmet, Blue	$ 12.03	Blue	$ 33.64	Sport-100	Helmets	Accessories
221	HL-U509-B	Sport-100 Helmet, Blue	$ 13.88	Blue	$ 33.64	Sport-100	Helmets	Accessories
222	HL-U509-B	Sport-100 Helmet, Blue	$ 13.09	Blue	$ 34.99	Sport-100	Helmets	Accessories
223	CA-1098	AWC Logo Cap	$ 5.71	Multi	$ 8.64	Cycling Cap	Caps	Clothing
224	CA-1098	AWC Logo Cap	$ 5.23	Multi	$ 8.64	Cycling Cap	Caps	Clothing

FIGURE 6.7: A flattened product table

Instead of creating separate tables, each row in this table contains hierarchical information about a single product: it belongs to a subcategory that belongs to a category.

DATE DIMENSIONS

Speaking of hierarchical data in a dimension table, let's talk about the most common dimension in likely 99 percent of dimensional data models: a date dimension.

Think about this for a second: what are the different ways that you can describe or format this single date value: 3/19/2023? I can think of about 25 right off the top of my head. Let me give you a few examples:

Different Versions of "3/19/2023"

20230319	3/19/2023	19 MAR 2023	19 MARZO 2023
2023-03-19	19 March 2023	19/03/2023	2023.03.19
March 19, 2023	03-19-2023	Sunday, March 19, 2023	19-03-2023

But that's just 12 ways of formatting the specific date value. However, there are other ways of thinking about this date. For instance, it is day 2 of the week. It is day 78 of the year. It is in week 12 of the year. It is in quarter 1 of the year. It is in some organizations' third fiscal quarter. It is in half 1 of the year, or half 2 of the fiscal year. And we haven't even broached the idea of the ISO-8601 date format of 2023-W11-7.[4] If we were to organize this hierarchically, you might drill down from the year to the quarter to the month to the day. Or, you might drill down from year to fiscal week. If you had all this on one row for each date, then you would enable your report users to use drill-down capabilities built right into Power BI visuals.

So, why all this discussion? For one, there is always a need to organize data in different date groupings and having a Date dimension enables that. Second, you don't have to worry about what might be needed from a data formatting perspective on every single report if you simply relate a date value (or ID) in your fact table to a Date dimension. Then when someone says they need to group the revenue report by 13-week intervals, you can tell them, "No sweat!" And if you need to add a new date format that you hadn't thought of, you won't need to rebuild your fact table; you will just add it to the end of your Date dimension. A very basic Date dimension might look something like this:

Date Dimension Example

DATEID	FULLDATE	DAYOFWEEK	DAYOFWEEKNUMBER	QUARTER	MONTH NUMBER	YEAR NUMBER
20000101	01/01/2000	Saturday	7	1	1	2000
. . .						
20230319	03/19/2023	Sunday	1	1	3	2023
20230320	03/20/2023	Monday	2	1	3	2023
20230321	03/21/2023	Tuesday	3	1	3	2023
. . .						
20401231	12/31/2040	Monday	2	4	12	2040

A Date dimension has one row for every day in the calendar starting with the first year for which you have data and extends to the last year for which you have data (*or* for which you expect to have data—depending on whether you need to project data into the future). The data should be contiguous days, meaning there should be no gaps in the data. If you limit the number of rows to the data you have, you will have to dynamically add a new row on a daily basis when new data is available.

POWER QUERY AND DATA MODELING

With that introduction, you may be wondering how this actually works in Power BI. How do you make sure that your data is arranged into a dimensional model? You must first have an idea of what the data looks like that you must work with. But then you need to *think* about how to arrange that

---

[4]See https://en.wikipedia.org/wiki/ISO_week_date.

data into tables that are either facts or dimensions. And the way you do that is by thinking along the lines we've discussed so far in this chapter. I find it very helpful to then use a diagramming tool to draw out what my data model will look like. You don't have to get fancy with this—PowerPoint or Excel would work for this. I personally like LucidChart, but Draw.io is free and does a great job as well. Once you have a visual to direct where you're heading, then you will work on cleanup steps with Power Query. Once you've cleaned up the data, then you'll use Power Query to *transform* your data into the model you've designed. In a sense, you can boil that down to a three-step process, as shown in Figure 6.8.

FIGURE 6.8: Transforming data into dimensions and facts

We're going to work with some more GDP data in this chapter. This time we have more data, and it is at the state level. Figure 6.9 gives you a peek at what we have to work with. If you'd like to download the file prior to cleanup, you can access it here: `https://tinyurl.com/SAGDP-97-21-dirty`.

	A GeoFIPS	B GeoName	C Region	D TableNam	E LineCode	F IndustryCl	G Description	H Unit	1997	1998	1999	2000	2001	2002	2003	2004	2005
1	"00000"	United States		SAGDP1	1 ...		Real GDP (millions of chained	Millions of chained 2012 dollars	11529157	12045824	12623361	13138035	13263417	13488357	13865519	14399696	14901269
2	"00000"	United States		SAGDP1	2 ...		Chain-type quantity indexes fc	Quantity index	70.931	74.11	77.663	80.83	81.601	82.985	85.305	88.592	91.678
3	"00000"	United States		SAGDP1	3 ...		Current-dollar GDP (millions o	Millions of current dollars	8577552	9062817	9631172	10250952	10581929	10929108	11456450	12217196	13039197
4	"00000"	United States		SAGDP1	4 ...		Compensation (millions of dol	Millions of current dollars	4713220	5075701	5409937	5854634	6046346	6143370	6362298	6729306	7077772
5	"00000"	United States		SAGDP1	5 ...		Gross operating surplus (millic	Millions of current dollars	3286531	3384012	3592863	3733598	3866804	4067108	4337585	4666176	5079950
6	"00000"	United States		SAGDP1	6 ...		Taxes on production and impc	Millions of current dollars	577806	603105	628376	662716	668981	718636	756561	821712	881527
7	"00000"	United States		SAGDP1	7 ...		Taxes on production and imp	Millions of current dollars	611614	639472	673585	708556	727691	760032	805618	868099	942438
8	"00000"	United States		SAGDP1	8 ...		Subsidies (millions of dollars)	Millions of current dollars	-33810	-36368	-45209	-45840	-58710	-41396	-49057	-46386	-60911
9	"01000"	Alabama	5	SAGDP1	1 ...		Real GDP (millions of chained	Millions of chained 2012 dollars	144501.2	149568.2	154900.2	157221.3	158853.2	160422.4	165134.7	176625	184369.5
10	"01000"	Alabama	5	SAGDP1	2 ...		Chain-type quantity indexes fc	Quantity index	76.356	79.034	81.851	83.078	82.883	84.769	87.26	93.331	97.423
11	"01000"	Alabama	5	SAGDP1	3 ...		Current-dollar GDP (millions o	Millions of current dollars	104811.9	110212	115680.1	119851.7	122915.5	127505	134152.6	147715.2	158846.0
12	"01000"	Alabama	5	SAGDP1	4 ...		Compensation (millions of dol	Millions of current dollars	61083.8	64168.6	67225.1	69764.4	72038.4	74152.3	77085	81588.9	86356.0
13	"01000"	Alabama	5	SAGDP1	5 ...		Gross operating surplus (millic	Millions of current dollars	37247.9	39368.1	41513.7	42583.4	43348.6	45807.1	49100.6	57547	63137
14	"01000"	Alabama	5	SAGDP1	6 ...		Taxes on production and impc	Millions of current dollars	6480.3	6675.4	6941.3	7503.9	7528.5	7545.6	7967	8579.2	9353
15	"01000"	Alabama	5	SAGDP1	7 ...		Taxes on production and imp	Millions of current dollars	6754.8	6968.3	7329.6	7868.6	8004.3	8050.2	8434.7	8995.7	9913.5
16	"01000"	Alabama	5	SAGDP1	8 ...		Subsidies (millions of dollars)	Millions of current dollars	-274.5	-292.9	-388.4	-364.7	-475.8	-504.7	-467.7	-416.4	-560.1
17	"02000"	Alaska	8	SAGDP1	1 ...		Real GDP (millions of chained	Millions of chained 2012 dollars	42211.3	41095.9	40590.5	39406.6	40958.7	42979	42355.3	44055	45657.2
18	"02000"	Alaska	8	SAGDP1	2 ...		Chain-type quantity indexes fc	Quantity index	72.424	70.51	69.643	67.612	70.275	73.741	72.671	75.587	78.330
19	"02000"	Alaska	8	SAGDP1	3 ...		Current-dollar GDP (millions o	Millions of current dollars	25810.8	24227.5	24744.3	26806.6	28494.1	29756.8	32037.9	35302.4	40356.6
20	"02000"	Alaska	8	SAGDP1	4 ...		Compensation (millions of dol	Millions of current dollars	12347.8	12889.6	13127.5	13893	14883.3	15703.7	16522	17454.3	18594.7
21	"02000"	Alaska	8	SAGDP1	5 ...		Gross operating surplus (millic	Millions of current dollars	11061.3	9388.7	9690.1	10455.7	11337.1	11963.7	13311.2	15436.6	19019.5

FIGURE 6.9: Sample GDP data

I have taken the time to design a data model given the limitations of the data in this file. Figure 6.10 shows where we're headed for a data model.

For the sake of brevity, I will skip the cleanup steps. The cleaned-up CSV file can be found here if you would like to download it: `https://tinyurl.com/SAGDP`. Let's start by discussing how we might build a Date dimension.

How to Build a Date Dimension

To build a Date dimension in Power BI, aside from already having access to one provided by your organization, there are three options:

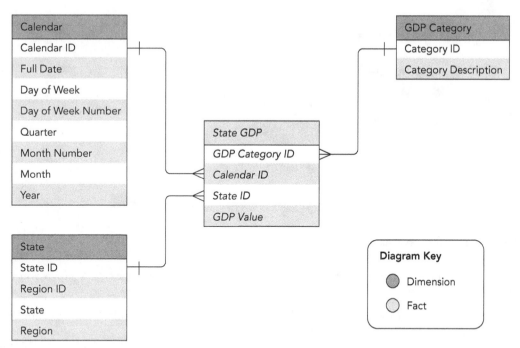

FIGURE 6.10: Sample GDP data model

- ➤ Maintain a file or database table outside of Power BI that you would import on a refresh schedule (see Chapter 9 for more information on refreshing data).

- ➤ Create a dynamic query in Power Query.

- ➤ Create a DAX-based table.

Import a Date Table from SQL Server Database

For the first option, let's connect to a database in the cloud where a Date dimension is maintained. This table is updated daily with new rows for each date. To begin, open a new report with Power BI Desktop. Once the report is open, click Import Data From SQL Server in the center. (If this is not obvious, click the Get Data drop-down button and select SQL Server.)

The window that appears will prompt you to enter a server name. Enter **bpbi.database.windows .net** in the Server field and **BPBI** in the Database field, as shown in Figure 6.11, and then click OK.

The next window that opens will prompt you for login credentials.

Enter the following username and password and click the Connect button (pay careful attention to what is a number and what is a letter in the password):

```
User Name: bpbiuser
Password:  Turn D@t@ Into Information 5o You Can Gain Ins1ght!
```

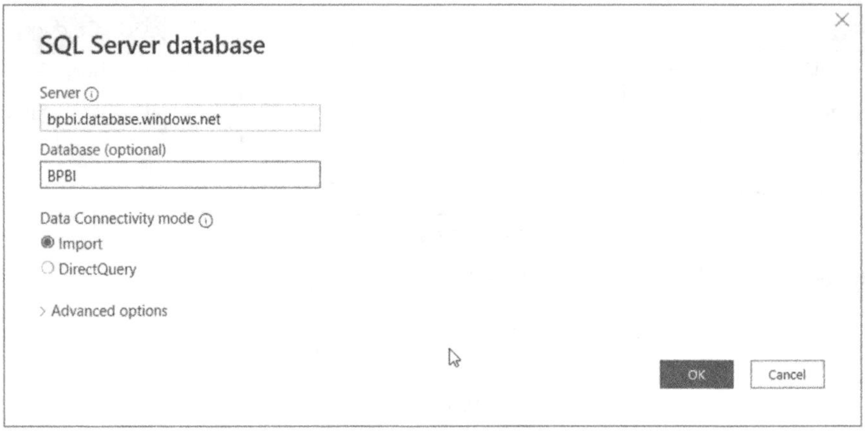

FIGURE 6.11: Enter the server name.

After a successful connection to the database, a Navigator window will appear that allows you to select the tables you want to import. Select the DW.DimDate table and click Load.

Once you click Load, Power BI Desktop will import the Date Dimension table. Click the Data View icon to view the contents of the table (see Figure 6.12).

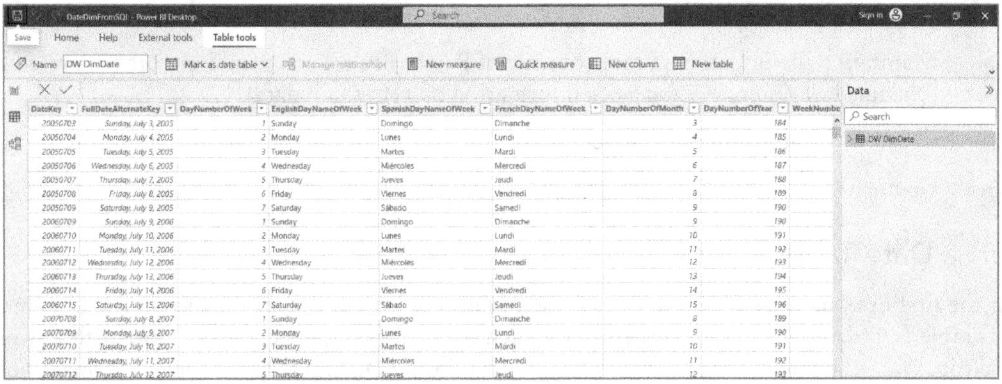

FIGURE 6.12: Viewing the Data Dimension table

This is the simplest way to bring a Date dimension into your report because you didn't have to build it or maintain it.[5] If your organization already has a data warehouse with a Date dimension and it is available for your consumption, then this is the ideal solution.

The organizational-level Date dimension is ideal because it ensures that everyone who is building Power BI data models is using the same date structures and formatting. However, if you don't have access to a database within your organization, the next two approaches are viable and actually very good options.

---

[5]Note, it might be tempting to use this Date Dimension table, but there is no guarantee on the performance of that database nor how long it will continue to be in existence.

Create a Date Dimension with Power Query

Creating a Date dimension with Power Query is an entirely code-based approach. Because the scope of this book is limited to business users, I do not want to dive into how to write M query language code. However, if this interests you, I heartily recommend Reza Rad's series of articles that explain how to do this: https://radacad.com/create-a-date-dimension-in-power-bi-in-4-steps-step-1-calendar-columns.

In the meantime, however, let's walk through using Reza's all-in-one Power Query script.[6]

1. Open a new Power BI Desktop report.

2. Close the default window that opens.

3. Open the Power Query window.

4. Click the New Source drop-down and select Blank Query.

5. Open the Advanced Editor window.

6. Delete the text that is in the Advanced Editor for Query1.

7. The following script can either be manually entered (though I would not recommend that) or be downloaded from this location and copied and pasted into the Advanced Editor Query1 window: https://tinyurl.com/RezaDates.

```
let
    // configurations start
    Today=Date.From(DateTime.LocalNow()), // today's date
    FromYear = 2018, // set the start year of the date dimension.
 // dates start from 1st of January of this year
    ToYear=2021, // set the end year of the date dimension. dates end
    // at 31st of December of this year
    StartofFiscalYear=7, // set the month number that is start of the
financial
        // year. example; if fiscal year start is July,
                          // value is 7
    firstDayofWeek=Day.Monday, // set the week's start day, values:
                          // Day.Monday, Day.Sunday....
    // configuration end
    FromDate=#date(FromYear,1,1),
    ToDate=#date(ToYear,12,31),
    Source=List.Dates(
        FromDate,
        Duration.Days(ToDate-FromDate)+1,
        #duration(1,0,0,0)
    ),
    #"Converted to Table" = Table.FromList(Source, Splitter.SplitByNothing(),
null, null, ExtraValues.Error),
    #"Renamed Columns" = Table.RenameColumns(#"Converted to Table",
{{"Column1", "Date"}}),
    #"Changed Type" = Table.TransformColumnTypes(#"Renamed Columns",
```

---

[6]These steps and this script can be found at https://radacad.com/all-in-one-script-to-create-date-dimension-in-power-bi-using-power-query.

```
{{"Date", type date}}),
    #"Inserted Year" = Table.AddColumn(#"Changed Type", "Year",
each Date.Year([Date]), Int64.Type),
    #"Inserted Start of Year" = Table.AddColumn(#"Inserted Year",
"Start of Year", each Date.StartOfYear([Date]), type date),
    #"Inserted End of Year" = Table.AddColumn(#"Inserted Start of Year",
"End of Year", each Date.EndOfYear([Date]), type date),
    #"Inserted Month" = Table.AddColumn(#"Inserted End of Year", "Month",
each Date.Month([Date]), Int64.Type),
    #"Inserted Start of Month" = Table.AddColumn(#"Inserted Month",
"Start of Month", each Date.StartOfMonth([Date]), type date),
    #"Inserted End of Month" = Table.AddColumn(#"Inserted Start of Month",
"End of Month", each Date.EndOfMonth([Date]), type date),
    #"Inserted Days in Month" = Table.AddColumn(#"Inserted End of Month",
"Days in Month", each Date.DaysInMonth([Date]), Int64.Type),
    #"Inserted Day" = Table.AddColumn(#"Inserted Days in Month", "Day",
each Date.Day([Date]), Int64.Type),
    #"Inserted Day Name" = Table.AddColumn(#"Inserted Day", "Day Name",
each Date.DayOfWeekName([Date]),
type text),
    #"Inserted Day of Week" = Table.AddColumn(#"Inserted Day Name",
"Day of Week", each Date.DayOfWeek([Date],firstDayofWeek), Int64.Type),
    #"Inserted Day of Year" = Table.AddColumn(#"Inserted Day of Week",
"Day of Year", each Date.DayOfYear([Date]), Int64.Type),
    #"Inserted Month Name" = Table.AddColumn(#"Inserted Day of Year",
"Month Name", each Date.MonthName([Date]), type text),
#"Inserted Quarter" = Table.AddColumn(#"Inserted Month Name", "Quarter",
each Date.QuarterOfYear([Date]), Int64.Type),
    #"Inserted Start of Quarter" = Table.AddColumn(#"Inserted Quarter",
"Start of Quarter", each Date.StartOfQuarter([Date]),
type date),
    #"Inserted End of Quarter" = Table.AddColumn(#"Inserted Start of Quarter",
"End of Quarter", each
Date.EndOfQuarter([Date]), type date),
    #"Inserted Week of Year" = Table.AddColumn(#"Inserted End of Quarter",
"Week of Year", each
Date.WeekOfYear([Date],firstDayofWeek),
Int64.Type),
    #"Inserted Week of Month" = Table.AddColumn(#"Inserted Week of Year",
"Week of Month", each
Date.WeekOfMonth([Date],firstDayofWeek)
, Int64.Type),
    #"Inserted Start of Week" = Table.AddColumn(#"Inserted Week of Month",
"Start of Week", each
Date.StartOfWeek([Date],firstDayofWeek,
 type date),
    #"Inserted End of Week" = Table.AddColumn(#"Inserted Start of Week",
"End of Week", each
Date.EndOfWeek([Date],firstDayofWeek),
type date),
FiscalMonthBaseIndex=13-
StartofFiscalYear,

adjustedFiscalMonthBaseIndex=if(
FiscalMonthBaseIndex>=12 or
```

```
FiscalMonthBaseIndex<0) then 0 else FiscalMonthBaseIndex,
    #"Added Custom" = Table.AddColumn(#"Inserted End of Week",
"FiscalBaseDate", each
Date.AddMonths([Date],
adjustedFiscalMonthBaseIndex)),
    #"Changed Type1" = Table.TransformColumnTypes(#"Added Custom",
{{"FiscalBaseDate", type date}}),
    #"Inserted Year1" = Table.AddColumn(#"Changed Type1", "Year.1", each
Date.Year([FiscalBaseDate]), Int64.Type),
    #"Renamed Columns1" = Table.RenameColumns(#"Inserted Year1",
{{"Year.1", "Fiscal Year"}}),
    #"Inserted Quarter1" = Table.AddColumn(#"Renamed Columns1", "Quarter.1",
each Date.QuarterOfYear([FiscalBaseDate]),
Int64.Type),
    #"Renamed Columns2" = Table.RenameColumns(#"Inserted Quarter1",
{{"Quarter.1", "Fiscal Quarter"}}),
    #"Inserted Month1" = Table.AddColumn(#"Renamed Columns2", "Month.1",
each Date.Month([FiscalBaseDate]), Int64.Type),
    #"Renamed Columns3" = Table.RenameColumns(#"Inserted Month1",
{{"Month.1", "Fiscal Month"}}),
    #"Removed Columns" = Table.RemoveColumns(#"Renamed Columns3",
{"FiscalBaseDate"}),
    #"Inserted Age" = Table.AddColumn(#"Removed Columns", "Age",
each [Date]-Today, type duration),
    #"Extracted Days" = Table.TransformColumns(#"Inserted Age",
{{"Age", Duration.Days, Int64.Type}}),
    #"Renamed Columns4" = Table.RenameColumns(#"Extracted Days",
{{"Age", "Day Offset"}}),
    #"Added Custom1" = Table.AddColumn(#"Renamed Columns4", "Month Offset",
each (([Year]-Date.Year(Today))*12)
+([Month]-Date.Month(Today))),
    #"Changed Type2" = Table.TransformColumnTypes(#"Added Custom1",
{{"Month Offset", Int64.Type}}),
    #"Added Custom2" = Table.AddColumn(#"Changed Type2", "Year Offset",
each [Year]-Date.Year(Today)),
    #"Changed Type3" = Table.TransformColumnTypes(#"Added Custom2",
{{"Year Offset", Int64.Type}}),
    #"Added Custom3" = Table.AddColumn(#"Changed Type3", "Quarter Offset",
each (([Year]-Date.Year(Today))*4)
+([Quarter]-Date.QuarterOfYear(Today))),
    #"Changed Type4" = Table.TransformColumnTypes(#"Added Custom3",
{{"Quarter Offset", Int64.Type}}),
    #"Added Custom4" = Table.AddColumn(#"Changed Type4", "Year-Month",
each Date.ToText([Date],"MMM yyyy")),
    #"Added Custom5" = Table.AddColumn(#"Added Custom4", "Year-Month Code",
each Date.ToText([Date],"yyyyMM")),
    #"Changed Type5" = Table.TransformColumnTypes(#"Added Custom5",
{{"Year-Month", type text},
{"Year-Month Code", Int64.Type}})
in
    #"Changed Type5"
```

8. After you've entered the code (I sure hope you copied and pasted it from the link!), there are four lines that you need to adjust for your situation (see Figure 6.13).

FIGURE 6.13: The area to be modified in the script

The FromYear and ToYear values determine the start date and end date. The StartOfFiscalYear variable indicates that the month number of the calendar is the first month of your fiscal year. Finally, the firstDayofWeek variable is usually Monday for businesses; however, if your first day of the week is Sunday, you will need to adjust that as well.

9. Close the Advanced Editor and rename Query 1 to **Calendar**.

As you can see, the complexities of this approach will be daunting if you are just beginning. That being said, this approach gives you more flexibility than the final approach I will demonstrate. At least now you have a great sample to work with as well as a goal to shoot for in terms of Power Query skills!

Create a Date Dimension with DAX

A third way to create a Date dimension, and the way we'll do it here in our GDP report, is to create a table with DAX. And just like in the previous chapter when we learned to create calculated columns using DAX before formally learning about DAX, I'll walk you through it, but don't put the expectation on yourself of fully understanding the DAX.

Excel formulas return a single result for a single cell.[7] DAX formulas can return either a single value or an entire table of data. Some very complex and sophisticated Date dimensions have been built that you might want to consider using in your own datasets someday. For example, Marco Russo has put together a fantastic example that can be used and adapted easily: www.sqlbi.com/articles/reference-date-table-in-dax-and-power-bi.

---

[7]In general this is true. Excel *can* return a range or array.

To begin, create another new Power BI report. (You might want to close other open reports because too many open instances of Power BI Desktop can affect performance of your computer.)

Once you are at a blank canvas in the new report, click the Model view. From there click New Table: a new table will appear in the model, and a formula bar will appear.

In the formula bar, enter the following DAX formula and then press Enter:

```
Calendar = Calendar( Date(1997, 1, 1), Date(2023,12,31))
```

After you hit Enter, you should see the new Calendar table (see Figure 6.14).

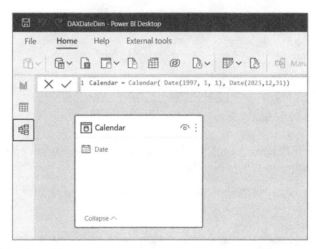

FIGURE 6.14: The new Calendar table

Click the Data view, and you will now see that the Calendar table has been created and has a row for every date between 1997 and 2023. On the Data Type field, select Date instead of Date/time (see Figure 6.15).

Next, let's add the other columns for this Date dimension. Each column will be a DAX calculated column. Remember, to add a calculated column, select Table Tools ⇨ New Column. For each of the following items, add a new column and enter the formula:

- ➤ Month = **Format('Calendar'[Date], "MMMM")**
- ➤ Quarter = **"Q" & Format(Calendar[Date], "q")**
- ➤ Year = **Format(Calendar[Date], "yyyy")**
- ➤ Month Number = **Format('Calendar'[Date], "M")**
- ➤ Quarter Number = **Format(Calendar[Date], "q")**
- ➤ Day Number = **WEEKDAY(Calendar[Date])**
- ➤ MonthYear = **Format(Calendar[Date], "yyyy-mm")**
- ➤ Day = **Format(Calendar[Date], "dddd")**
- ➤ CalendarID = **CONVERT(FORMAT ('Calendar'[Date], "YYYYMMdd"), INTEGER)**

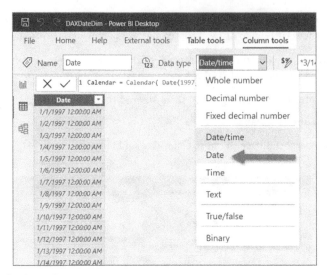

FIGURE 6.15: Selecting the Date data type

From the Column Tools ribbon, change the data type for the Year, Month Number, Quarter Number, and Day Number columns to Whole Number.

You should now have a basic Date dimension that is built simply with formulas. It should look something like Figure 6.16.

Date	Month	Quarter	Year	Month Number	Quarter Number	Day Number	MonthYear	Day	CalendarID
Wednesday, January 1, 1997	January	Q1	1997	1	1	4	1997-01	Wednesday	19970101
Thursday, January 2, 1997	January	Q1	1997	1	1	5	1997-01	Thursday	19970102
Friday, January 3, 1997	January	Q1	1997	1	1	6	1997-01	Friday	19970103
Saturday, January 4, 1997	January	Q1	1997	1	1	7	1997-01	Saturday	19970104
Sunday, January 5, 1997	January	Q1	1997	1	1	1	1997-01	Sunday	19970105
Monday, January 6, 1997	January	Q1	1997	1	1	2	1997-01	Monday	19970106
Tuesday, January 7, 1997	January	Q1	1997	1	1	3	1997-01	Tuesday	19970107
Wednesday, January 8, 1997	January	Q1	1997	1	1	4	1997-01	Wednesday	19970108
Thursday, January 9, 1997	January	Q1	1997	1	1	5	1997-01	Thursday	19970109
Friday, January 10, 1997	January	Q1	1997	1	1	6	1997-01	Friday	19970110
Saturday, January 11, 1997	January	Q1	1997	1	1	7	1997-01	Saturday	19970111
Sunday, January 12, 1997	January	Q1	1997	1	1	1	1997-01	Sunday	19970112
Monday, January 13, 1997	January	Q1	1997	1	1	2	1997-01	Monday	19970113
Tuesday, January 14, 1997	January	Q1	1997	1	1	3	1997-01	Tuesday	19970114
Wednesday, January 15, 1997	January	Q1	1997	1	1	4	1997-01	Wednesday	19970115
Thursday, January 16, 1997	January	Q1	1997	1	1	5	1997-01	Thursday	19970116
Friday, January 17, 1997	January	Q1	1997	1	1	6	1997-01	Friday	19970117
Saturday, January 18, 1997	January	Q1	1997	1	1	7	1997-01	Saturday	19970118
Sunday, January 19, 1997	January	Q1	1997	1	1	1	1997-01	Sunday	19970119
Monday, January 20, 1997	January	Q1	1997	1	1	2	1997-01	Monday	19970120
Tuesday, January 21, 1997	January	Q1	1997	1	1	3	1997-01	Tuesday	19970121

FIGURE 6.16: A basic Date dimension

Sort by Column

For all three approaches to a Date dimension, you need to do this next step.

First, if you were to use this Date dimension in a visual, say a stacked column chart, and put the Month column across the x-axis, it would sort the Month values alphabetically. That's not what we want to happen when we're working with date values. We need to control how that Month column and also the Day column are sorted. To do this, select the Month column. Then click the Sort By button in the toolbar.

The Sort By button tells you which column controls the sorting for the column you have selected. By default, it will always sort by itself. However, with this button, you can change that to sort by something else. In our case, we want the Month column, which contains the month names to be sorted by the Month Number column. So, select Month Number. Do the same thing for Day (select Day and then control the sort by selecting Day Number).

Mark It as a Date Table

The final step we need to do for any of the three types of Date dimensions we've utilized is to tell Power BI that this is a Date dimension. There is no feature in Power BI that marks tables as fact tables or dimension tables or anything else, except this one thing: a Date table. This is an important step because it helps Power BI know how to enable *time intelligence*. Time intelligence is the ability through many different DAX functions available to perform date calculations such as calculating what the date was exactly one year prior to the current date. That's not as simple as subtracting 365 from a Date value because you have leap years occasionally. There are also other complications that can arise when trying to do things like rolling averages over the last *x* periods. If Power BI doesn't know which table is your Date dimension table, it will not be able to perform the time intelligence functions.

To mark a table as a Date table, make sure you are in the Data View and select Table Tools ⇨ Mark As Date Table. Once you click that, a window will pop up that will ask you to identify what the main Date value is in the table. (Our table has only one column that is actually a Date data type, but you could have other date values in your table that are not your primary date. For example, you might want to include a date value that is six months ahead or six months behind.)

How to Arrange into a Star-Schema

Let's walk through what it looks like to arrange your data into a star schema with Power Query. It's worth noting that there are many different ways you could approach these transformations using Power Query. As you may have deduced when playing with Power Query, there are many possibilities of arranging and transforming your data.

Begin by using the same Power BI report that has our DAX Date table. On the Get Data drop-down, select Text/CSV.

You will be prompted to enter the location of a file. Enter the `https://tinyurl.com/SAGDP` path into the location field.

When you select Open, Power BI will download the CSV file to a temporary area on your computer. This will be a problem for us if we just published our report to Power BI Service because your query will reference a specific location on your computer. We'll remedy that first thing.

Click Transform Data on this window, and then we'll see the data brought into the Power Query tool. To force the query to not reference a file on your computer, click the little gear to the right of the source in Applied Steps (see Figure 6.17).

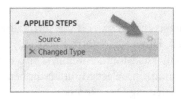

FIGURE 6.17: Changing the query source

As you'll notice, the path to the file is not the URL we specified: `https://tinyurl.com/SAGDP`. It is some path on your computer. Change the File Path property back to `https://tinyurl.com/SAGDP`. Then, click OK.

The query name might have gotten renamed to SAGDP[1]. If so, rename it to **SAGDP**.

Now let's work our newly found dimensional modeling magic!

1. On the Transform ribbon, click Use First Row As Headers.

2. Right-click the SAGDP query and duplicate it twice.

3. Rename the first duplicate **State**.

4. Rename the second duplicate **GDP Category**.

Create a State Dimension

Follow these steps:

1. On the State query, select the first three columns (holding the Ctrl key will let you select multiple columns).

2. Right-click the first selected column and select Remove Other Columns. This will remove everything except the three selected.

3. Under the Remove Rows drop-down button on the Home ribbon, select Remove Duplicates. This will reduce the rows to 51 rows (50 states + the District of Columbia).

4. On the Add Column ribbon, click the Index Column button. (It's up to you whether you use the drop-down and start the index at zero or one.)

5. Rename the new Index column **StateID**.

6. Rename the GeoName column **State**.

Create a GDP Category Dimension

Follow these steps:

1. For the GDP Category, we have fewer steps to take because this column already comes with an index value (an ID). Select the GDP Category query.

2. Select the Line Code And Description columns.

3. Remove all other columns.

4. Remove the duplicate rows. This should result in six rows. In the cleaning process, I removed two of the categories because the values for those rows were not dollar values but quantity values. If we were going to use those, they would possibly be placed into a separate fact table. If not a separate fact table, the value column would at least need to be put into a separate column in our fact table.

5. Select the Transform ribbon. Then select the Description column, and under the Extract drop-down, select Text Before Delimiter.

6. In the Extract window, enter (and click OK. This will remove the *(millions of dollars)* value from each entry. The reason for that is because we are going to reset the GDP values to their unabbreviated values later.

7. Reselect the SAGDP query.

8. Rename the GeoName column to **State**.

Add a New StateID Foreign Key to Our Fact Table

Follow these steps:

1. On the Home ribbon, click the Merge Queries button.

2. In the Merge window that opens, select the State table as the second table to merge to. In both tables, select the State column, as shown in Figure 6.18. Then click OK.

3. The Merge process will add a new column to the end of the SAGDP query. Click the Expand button on the new column that was added.

4. When you click the Expand button, it will ask you which columns from the merged query you want to include in this query. We want to keep only the StateID column because that is our new foreign key, so be sure to unselect the Use Original Column Name As Prefix.

5. The new StateID column now exists on our fact table, but it's located at the end of our table. We need to move that column up to the front. To do that, right-click the StateID column and select Move ⇨ To Beginning.

6. Remove the State, Region, and Region Name columns from the SAGDP table. The reason we can remove them is because now they're set apart into a State dimension and our fact table references the State dimension via the new StateID column.

7. In the State table, rename Region to **Region Number**.

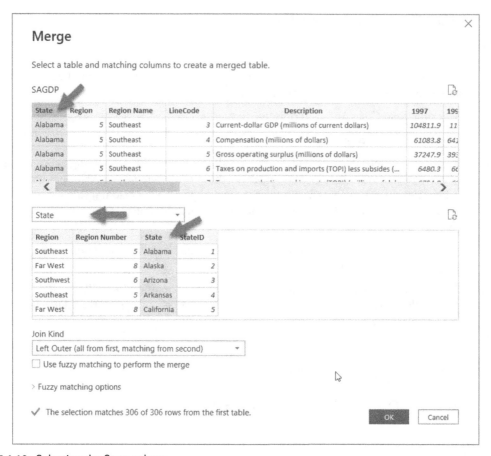

FIGURE 6.18: Selecting the State column

8. Rename Region Name to **Region**.

9. Unlike the State dimension, we don't have to merge the GDP Category dimension into the SAGDP fact table because the Line Code column is already on the table. We just need to rename it to GDPCategoryID. Do that now in the SAGDP table.

10. Remove the Description column.

Unpivot the GDP Year Values

Follow these steps:

1. In the SADGP table, select StateID and GDPCategoryID columns.

2. Select Unpivot Other Columns (see Figure 6.19).

3. The resulting view should have only four columns now: StateID, GDPCategoryID, Attribute, and Value. Rename the Attribute column to **Year**.

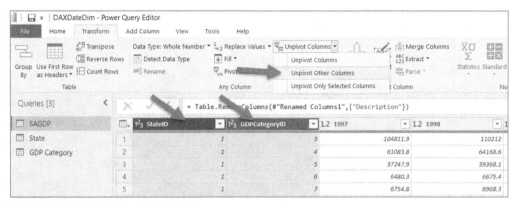

FIGURE 6.19: Selecting Unpivot Other Columns

4. Notice that the Year column is just a Text data type (it's not a Date or Number data type). This next step is possible because the column is textual at this point. Now, with the Year column selected, click the Format button on the Transform ribbon and select Add Suffix.

5. In the Suffix window, enter the following value and click the OK button: 1231. This will make all the values in the Year column appear to be a numerical date value that would match up to our Date dimension's CalendarID column. But remember, they are still a Text data type.

6. With the Year column still selected, convert the data type to Whole Number.

7. Rename the Year column **CalendarID**.

8. Rename the Value column **GDPValue**.

9. Since the unit value is one million, let's convert the values to not be shortened. To do that, select the GDPValue column. Then, from the Transform ribbon, click the Standard button and choose Multiply. Enter **1000000** in the Value field.

10. Finally, rename the SADGP query **State GDP**.

We now have two dimension tables in Power Query and a fact table that closely align to the diagram I laid out earlier. Notice that there are no textual values in our fact table. This won't always be the case, but you want to strive for as few textual values in your fact tables as possible because it will help with the performance of your dataset. Also, do your best to make the foreign key ID values that link back to your dimension tables be Whole Number data types instead of text (again because of performance).

Close and apply the changes to your model and then save your changes. Navigate to the Model view, and you should have a model that closely resembles Figure 6.20.

I have hidden all of the ID values in my model on purpose. The reason I hid those columns is because they provide no real value to my report consumers. They're simply there to provide links to create the relationships between the tables.

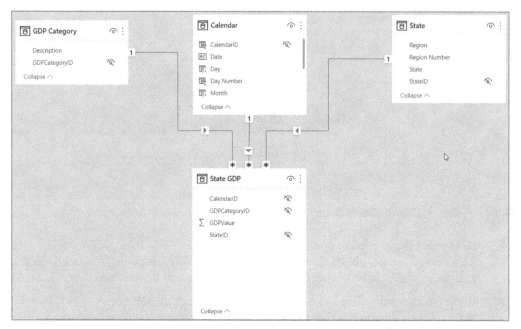

FIGURE 6.20: Model view showing changes

PUTTING IT ALL INTO ACTION

Now let's see this very fast-performing model in action. In the Report view, on the blank canvas, add three short slicers to the top of your canvas. Then add a Matrix visual (looks a like a Table visual and is set right next to the Table visual in the Visuals pane) to fill up the rest of the screen.

To the first slicer, add the Year value from the Calendar. (Note: with this dataset, we won't be able to see that Date dimension table work its power, because our GDP fact table only has one particular date value for each year.) To the second slicer, add the region from the State dimension table. On the third slicer, add GDP Description.

To the matrix, add *both* Region and State to the Rows property. Add GDP Description to the Columns property. And to the Values property, add the GDP Value field.

The resulting report should look something like Figure 6.21.

To help you out a little, I highlighted how the properties of the matrix should be configured. Play around with this report, and notice a few new things we haven't covered.

➤ The State Dimension has the Region hierarchy built into the rows. By adding *both* Region and State to the Rows property, Power BI automatically collapsed the regions but allows you to expand each region to see the constituent states.

➤ The matrix subtotals by *both* rows and columns. In the Formatting pane for the Matrix visual, you can change that so that it shows only rows, columns, or neither.

➤ As you select the different slicer values, you will see the matrix dynamically and very quickly respond to those changes, calculating values into the trillions.

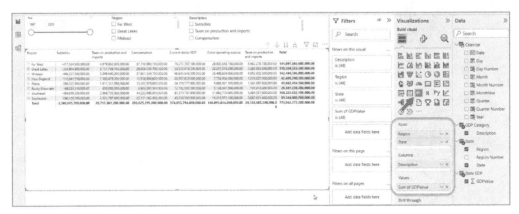

FIGURE 6.21: The completed report

CONCLUSION

In this chapter, you learned two key skills that are essential for following the proven method: dimensional modeling and how to use Power Query to arrange your data into a dimensional model.

We learned that there are ultimately two types of tables in the dimensional modeling world: dimensions and facts. Dimensions support the ability to filter and group your data: the who, when, where, what. Facts support the ability to do math on your data such as summarization or averages: the how much.

If this chapter has intrigued you to learn more, a great place to start is https://learn.microsoft .com/en-us/power-bi/guidance/star-schema.

PART 3
Going Deeper into Power BI

- ➤ **Chapter 7:** Relationships and Filtering

- ➤ **Chapter 8:** Enhancing Your Report

- ➤ **Chapter 9:** Refreshing, Sharing, and Collaborating

- ➤ **Chapter 10:** Introducing DAX

- ➤ **Chapter 11:** Conclusion

7

Relationships and Filtering

If you've come this far in the book, you're now able to build some amazing content that will unleash some deep insights into your business's data. That must feel good!

In the previous chapters, we've walked step-by-step through understanding the big picture and building content. Now that you have those tools under your belt, the approach to the remaining chapters will be more topical, intended to help you answer general "How do I do _____?" topics. In this chapter, we'll look at several ways to take your report to the next level. So, let's dive in!

FILTERING *THROUGH* RELATIONSHIPS

We've talked quite a bit about how important relationships are in your data model, but let's take some time to understand how they affect your report visualizations.

To understand how relationships work, let's go back to the Power BI report we built in Chapter 6. Open that report and save the report as a new file. To do that, click File and then Save As. (Otherwise, you can also just open the Chapter 7 example PBIX file from the book resources. Doing that will ensure you are starting at the same point I am in this chapter!)

Once you have the new report opened, it should look something like Figure 7.1.

In the top section of the report, we have three slicers: Year from the Calendar dim (going forward, I'll sometimes refer to a dimension table as a *dim*), Region from the State dim, and Description from the GDP Category dim. We have not selected anything from those slicers directly. In the matrix across the bottom of the report, we have Region and State on the rows, GDP Category Description on the columns, and the State GDP value in the values section.

Right-click the Far West region in the matrix and select Exclude (see Figure 7.2).

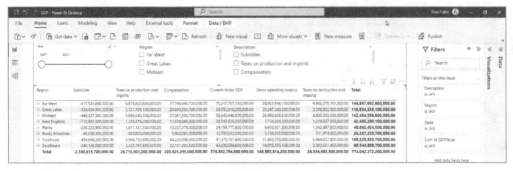

FIGURE 7.1: Gross domestic product (GDP) report with date and region slicers

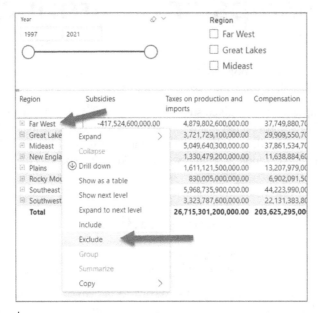

FIGURE 7.2: Excluding a value

By excluding that Region value, you automatically created a new filter on *just that Matrix visual*. Notice in the Filters pane that you have a new Excluded section for the Matrix filters (see Figure 7.3).

FIGURE 7.3: Excluded section

What this is doing is telling Power BI to filter rows *in the matrix* that have a Region value of Far West. While this may seem a very obvious statement, understand that this excluding is filtering only the rows in the matrix, not in any other visual on the report. This is evidenced by the fact that the Region slicer still displays "Far West" (see Figure 7.4).

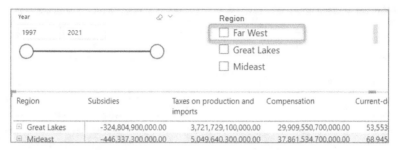

FIGURE 7.4: Region slicer displaying "Far West"

Now, select the Far West region in the slicer. When you do that, you'll see that now *nothing* shows up in the matrix (see Figure 7.5). Think about that for a second. Why did that happen?

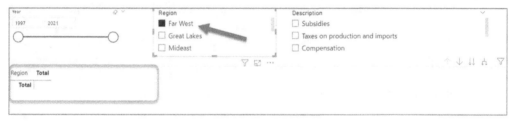

FIGURE 7.5: Nothing displayed in the Far West region

The reason all the rows disappeared from the matrix is because you have an existing filter on the matrix that excludes the Far West region. When you selected the Far West value from the slicer, it filtered every visual that contains data related to the State table where the State rows have a Region value of Far West. It's important that you notice that I did not say "every visual that has the value Far West in it." Let me demonstrate what I'm saying.

First, uncheck the Far West value in the slicer. Select the Matrix visual. Then remove the Region field from the Rows section of the Matrix properties (see Figure 7.6).

FIGURE 7.6: Removing the Region field in the Rows section

In Figure 7.7 you can see the before and after, after having removed the region from the Rows property. Notice that the Total row values match exactly between the before and after. This is because the Excluded filter still exists on this Matrix visual and is causing all rows related to the State rows in the State dim with a Far West region value to be excluded. The other evidence here that we are filtering out rows that are *related* is that between the Arkansas and Colorado rows you don't see the California row.

Before

Region	Subsidies	Taxes on production and imports	Compensation	Current-dollar GDP	Gross operating surplus	Taxes on production and imports	Total
Great Lakes	-324,804,900,000.00	3,721,729,100,000.00	29,909,550,700,000.00	53,553,816,200,000.00	20,247,340,200,000.00	3,396,923,800,000.00	110,504,555,100,000.00
Mideast	-446,337,300,000.00	5,049,640,300,000.00	37,861,534,700,000.00	68,945,646,500,000.00	26,480,809,600,000.00	4,603,303,000,000.00	142,494,596,800,000.00
New England	-110,841,500,000.00	1,330,479,200,000.00	11,638,884,600,000.00	20,592,826,500,000.00	7,734,304,300,000.00	1,219,637,000,000.00	42,405,290,100,000.00
Plains	-268,222,900,000.00	1,611,121,500,000.00	13,207,979,000,000.00	24,159,777,800,000.00	9,608,901,300,000.00	1,342,897,800,000.00	49,662,454,500,000.00
Rocky Mountain	-88,030,300,000.00	830,005,000,000.00	6,902,091,500,000.00	12,782,632,500,000.00	5,138,567,000,000.00	741,974,000,000.00	26,307,239,700,000.00
Southeast	-484,698,200,000.00	5,968,735,900,000.00	44,223,990,000,000.00	81,370,797,600,000.00	31,662,770,600,000.00	5,484,037,800,000.00	168,225,633,700,000.00
Southwest	-240,156,000,000.00	3,323,787,600,000.00	22,131,383,800,000.00	43,230,589,800,000.00	18,015,573,100,000.00	3,083,631,400,000.00	89,544,809,700,000.00
Total	-1,963,091,100,000.00	21,835,498,600,000.00	165,875,414,300,000.00	304,636,086,900,000.00	118,888,266,100,000.00	19,872,404,800,000.00	629,144,579,600,000.00

After

State	Subsidies	Taxes on production and imports	Compensation	Current-dollar GDP	Gross operating surplus	Taxes on production and imports	Total
Alabama	-22,9 200,000.00	272,946,400,000.00	2,394,116,600,000.00	4,333,967,400,000.00	1,689,859,000,000.00	249,992,100,000.00	8,917,9 7,300,000.00
Arizona	-34,7 800,000.00	445,079,500,000.00	3,492,548,800,000.00	6,414,288,600,000.00	2,511,377,400,000.00	410,362,000,000.00	13,238,9 3,500,000.00
Arkansas	-23,5 200,000.00	188,381,000,000.00	1,372,727,600,000.00	2,494,995,900,000.00	957,423,100,000.00	164,845,400,000.00	5,154,8 7,800,000.00
Colorado	-42,7 700,000.00	418,120,200,000.00	3,657,892,900,000.00	6,618,521,400,000.00	2,585,252,000,000.00	375,376,500,000.00	13,612,4 9,300,000.00
Connecticut	-25,4 2,100,000.00	393,896,500,000.00	2,977,507,900,000.00	5,586,546,400,000.00	2,240,624,300,000.00	368,414,300,000.00	11,541,5 7,300,000.00
Delaware	-6,9 5,800,000.00	75,341,900,000.00	651,149,100,000.00	1,449,753,400,000.00	730,208,500,000.00	68,396,000,000.00	2,967,9 4,100,000.00
District of Columbia	-21,6 2,400,000.00	92,518,900,000.00	1,736,514,100,000.00	2,515,000,700,000.00	707,629,900,000.00	70,856,800,000.00	5,100,8 1,000,000.00
Florida	-119,6 9,500,000.00	1,718,589,400,000.00	10,445,688,300,000.00	19,176,302,800,000.00	7,131,634,700,000.00	1,598,979,900,000.00	39,951,5 5,600,000.00
Georgia	-62,1 0,300,000.00	678,468,900,000.00	5,849,897,700,000.00	10,947,746,500,000.00	4,481,519,900,000.00	616,329,000,000.00	22,511,8 2,700,000.00
Idaho	-11,1 5,500,000.00	91,545,800,000.00	754,751,300,000.00	1,404,012,800,000.00	568,842,500,000.00	80,419,000,000.00	2,888,4 1,900,000.00
Illinois	-119,0 5,900,000.00	1,239,400,300,000.00	9,276,694,200,000.00	16,668,032,100,000.00	6,270,946,400,000.00	1,120,391,200,000.00	34,456,4 5,300,000.00
Indiana	-41,6 5,600,000.00	435,019,700,000.00	3,744,778,600,000.00	7,036,045,700,000.00	2,897,873,600,000.00	393,392,900,000.00	14,465,4 0,900,000.00
Iowa	-46,2 5,600,000.00	229,833,600,000.00	1,810,472,500,000.00	3,558,912,400,000.00	1,565,379,700,000.00	183,059,700,000.00	7,300,8 9,300,000.00
Kansas	-36,4 5,800,000.00	229,000,300,000.00	1,737,194,000,000.00	3,193,283,700,000.00	1,263,546,400,000.00	192,543,500,000.00	6,579,1 1,100,000.00
Total	-1,963,091,100,000.00	21,835,498,600,000.00	165,875,414,300,000.00	304,636,086,900,000.00	118,888,266,100,000.00	19,872,404,800,000.00	629,144,579,600,000.00

FIGURE 7.7: Before and after having removed the region from the Rows property

Here's the principle to understand: *Power BI filtering works through the relationships defined between the tables. If there is no relationship defined between two tables, filtering one table will not affect the other tables.*

VISUALS INTERACT INDEPENDENTLY

Let's explore this a little further. Make the Matrix visual shorter and add a Table visual below. Then add the region to the Columns property as well as the GDPValue (see Figure 7.8). Notice that even on a Table visual, the Fact value is automatically aggregated. But observe what is happening: the Matrix visual is still filtered to exclude Far West rows from the State dim, but this Table visual does not have the same filter. As such, it includes Far West, and consequently, the total GDPValue is different from the Matrix total displayed.

What do you think will happen now if you select Far West from the Region slicer? If you select the Far West region in the Region slicer, both the Matrix and Table visuals react. The Matrix visual behaved as before—the Far West value is already excluded. The Table visual reduces the rows to only those rows that have Far West in the region (see Figure 7.9).

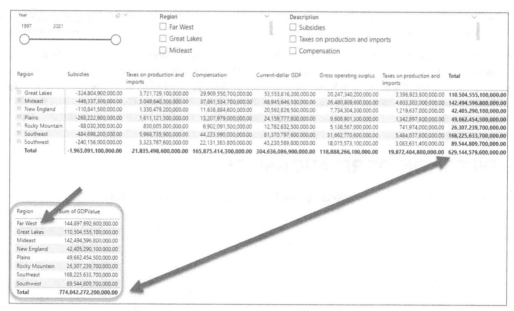

FIGURE 7.8: Region and GDPValue added to new matrix and totals not matching because of filters

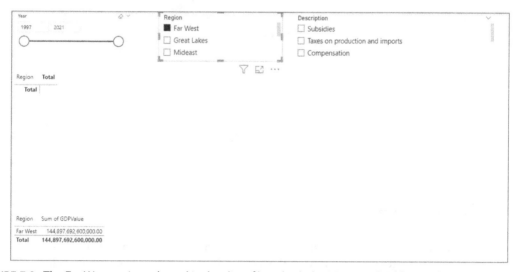

FIGURE 7.9: The Far West region selected in the slicer filters both the Matrix and Table visuals.

What is likely not obvious is that these Slicer filters are actually working upon the underlying table in the data model and technically not in the visual itself. (The Exclude filtering function is an exception to this rule that I'll explain in a little bit.) Even though it appears that the visuals are dependent on each other, in fact all the visuals act independently of each other. What they are dependent upon is the underlying data model that you created. *This is why it is so imperative to first understand your data model and the relationships between tables before trying to build a report for consumption by others.*

If you do not understand how the tables relate to each other, then you will not be able to understand why visuals behave the way they do in a report.

For example, when you select a value in the slicer, it is ultimately filtering the State table itself and not the visual. The visuals on the report then respond to the reality that the State table now only has rows visible that have Far West in the Region field. But that doesn't really answer how it is that the Table and Matrix visuals responded since *just* the State dim has been filtered. This brings us to the direction that filtering *flows*.

THE DIRECTION OF RELATIONSHIPS

Observe the arrows on each relationship line between the tables in Figure 7.10.

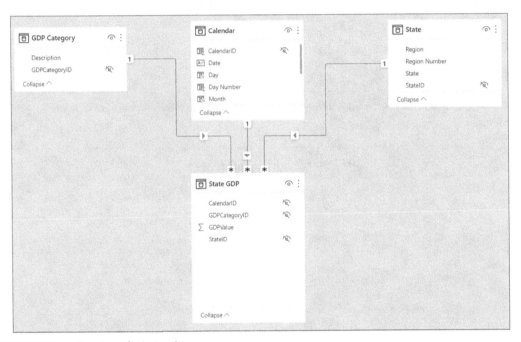

FIGURE 7.10: The direction of relationships

Notice that all the arrows point toward our State GDP Fact. This means that as filtering occurs on a dim, the effect of the filter will flow toward the fact. (It doesn't matter to Power BI whether a table is a fact or a dim; it simply depends on the relationship configuration.) As rows are filtered in one table, the tables to which that table is related *will also be filtered*. In other words, if we filtered the State table, all rows in the State GDP fact table that are related will also be filtered. You could think of it as hiding the rows in one table and hiding any rows that are in related tables. In our example earlier, if we filtered Far West from the State dim, then all State GDP fact rows that have a StateID value of 5 (California is in the Far West region and has a StateID value of 5) will also be hidden.

An important thing to understand about that directional arrow is that filtering does not flow in the opposite direction. So, for example, if I filtered rows from the State GDP fact where StateID does not equal 5, then the State dim would *still* have the California state row visible. To demonstrate this, go into the Model view and unhide the StateID value in the State GDP fact (see Figure 7.11).

FIGURE 7.11: Unhiding the StateID value

Then add a slicer to your report and add the State field to the slicer. I added my State slicer to the upper-right corner of the report, as shown in Figure 7.12.

Region	Subsidies	Taxes on production and imports	Compensation	Current-dollar GDP	Gross operating surplus	Taxes on production and imports	Total
Far West	-417,524,600,000.00	4,879,802,600,000.00	37,749,880,700,000.00	70,217,707,100,000.00	28,005,548,100,000.00	4,462,278,700,000.00	144,897,692,600,000.00
Great Lakes	-324,804,900,000.00	3,721,729,100,000.00	29,909,550,700,000.00	53,553,816,200,000.00	20,247,340,200,000.00	3,396,923,800,000.00	110,504,555,100,000.00
Mideast	-446,337,300,000.00	5,049,640,300,000.00	37,861,534,700,000.00	68,945,646,500,000.00	26,480,809,600,000.00	4,603,303,000,000.00	142,494,596,800,000.00
New England	-110,841,500,000.00	1,330,479,200,000.00	11,638,884,600,000.00	20,592,826,500,000.00	7,734,304,300,000.00	1,219,637,000,000.00	42,405,290,100,000.00
Plains	-268,222,900,000.00	1,611,121,500,000.00	13,207,979,000,000.00	24,159,777,800,000.00	9,608,901,300,000.00	1,342,897,800,000.00	49,662,454,500,000.00
Rocky Mountain	-88,030,300,000.00	830,005,000,000.00	6,902,091,500,000.00	12,782,632,500,000.00	5,138,567,000,000.00	741,974,000,000.00	26,307,239,700,000.00
Southeast	-484,698,200,000.00	5,968,735,900,000.00	44,223,990,000,000.00	81,370,797,600,000.00	31,662,770,600,000.00	5,484,037,800,000.00	168,225,633,700,000.00
Southwest	-240,156,000,000.00	3,323,787,600,000.00	22,131,383,800,000.00	43,230,589,800,000.00	18,015,573,100,000.00	3,083,631,400,000.00	89,544,809,700,000.00
Total	-2,380,615,700,000.00	26,715,301,200,000.00	203,625,295,000,000.00	374,853,794,000,000.00	146,893,814,200,000.00	24,334,683,500,000.00	774,042,272,200,000.00

Region	Sum of GDPValue
Far West	144,897,692,600,000.00
Great Lakes	110,504,555,100,000.00
Mideast	142,494,596,800,000.00
New England	42,405,290,100,000.00
Plains	49,662,454,500,000.00
Rocky Mountain	26,307,239,700,000.00
Southeast	168,225,633,700,000.00
Southwest	89,544,809,700,000.00
Total	774,042,272,200,000.00

FIGURE 7.12: Adding the State field to the slicer

To first demonstrate my point that a slicer is not really filtering the visuals themselves, but the underlying data model, select Alabama in the slicer and see what happens to the Region slicer you already have on the report (see Figure 7.13).

FIGURE 7.13: Selecting Alabama

When you selected Alabama, the Region slicer reflected the reality that the State dim itself in the underlying data model was filtered down to the row for Alabama, which is in the Southeast region. All that the Region filter can see is the rows that are visible in the State table, which in this case is only Alabama. Now uncheck Alabama in the slicer so that the report shows everything. I also have removed the *Far West* Excluded filter on the matrix (see Figure 7.14).

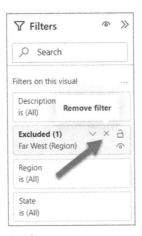

FIGURE 7.14: Removing the *Far West* Excluded filter

Let me clarify what is happening with the Exclude filter. I mentioned earlier that this filter type is an exception to the rule. It is somewhat different than other filtering in that it is *not* filtering the underlying table itself, but only the data coming into the visual. To see that, right-click Far West in the Region slicer and exclude it, as shown in Figure 7.15.

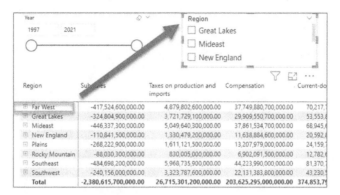

FIGURE 7.15: Excluding the Far West region

Notice that while Far West is no longer visible in the Region slicer, the value of Far West is still visible in the matrix. Go ahead and remove that Excluded filter by removing it from the Filters pane.

BIDIRECTIONAL FILTERING

Let's go back to the idea of the filter flowing only one way. As I mentioned, the filtering flows in the direction of the arrow toward the related table. Now that we made the StateID field visible in our State GDP fact, let's filter out California from the State GDP fact. To do this, we need to take the critical step of changing the behavior of the relationship itself.

Go to the Model view and double-click the relationship between the State GDP fact and the State dim (see Figure 7.16).

In the Edit Relationship window that opens, change the Cross-filter Direction property from Single to Both. Then click OK.

After you've closed the Edit Relationship window, you'll notice that the arrow indicating the flow of the filters has changed to point in *both directions* (see Figure 7.17).

Now, go back to the Report view and make sure no visual is selected on your report canvas. Then drag StateID from the State GDP fact to the Filters On This Page section in the Filters pane.

By adding the StateID to Filters On This Page, we are not filtering a specific visual but directly filtering the underlying table. And by applying it to the Page level, we are saying that this filter will apply to everything on the page. The reason it will apply to everything is because we are directly filtering the underlying table itself.

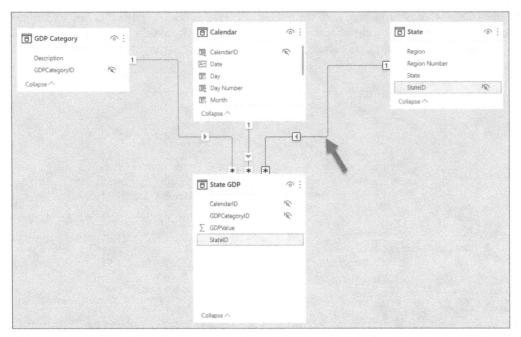

FIGURE 7.16: Selecting the relationship between the State GDP fact and the State dim

Once you have the StateID field added to the Filters On This Page, select Is Not from the Show Items When The Value field. Then specify the value of 5 (since California has a StateID of 5). Then hit the Apply button.

What happened when you applied that filter? Under the hood, the State GDP fact was filtered to not show any rows where the StateID equals 5. On the surface, you may have noticed that the Far West region values all decreased since California has been removed. But that's just filtering the fact. Since the filter direction has been changed to Both, though, that has caused something else to happen that didn't happen before when we filtered the State GDP fact. Look in the State slicer and scroll down past Arkansas, and you will see that the list now goes from Arkansas to Colorado, and California is no longer in the list. This is because the filtering now flows from the fact to the dimension and vice versa. This both-direction filtering is sometimes called *bidirectional filtering* or *cross-filtering*.

> **NOTE** It is advised to avoid bidirectional filtering because it can produce unexpected or complicated results that are difficult to understand. Furthermore, Microsoft provides the following caution: "Generally, we recommend minimizing the use of bi-directional relationships. They can negatively impact on model query performance, and possibly deliver confusing experiences for your report users." (See `https://learn.microsoft.com/en-us/power-bi/guidance/relationships-bidirectional-filtering`.)

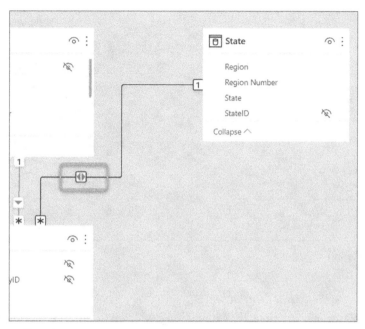

FIGURE 7.17: The cross-filter direction property is now Both.

REPORT FILTER TYPES

In that previous exercise you might have thought to yourself, "What is the difference between adding a filter to the page and to a visual?" That's a great question! In Power BI, beyond the Filters pane, there are many different filter types. Nine to be exact (`https://learn.microsoft.com/en-us/power-bi/create-reports/power-bi-report-filter-types`). However, some of those are beyond the scope of this book. A few of them (drill through and drill down) will be utilized in the next chapter. We have already discussed, as early as Chapter 3, *automatic filters* and *manual filters*. Automatic filters are those that get created for each field you add to a visual. Manual filters are those that you manually create by adding them to the Filter pane. In this section, let's just look at the three types of filters that are used on the Filter pane: Visual, Page, and Report.

Visual Filters

Visual filters apply filtering to just a single visual on your report. These filters are filtering the data as it comes into the visual but do not affect the underlying tables. If you apply a filter on a specific visual such as a State name, the same State name filter would not flow through to another visual because you are not filtering the table but are filtering what is displayed in the visual.

As demonstrated earlier, how you are able to filter data within the Filter pane depends on the type of data you are working with. If you are filtering with a date data type, then you have many different filtering options.

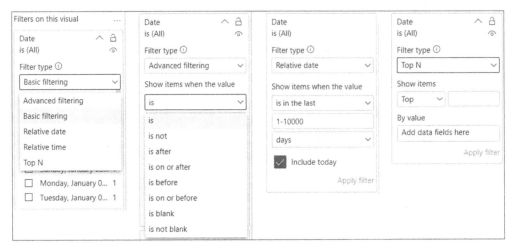

FIGURE 7.18: Date filtering

Date Filtering

Figure 7.18 shows the many options for date filtering, which falls into several categories.

➤ *Basic Filtering* allows you to specify one or more specific dates.

➤ *Advanced Filtering* allows you to pick an operator such as "is on or after 3/1/2023" (which is the equivalent of $x \geq 3/1/2023$).

➤ *Relative Date and Relative Time Filtering* allows you to filter the date (or time if the data type includes time values versus just a simple date) relative to right now. You can choose an operator (in the last, in this, or in the next), then pick a control number, and finally choose an interval such as days, weeks, months, or years. For example, you could filter a date field to just dates in the last 6 months.

➤ *Top N Filtering* allows you to pick the top number of dates (you specify the N value) based on the value of a measure (explicit or implicit). We'll finish up this section with an example of that, but with a different data type.

Numeric Filtering

Filtering on numeric values is the simplest form of filtering and has the least set of options. The filtering operators are mathematical.

➤ "is less than" $(x < 10)$

➤ "is less than or equal to" $(x \leq 10)$

➤ "is greater than" $(x > 10)$

➤ "is greater than or equal to" $(x \geq 10)$

➤ "is" $(x = 10)$

➤ "is not" $(x \neq 10)$

➤ "is blank" $(x = \emptyset)$

➤ "is not blank" $(x \neq \emptyset)$

Text Filtering

Filtering with text data types has the ability to do *basic filtering* where you pick specific values from a list of values in that column and *advanced filtering* with all the filtering operators that are seen in filtering the other data types. But text filtering also adds the Top N Filtering option such as the date types offered.

In the new table I added to the bottom of the report, I changed the first column from Region to State (see Figure 7.19).

State	Sum of GDPValue
Alabama	8,917,927,300,000.00
Alaska	2,346,045,300,000.00
Arizona	13,238,938,500,000.00
Arkansas	5,154,837,800,000.00
California	104,438,617,000,000.00
Colorado	13,612,419,300,000.00
Connecticut	11,541,507,300,000.00
Delaware	2,967,903,100,000.00
District of Columbia	5,100,858,000,000.00
Total	**774,042,272,200,000.00**

FIGURE 7.19: Changing the first column from Region to State

I'd like to find what the Taxes on Production and Imports (TOPI) are for the top five states with the highest GDP. With the table selected, open the Filters pane and find the State filter on this visual. Change Filter Type to Top N. To do that, I'm going to teach you just a tad more DAX without any explanation.

In the Data pane, right-click the State GDP table and select New Measure (see Figure 7.20).

FIGURE 7.20: Selecting New Measure

When you add a measure to a table, a formula bar appears at the top of the report canvas. Enter the following DAX code in that formula bar:

```
TOPI = CALCULATE ( SUM ( 'State GDP'[GDPValue] ) ,
                   'GDP Category'[GDPCategoryID] = 7 )
```

Now in the State GDP table, you should see what appears to be a new field but is in fact a measure (as indicated by the calculator icon) called TOPI (see Figure 7.21).

FIGURE 7.21: New measure displayed

Now, remove the GDP Value column from the Table visual and drag the TOPI measure into the table. Your table should now have a State column and a TOPI column and look something like Figure 7.22.

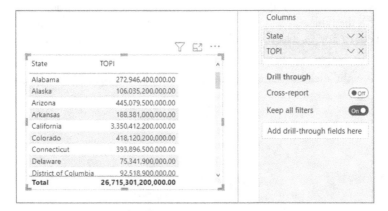

FIGURE 7.22: Table showing State and TOPI columns

Now let's apply that Top N filter. We want to identify the top five states with the highest GDP, but then simply display the TOPI value for each of those states. We already have the TOPI value in our table. So all we need to do is filter down our table to the states with the highest GDP.

With the Table visual selected, open the Filters pane. Then in the State filter, select the Top N filter type. Enter the value of 5 for the Show Items property. Then drag the GDPValue column from the State GDP table into the By Value property. This is saying, show only the top five states *by GDPValue*. The reason this works is because the GDPValue is numeric and can be interpreted as an implicit measure (remember, the Σ icon next to the field tells you that this numeric value is an implicit measure). In the Show Items property, you can only drag measures, but those measures can be implicit or explicit measures. Finally, click the Apply Filter button.

The resulting view in the table should have only five rows, which should have unsurprisingly the following states: California, Florida, Illinois, New York, and Texas (see Figure 7.23).

FIGURE 7.23: View with only five rows

If we add the GDPValue back into the Table visual, you'll be able to see the top five GDPValues.

Page and Report Filters

All the options I described in the previous section on visual filters apply here except that the Top N filtering is not available. The key difference between Visual filters and Page and Report filters is the *scope* of the filtering. The scope is obvious by the name: filters that you place on pages are scoped to everything on that page, and filters on reports apply across all pages of the report.

What is important to know is that, as we saw earlier in this chapter, these filters apply to the data model itself so that all visuals within the scope (page or report) are affected. The only way to bypass filters applied at those levels is through DAX measures.

Controlling the Use of Filters

Any filter that exists in the report, whether automatic or manual, will be visible to your report consumers when they use the report *unless you take advantage of the filter controls.*

There are two kinds of controls, editability and visibility, as shown in Figure 7.24.

If you lock the filter, the user can see the filter but not change its values. If you hide the filter, the user cannot even see the filter though the filter remains in effect.

FIGURE 7.24: Editability and visibility

Controlling the filters so that your users cannot adjust the values may sometimes be needed because adjusting the filter value may affect the report data in such a way that the message is not accurately portrayed. For example, if there are certain rows that need to be removed to make business sense of the values and adding them back in portrays an inaccurate value, then you should lock the filter. Hiding the filters, however, is not *usually* a good thing to do because transparency in analytical reporting is always essential.

CONCLUSION

Well, once again we covered a ton of ground on just one simple topic. However, as you can see, there is much involved here that can make your reporting incredibly powerful.

If there are only two things you take away from this chapter, it should be these two critical points:

➤ Slicer filters are actually working upon the underlying table in the data model and technically not in the visual itself.

➤ It is thus imperative to first understand your data model and the relationships between tables before trying to build a report for consumption by others.

8

Enhancing Your Report

Believe it or not, we have only a few more topics to cover regarding creating reports for your business consumers. But that's not to say that this is the final word on report development. After you've finished this chapter, you'll have covered enough ground to create plenty of useful content, but this is just the beginning of your Power BI journey. And even here in this book we have some more topics to cover that I'm sure you're still scratching your head about, such as, "How do I share this content with others?" We'll get there!

In this chapter, we're going to cover some loosely related topics that will help you enhance the overall behavior of your report. We'll hit on configuring drill-down capabilities, configuring the ability to drill through into other reports, adding buttons, creating bookmarks, and controlling visibility of items on your reports.

CONFIGURING DRILL-DOWN

In Power BI we talk about two kinds of "drilling." Let's talk first about *drilling down*. Drilling down in Power BI is taking data that is hierarchical (such as product category and subcategory) and is aggregated to some level and then expanding down into that hierarchy to see what makes up that hierarchy. Several visuals within Power BI support drill-down such as bar charts and the matrix. If a visual supports drill-down, then you will see these icons in the upper-right corner of the visual once the visual is placed on the report canvas:

The up arrow allows you to navigate up (to *drill up*) after drilling down. The down arrow unintuitively does *not* cause a drill-down action but rather turns on the drill-down mode. If you click this button, the visual will turn on Drill Mode. The benefit here is that it allows you to drill down by field in the visual as you click that field. The two down arrows expand the data into the next level of the hierarchy across all rows. Each time you click that button, the data in the visual will reflect all the data expanded at the next level down in the hierarchy. How these interact together will make sense as we work with the following example, but this link is also very helpful: `https://learn.microsoft.com/en-us/power-bi/consumer/end-user-drill`.

To enable drill-down functionality, you need to add hierarchical data. Let's go back to the report we created in Chapter 4, but with a new report page. Use Chapter 8 PBIX from the book resources file to get started.

On the first report page called Overview, select the Sales Variance From Target By District Manager matrix in the lower-right corner. On that visual we have the District Manager (DM) on the Rows property (see Figure 8.1).

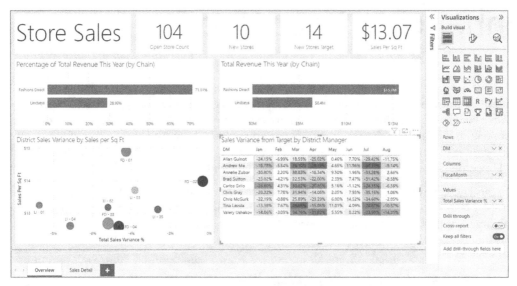

FIGURE 8.1: Selecting the Sales Variance From Target By District Manager matrix

From the District table, drag the District field to the Rows property in the visual, but put the field *above* the DM field. After doing that, your visual should look like Figure 8.2.

Many changes happened to the visual all at once. The first column is now District but also has a plus sign (+) by each district name. In addition, the upper-right corner now has those drill-mode icons. Now, do the following:

1. Add the Territory field in between the District and DM fields on the Rows property.

2. Remove the Fiscal Month field from the Columns property.

3. Add the Date Hierarchy field from the Time table to the Columns property.

After you add the Date Hierarchy field to the Columns property, the complete date hierarchy (Year, Quarter, Month, Day) gets expanded. Remove the Year field from the Columns property so that the data will be aggregated to the Quarter level first (see Figure 8.3).

FIGURE 8.2: District field added above DM field in Rows property and reflected in visual

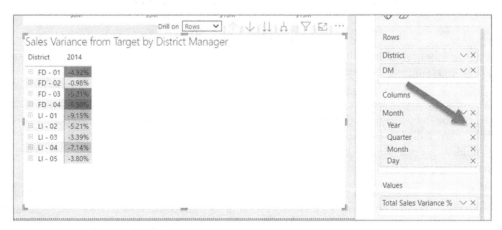

FIGURE 8.3: Removing the Year field

After you remove the Year field, it should look like Figure 8.4. Also notice that now a new field appears next to the Drill Mode icons. The Drill On [Rows] property allows you to control which part experiences drilling. The reason this appeared is because we have *two* hierarchical fields on our matrix: the District|Territory|DM on the rows and the date hierarchy on the columns.

Explore how the drill-down behavior works as you use the different Drill Mode buttons and as you change the Drill On property from Rows to Columns.

Next, let's look at the concept of *drill-through*.

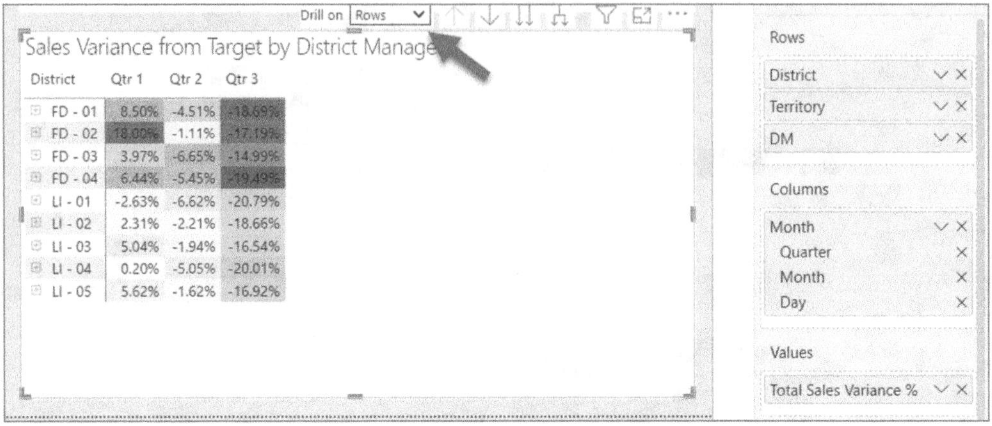

FIGURE 8.4: Drilling on Rows property displayed next to the Drill Mode icons

CONFIGURING DRILL-THROUGH

You may have noticed in our new PBIX for this chapter that I have added a second report page that has a detailed view of all the sales for each district manager. At the top of the screen is a Table visual that lists all the district managers. I intentionally made the table height the size of only one row (see Figure 8.5).

Below the top table, there are five cards with metrics in which the DMs are interested. Below the cards is a table with sales details for all the DMs. If you think about it, this report isn't very useful unless you start filtering the data. What would be ideal is if from the first page when looking at the sales variances for a DM, you could zoom in to see more detailed information. That's really what *drill-through* enables you to do. Drill-through allows you to navigate from a certain data point on one page through to a separate report page *automatically filtered to that same data point*. With this example, if we drilled down to Annelie Zubar's Sales Variance data on the first page, it would be great if we could click something and be taken to the Sales Detail page filtered to just her data. Let's make that happen!

On the Sales Detail page, open the District table on the right and find the DM field. Then drag the DM field to the Add Drill-Through Fields Here area in the Values pane. When you add fields to this area, this tells Power BI that on *any other* report page where these fields are used, allow the user to *drill-through* to this page and filter by the data point in that field. This has the effect of adding a filter to the Filters On This Page filter section of the detail page.

Now, go back to the Overview page. In the Sales Variance visual, click the double down arrows button (see Figure 8.6), which is the Go To The Next Level In Hierarchy button.

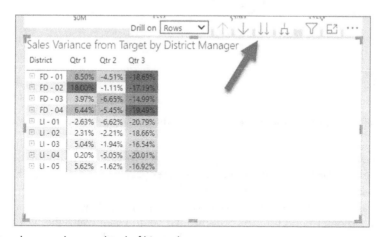

Allan Guinot

Lindseys Sales for District LI - 01

$23M	$22M	$23M	7.41M	-4.67%
Last Year Sales	This Year Sales	This Year Sales Goal	# Units Sold	Total Sales Variance %

Store	Territory	This Year Sales	Last Year Sales	Average Unit Price Last Year	Average Unit Price	Gross Margin Last Year %	Gross Margin This Year %	Total Units Last Year
Akron Fashions Direct	OH	$453,623	$462,784	$4.75	$5.20	41.50%	42.89%	$97,508
Alexandria Lindseys	VA	$141,971	$150,476	$7.43	$7.84	46.01%	45.29%	$20,251
Altoona Fashions Direct	PA	$410,079	$416,648	$4.21	$4.91	40.00%	41.12%	$98,934
Anderson Lindseys	SC	$111,359	$110,420	$6.56	$6.84	41.80%	43.22%	$16,820
Asheville Lindseys	NC	$112,270	$127,052	$6.90	$7.07	44.65%	44.86%	$18,414
Athens Lindseys	GA	$90,303	$97,186	$6.81	$6.54	43.09%	43.32%	$14,263
Augusta Lindseys	GA	$88,351	$88,345	$6.47	$6.66	42.67%	41.28%	$13,663
Beavercreek Fashions Direct	OH	$377,800	$389,253	$5.05	$5.10	40.65%	41.73%	$77,044
Beckley Fashions Direct	WV	$403,603	$442,276	$4.79	$5.34	39.96%	41.25%	$92,259
Bel Air Fashions Direct	MD	$515,557	$582,592	$4.95	$5.09	42.61%	42.81%	$117,750
Belle Vernon Fashions Direct	PA	$367,434	$384,213	$4.02	$4.53	38.82%	39.87%	$95,493
Boardman Fashions Direct	OH	$502,966	$534,610	$4.67	$5.00	40.95%	41.89%	$114,388
Bowie Lindseys	MD	$88,251	$94,017	$6.66	$6.73	41.07%	41.84%	$14,108
Bowling Green Lindseys	KY	$84,893	$80,218	$6.82	$6.82	44.12%	44.39%	$11,759
Buford Lindseys	GA	$83,489	$92,727	$6.32	$6.75	41.18%	42.62%	$14,677
Cartersville Lindseys	GA	$102,447	$106,914	$6.40	$7.14	41.44%	42.03%	$16,704
Cary Lindseys	NC	$70,595	$68,885	$5.91	$6.49	36.77%	39.71%	$11,655
Century III Fashions Direct	PA	$486,689	$518,391	$4.56	$4.55	40.31%	41.69%	$113,625
Chambersburg Lindseys	PA	$74,008	$76,480	$6.76	$6.92	40.60%	41.53%	$11,309
Total		**$22,051,952**	**$23,132,601**	**$5.19**	**$5.49**	**41.69%**	**42.29%**	**$4,461,252**

Overview   Sales Detail

FIGURE 8.5: Table visual configured to show only one row

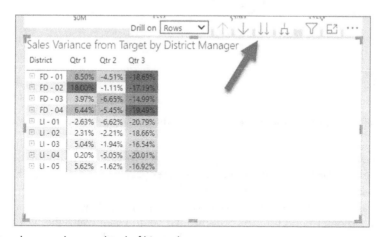

FIGURE 8.6: Moving down to the next level of hierarchy

When you drill down to the next level in the hierarchy, it drills down to show *every row* in the hierarchy at that second level (Territory), as shown in Figure 8.7.

Click the next-level-down button one more time, as shown in Figure 8.8.

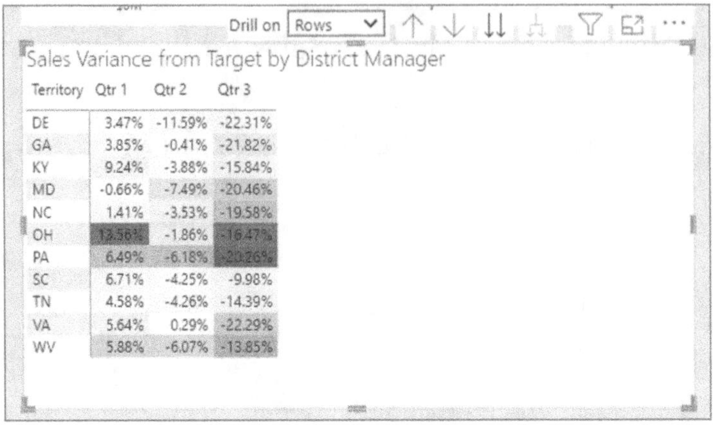

FIGURE 8.7: Every territory in the second level of the hierarchy displayed after drilling down

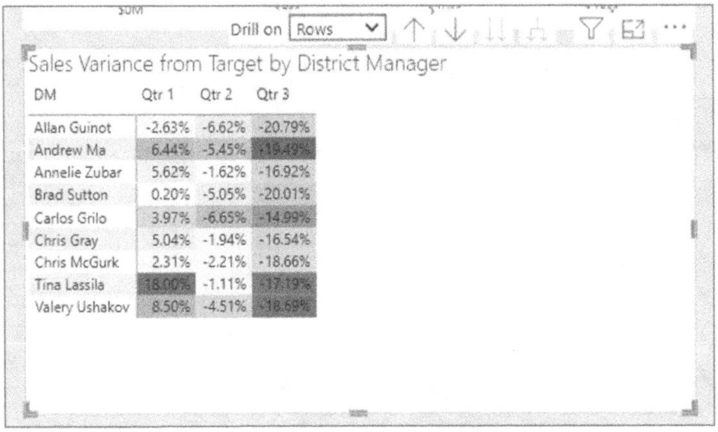

FIGURE 8.8: Every salesperson displayed in the third level of the hierarchy displayed after further drilling down

Now right-click Annelie Zubar. When you right-click the DM value in that visual, the right-click menu will now have a Drill Through option. Every other page in this report that has the DM field added to the Drill-Through Fields property will be listed. In our case, we have only one page. But, if you had other pages with that field listed as a drill-through field, they would show up here. In addition, if you had other fields listed as drill-through fields, when you right-click those fields on other report pages, you would see the Drill Through menu as well.

Go ahead and click the Sales Detail option on the Drill Through menu (see Figure 8.9). This will take you to the Sales Detail page, but it will be filtered for Annelie Zubar and show you just her Sales Detail information.

If you look at the Filters pane, you will not see the DM filter for Annelie. However, if you look at the Filter icon (∇) in the upper-right corner of the visuals, you'll see that it shows that the page is filtered by DM = Annelie Zubar.

Annelie Zubar **Lindseys Sales for District LI - 05**

$1M	$1M	$1M	335.10K	-3.80%
Last Year Sales	This Year Sales	This Year Sales Goal	# Units Sold	Total Sales Variance %

Store	Territory	This Year Sales	Last Year Sales	Average Unit Price Last Year	Average Unit Price	Gross Margin Last Year %	Gross Margin This Year %	Total Units Last Year
Athens Lindseys	GA	$90,303	$97,186	$6.81	$6.54	43.09%	43.32%	$14,263
Augusta Lindseys	GA	$88,351	$88,345	$6.47	$6.66	42.67%	41.28%	$13,663
Bowling Green Lindseys	KY	$84,893	$80,218	$6.82	$6.82	44.12%	44.39%	$11,759
Buford Lindseys	GA	$83,489	$92,727	$6.32	$6.75	41.18%	42.62%	$14,677
Cartersville Lindseys	GA	$102,447	$106,914	$6.40	$7.14	41.44%	42.03%	$16,704
Chattanooga Lindseys	TN	$123,247	$129,471	$6.98	$7.03	44.54%	45.00%	$18,548
Cookeville Lindseys	TN	$110,806	$115,965	$6.73	$7.09	42.42%	42.22%	$17,223
Duluth Lindseys	GA	$118,947	$114,527	$6.64	$7.09	43.25%	45.38%	$17,241
Elizabethtown Lindseys	KY	$101,119	$102,881	$6.84	$7.04	45.02%	44.59%	$15,051
Ft. Oglethorpe Lindseys	GA	$61,278	$70,611	$6.88	$6.79	43.23%	44.59%	$10,266
Gallatin Lindseys	TN	$139,576	$135,800	$6.88	$7.28	44.47%	44.52%	$19,735
Johnson City Lindseys	TN	$99,376	$106,063	$6.46	$7.09	43.96%	44.13%	$16,418
Knoxville Lindseys	TN	$49,161	$59,568	$6.12	$6.49	42.30%	40.81%	$9,739
Newnan Lindseys	GA	$81,101	$86,516	$6.31	$6.89	42.58%	41.44%	$13,710
Total		$1,334,093	$1,386,792	$6.64	$6.95	43.25%	43.49%	$208,997

FIGURE 8.9: Drill-through report filtered to value selected on previous page

What you might not have noticed that happened when you added the Drill Through field to the page was that an arrow button appeared at the top of the report in the upper-left corner. In Power BI Desktop, you have to hold the Ctrl key, and then when you click that button, it will navigate back to where you previously were. Once you publish this report to the Power BI service, when it's displayed in a web browser, this button will behave like any other button on a web page, meaning you won't have to hold the Ctrl key there.

What's really cool is that you can add different kinds of buttons to your report. Let's look into that for a minute.

BUTTONS

Select the arrow button in the upper-left corner (see Figure 8.10), and then look at the Format pane to see the properties (see Figure 8.11).

FIGURE 8.10: Arrow button in upper-left corner selected

There are all the usual suspects with the properties that you can modify such as style, shape, color, text, etc. But the key property you need to see of a Button control is the Action property. Open the property details (see Figure 8.12).

FIGURE 8.11: Button properties in Format pane

FIGURE 8.12: Options for the action property displayed

Buttons have eight different kinds of *actions* that can be specified. The action for this button that got set automatically when you set the Drill-Through field property was set to Back. The Back action will allow your report consumers to navigate back to the report page from where they came. The Bookmark action will let you navigate to a bookmarked view (we'll look at creating Bookmarks next). The Drill Through action will let your users perform the drill-through action without having to right-click. The Q&A action will (if you have imported data versus connecting to a Power BI dataset like we're doing in this report) pop up a window that will let your users ask natural language questions about your data (such as "How much were our sales last year for the X product?"). The Web URL action allows you to embed a hyperlink into your report that will let your users navigate to a link outside of your report. Finally, the Apply All Slicers and Clear All Slicers actions do exactly what they sound like!

Take some time to play with those and then let's look at what those bookmarks are all about.

BOOKMARKS

Bookmarks function somewhat like a browser bookmark that saves your place in browsing. However, take that idea a step further. Imagine if you set different properties on a page and then could bookmark not just the page but all the property values at that point in time. That's what Power BI bookmarks do. They allow you to capture exactly all the filters, slicers, and highlighting just as they are and then give it a name. So, let's try that.

Go back to the Overview page if you're not there already. Then on the upper-left Percentage Of Total Revenue This Year (By Chain) visual, select the Lindseys chain (see Figure 8.13).

FIGURE 8.13: Overview page with the Lindseys chain highlighted

This will highlight all the Lindseys-related data throughout the report because we have the relationships defined clearly through our data model. Now click the View ribbon and then the Bookmarks button. This will open a new pane you haven't seen before, the Bookmarks pane (see Figure 8.14).

The pane states two steps: Filter and Add. We've already highlighted the data we want (which, as I mentioned, covers both filters *and highlighting*). So, let's click Add. As soon as you click Add, it will create a bookmark called Bookmark 1. Then click the ellipsis next to that bookmark, and you'll see the options for each bookmark (see Figure 8.15).

Interestingly, bookmarks can bookmark data values (such as selecting the Lindseys value) and/or display settings (such as a color setting). In this case, click Rename and rename the bookmark to **Lindsey's**.

FIGURE 8.14: The Bookmarks pane

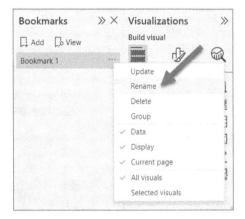

FIGURE 8.15: Bookmark options

Next, highlight the Fashions Direct bar in the upper-left corner. Then create another bookmark and name it **Fashions Direct**.

Now, click each bookmark, and you will see that your selections get applied as you select each bookmark.

Let's try applying the concept of buttons that we just learned to bookmarks. First, since we have some extra whitespace in our Sales Variance visual, let's shrink it to free up a little room (as shown in Figure 8.16).

Now, click the Insert ribbon and then open the Buttons menu. On the menu of Button options, choose Bookmark (see Figure 8.17).

This will position a new button with a bookmark icon in the upper-left corner. Drag that visual to the lower-right corner next to the Sales Variance visual (see Figure 8.18).

With the new button selected, go to the Format pane and open the Action property. Since the Action type of Bookmark is already selected, we just need to select the Bookmark we want to load. Select Lindsey's, as shown in Figure 8.19.

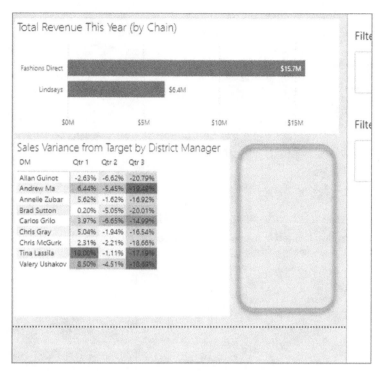

FIGURE 8.16: Extra whitespace where buttons are going to be placed

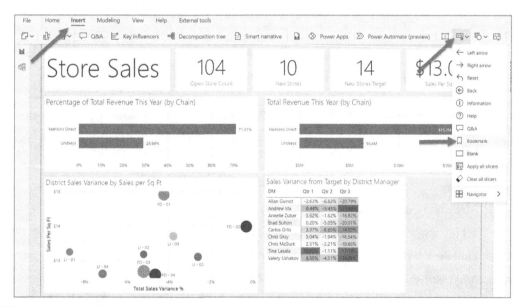

FIGURE 8.17: Bookmark menu item location

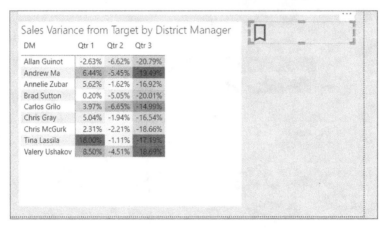

FIGURE 8.18: Bookmark button located in available whitespace

FIGURE 8.19: Configuring the bookmark action properties

Now let's change the formatting a little. In the Format pane, apply the following property values:

1. On the Button tab, in the Style section, open the Text property group and set the text to **Lindsey's.**

2. Change the font to Segoe UI Light and set the size to 16.

3. Make sure the Text color is black.

4. Set the text alignment to Center.

5. Find the Fill property group and toggle it On.

6. Make sure the Color property value is set to White.

We did all that just to make sure that the look and feel of your buttons match the rest of the text on the report. A mix of fonts and font sizes is not good practice, as we learned earlier in this book.

Now, copy the Lindsey's button and paste it. Change the Title property on the new button to say **Fashion Direct.** Then select the Fashion Direct bookmark for the Action property. Your report's lower-right corner should now look something like Figure 8.20.

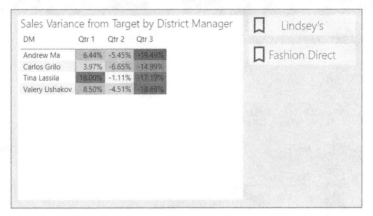

FIGURE 8.20: Bookmark buttons created and renamed

Publish your report to My Workspace. (Remember, since it's probably been a while since we've published a report, the Publish button is at the far right of the Home ribbon. When it's clicked, it will ask to which workspace you want it published.)

Personal Bookmarks vs. Report Bookmarks

The reason I want us to publish this report is that we need to talk a minute about the difference between personal bookmarks and report bookmarks. We just took time to build two bookmarks directly into our report, Lindsey's and Fashion Direct, which highlight their corresponding chain data.

When your report consumers are using your report, they can have their own personal bookmarks saved in the workspace that no one else can see. But when they are in the Power BI service using your report, they will also be able to see your predefined report bookmarks.

Open your browser and navigate to `https://app.powerbi.com/groups/me/list` to find the report you just published. I named mine `c08report` (a very exciting name). Click your report to display it (see Figure 8.21).

Once you're there in your newly published report, try using the bookmark buttons we created to see how they work.

Next, in the upper-right corner, you should see the Bookmark button. Clicking this button will give your user the option to add their own bookmarks or to look at the report bookmarks (under Show More Bookmarks) that you created already (see Figure 8.22).

Let's take these buttons and bookmarks features just one step further before we wrap up this chapter.

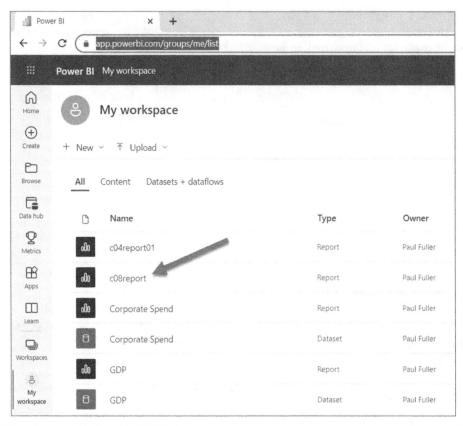

FIGURE 8.21: c08report displayed In My Workspace

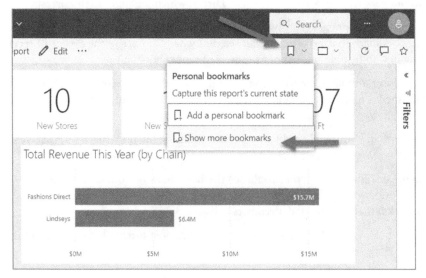

FIGURE 8.22: Show More Bookmarks menu item displayed

SELECTIONS AND VISIBILITY

Let's go back to this report in Power BI Desktop on our report. Drill up on our Sales Variance visual all the way up to the highest level. Then, copy and paste the visual. This will result in two visuals right on top of each other, maybe staggered a little, as shown in Figure 8.23.

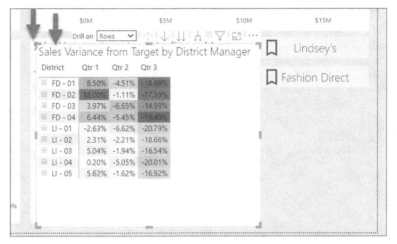

FIGURE 8.23: Copied and pasted visuals overlapping

Now open the Visualization pane and Data pane and drag the Total Sales Variance measure from the Sales table into the Values property for the matrix (see Figure 8.24). Then remove the Total Sales Variance percent measure.

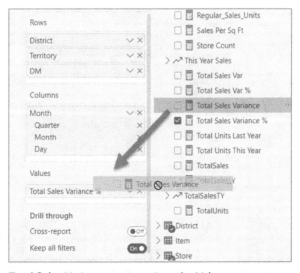

FIGURE 8.24: Dragging the Total Sales Variance measure into the Values property

Now your Matrix visual on top of the original one should look something like Figure 8.25, with just dollar values in the grid instead of percentage values.

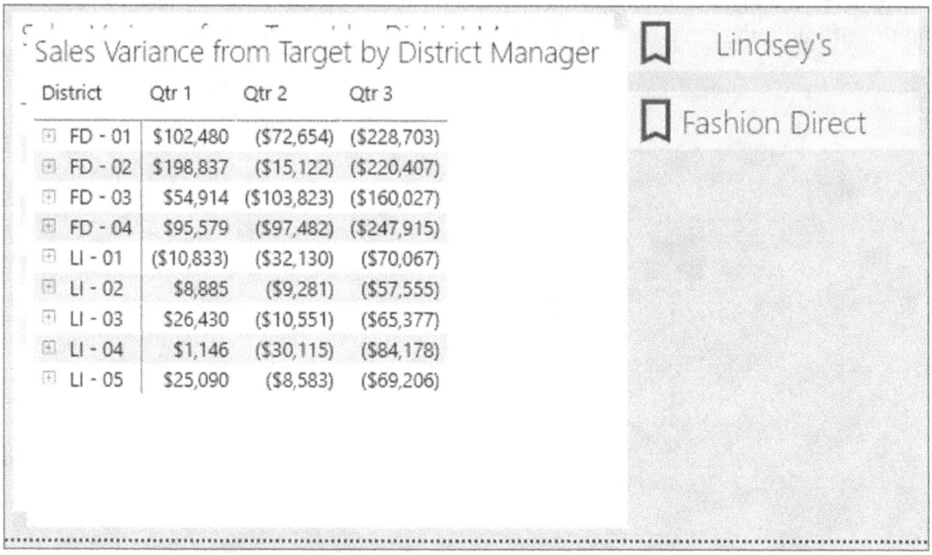

District	Qtr 1	Qtr 2	Qtr 3
FD - 01	$102,480	($72,654)	($228,703)
FD - 02	$198,837	($15,122)	($220,407)
FD - 03	$54,914	($103,823)	($160,027)
FD - 04	$95,579	($97,482)	($247,915)
LI - 01	($10,833)	($32,130)	($70,067)
LI - 02	$8,885	($9,281)	($57,555)
LI - 03	$26,430	($10,551)	($65,377)
LI - 04	$1,146	($30,115)	($84,178)
LI - 05	$25,090	($8,583)	($69,206)

Sales Variance from Target by District Manager — Lindsey's — Fashion Direct

FIGURE 8.25: Copied and pasted visuals overlapping

Go back to the Visualizations pane, go to the Format Visual tab, and find the General tab. Change the Title property of our new visual to **Sales Variance ($) from Target by DM** (see Figure 8.26).

Sales Variance ($) from Target by DM

District	Qtr 1	Qtr 2	Qtr 3
FD - 01	$102,480	($72,654)	($228,703)
FD - 02	$198,837	($15,122)	($220,407)
FD - 03	$54,914	($103,823)	($160,027)
FD - 04	$95,579	($97,482)	($247,915)
LI - 01	($10,833)	($32,130)	($70,067)
LI - 02	$8,885	($9,281)	($57,555)
LI - 03	$26,430	($10,551)	($65,377)
LI - 04	$1,146	($30,115)	($84,178)
LI - 05	$25,090	($8,583)	($69,206)

FIGURE 8.26: Title changed on pasted visuals

Now align the new visual directly over the top of the other visual. You may be wondering, "What in the world are we doing?" Fair enough. Here's a common ask of users: "Hey! I really like seeing those percentage values there, but it'd be really nice to be able to toggle the table so that I can see the dollar values those percentages represent. Can you do that for me?" The answer you need to give them is, "For sure!" (Since that's what we're learning here now!)

Now let's look at yet *another new pane!* On the View ribbon, click the Selection button to open the Selection pane. The Selection pane lets you control several things, but one particular area of interest to us right now is the *visibility* of the controls on your report page. Notice that each visual is listed. Some of the visuals have obvious names and others don't (see Figure 8.27).

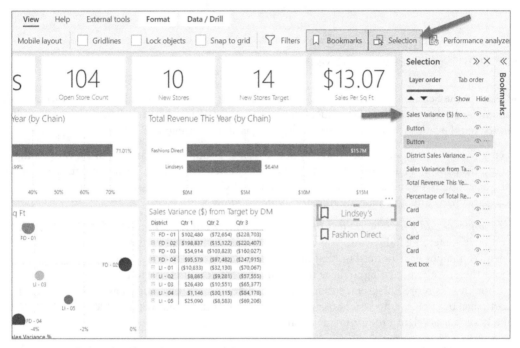

FIGURE 8.27: Visuals listed in the selection pane

At the top of my list of visuals in the Selection pane is the new Sales Variance ($) item. Now let's add a new bookmark button just like we did before. We can do that by copying and pasting our Fashion Direct button. Change the text on the new button to **Show percent**. Again, copy and paste the new button and change its text to **Show $**. Your bottom-right corner should look something like Figure 8.28.

Sales Variance ($) from Target by DM			
District	Qtr 1	Qtr 2	Qtr 3
FD - 01	$102,480	($72,654)	($228,703)
FD - 02	$198,837	($15,122)	($220,407)
FD - 03	$54,914	($103,823)	($160,027)
FD - 04	$95,579	($97,482)	($247,915)
LI - 01	($10,833)	($32,130)	($70,067)
LI - 02	$8,885	($9,281)	($57,555)
LI - 03	$26,430	($10,551)	($65,377)
LI - 04	$1,146	($30,115)	($84,178)
LI - 05	$25,090	($8,583)	($69,206)

Lindsey's

Fashion Direct

Show %

Show $

FIGURE 8.28: Two bookmark buttons created

FIGURE 8.29: Hiding the Sales Variance ($) visual

Go back to the Selection pane and find the Sales Variance ($) visual listed. Immediately to the right of that name you'll see a visibility icon just like we've seen before in the Model view. Click the visibility icon so that the Sales Variance ($) visual is hidden (as shown in Figure 8.29).

When you click it, you should see that our new $ Visual disappears. That's good! Now open the Bookmarks pane and add a new bookmark. Name that new bookmark **Show percent**. Next, go back to the Selection pane and unhide the Sales Variance ($) visual. For the last time, go back to the Bookmarks pane and add a new bookmark. Name it **Show $**.

Every time you add a bookmark, it is like taking a snapshot of what things look like at that moment. If you have something hidden and you create a bookmark, that will by default remember what was hidden. You might have noticed on that menu where you rename the bookmarks that there are other options there. We're not going to delve into them, but it's good for you to know that you can make your bookmarks more fine-grained than what we're doing here. Our bookmark looks at the whole report page, but you can make a bookmark relative to just the visual you have selected. You can also make bookmarks relative to just the data values you've selected.

Let's do one more thing to wrap this up before we republish. Go back to our new Show percent Button in the lower-left corner and select it. On the Format pane, find the Action property. Notice that the action is set to open Fashions Direct (or Lindsey's if you copied the Lindsey's button). Change it to point to the Show percent bookmark. Do the same thing for the Show $ button: make it point to the Show $ bookmark (see Figure 8.30).

What we have done here is tied our bookmarks, which take into consideration the visibility of visuals, to button actions. That's getting pretty sophisticated for a new Power BI developer! You're well on your way to knocking the socks off your users!

Let's wrap this up by republishing your report. When you click the Publish button and reselect My Workspace, you are going to be alerted that this report already exists. Choose Replace to update your report as it is published.

Once your report is republished, go back out to the Power BI service on the Web and check out how your new buttons allow you to toggle whether the percentages or dollars are shown.

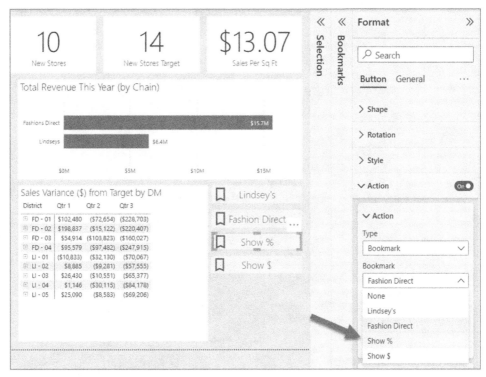

FIGURE 8.30: Selecting the Show % bookmark

CONCLUSION

At this point, you have learned enough to create very useful content. There are many kinds of visualizations in Power BI that you can explore and different techniques that you can explore in creating reports. At the end of this book, I will provide some favorite websites I use that will provide you with additional resources for Power BI report development. But, at this point we have several other Power BI topics we need to cover that aren't about creating reports.

Refreshing, Sharing, and Collaborating

I'm sure you're still scratching your head about how you'll share this content with others! Well, we're here now!

In this chapter, we'll cover three topics: refreshing the data in your report, sharing your reports, and collaborating with others in report development.

Before we jump into the sharing aspect, we'll examine how to keep that report up-to-date with the most recent data.

REFRESHING DATA

Let's talk about your old process of building reports with something like Excel. Typically, you'd be presented with the need to create a report, and you would need to find where that data was. Once you found or received the data, you would somehow import that data into Excel, probably by copying and pasting from an original source. Ideally you're not keying it in manually. Then you arranged the data in a way that would be presentable for your report consumers. Next, you'd disseminate that report in some way. People would use your report, and everyone would be able to analyze to their hearts' content. Then what happens? You get more data. Either a new financial period (like next month) or updated data comes in. At that point you must decide: am I going to create a new report or update my previous report? If I create a new one, then at least I'd be able to keep track of historical data. But maybe I want to just add a new worksheet to my Excel document, rearrange it, and then redistribute it. Either way, I need to create or update the report. And the cycle will go on, as shown in Figure 9.1.

Part of the reason you're reading this book is that maybe you've heard that you can get out of that perpetual cycle! Well, that's definitely true. Even with what we've done so far, you have simplified your report creation process.

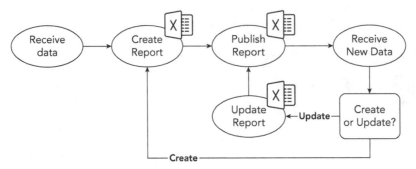

FIGURE 9.1: The manual process of updating and publishing Excel reports

Now when you receive new data, as long as the data comes in with the same structure in its source (that is, the same number of columns and same data types in each column), you should be able to just open your Power BI Desktop app, open the report you created, and click the Refresh button at the top. This would work as long as your filename (if you're using a file as the data source) is the same as before and if you put that file in the same location as before. Once you hit that Refresh button, it will open the file, repeat all the same steps you created in preparing your data in Power Query, and refresh the data model. You should not have to do anything in your report visualizations. The only step you would have to do so far is to just republish the report (see Figure 9.2).

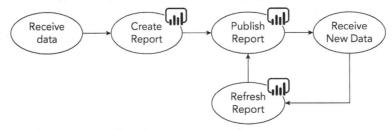

FIGURE 9.2: The manual process of refreshing a Power BI report

So, we eliminated a little bit of the process. That's helpful so far, but still not all that glamorous. It would be nice if all you had to do was refresh the report within the Power BI Service without even opening Power BI Desktop. Well, as you might imagine, that's the magical case.

Remember that when you publish a report that has imported data (versus using a shared dataset), it publishes two components: a report and a dataset (see Figure 9.3).

When you click Refresh in Power BI Desktop, technically the only thing getting refreshed is the dataset component. Once you have published a report to the Power BI Service, that dataset can simply be refreshed by clicking the Refresh button (see Figure 9.3) as you hover over the dataset where it is located in a Power BI Workspace. In this case, you don't even have to republish the report (see Figure 9.4).

This all sounds great; however, it works only if your source of data is in the cloud. What do I mean by that?

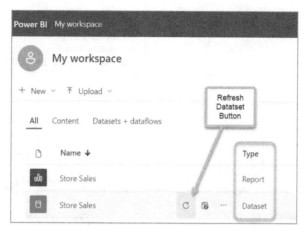

FIGURE 9.3: Distinguishing between a report and a dataset and the location of the Refresh button

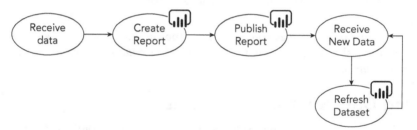

FIGURE 9.4: The automatic process of refreshing a Power BI dataset

Most of the reports we've built so far (except ones where we connected to an existing Power BI dataset, which, for those datasets are also confined to this prerequisite) have been importing data from some source. That data source in our book has always been a file except for the one time we connected to a SQL database to build our Date dimension. That file must reside *somewhere*. For the Power BI Service (on the Web) to refresh a dataset, it must be able to "see" that source of data. For it to "see" that source, it must have two things: connectivity and accessibility.

Connectivity means that the source exposes itself to the Internet *and* that there is nothing blocking the Power BI Service from accessing it. Something that might block the service from accessing it would be a firewall. *Accessibility* means that Power BI has the appropriate security credentials necessary to connect to the data.

Many data sources today are available in the cloud, such as online services like Survey Monkey and Salesforce, and databases like Azure SQL Database, Google BigQuery, and Amazon Redshift. But cloud file storage providers such as OneDrive, SharePoint Online, or Google Sheets are also ways to access your data in the cloud (see Figure 9.5). All of these methods have connectivity, because they all reside within the Internet (the cloud). Furthermore, they each provide a way to authenticate with them, so therefore, they're accessible.

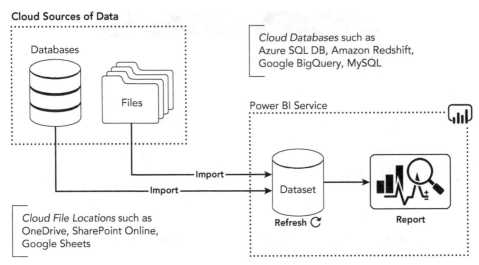

FIGURE 9.5: Accessible file and database cloud-based sources of data

For cloud sources of data, as long as you provide the appropriate credentials (which we'll look at shortly), you can refresh your datasets in the Power BI Service *without republishing the report every time you receive new data.*

Configuring Data Source Credentials

Data sources in Power BI Desktop and the Power BI Service must be configured with the appropriate credentials required to access the data source. There are different modes of authentication for the different types of data sources, so it would be too difficult to explain all the possibilities. However, what I will show you is how to configure the credentials for your data source once it's published to the Power BI Service.

Within the workspace, click the ellipsis next to a dataset and select Settings (see Figure 9.6).

There are many settings you can learn about for datasets, but what we're interested in here is the data source credentials. Find that setting and click the little triangle pointing to Data Source Credentials (see Figure 9.7).

You'll notice in Figure 9.7 that it says *Web*. This means the data source type is a file located at a specific location on the Web; that is, a URL is specified. If this dataset imported multiple sources, they would each be listed here. Click Edit Credentials.

The Edit Credentials link opens the Configure window for that dataset's data source. Notice the Url field at the top in my example in Figure 9.8? That helps you see where the source is located. The Authentication Method field tells you the way the source allows you to connect with credentials. In this example, I'm using Anonymous because the file is located in a public area and does not require credentials.

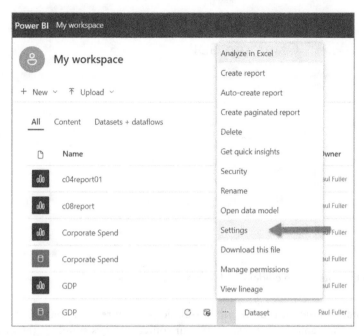

FIGURE 9.6: Finding the Settings menu for a dataset

FIGURE 9.7: The location of the link to edit data source credentials

FIGURE 9.8: Editing the data source credentials for an anonymous source

However, if I change Authentication Method to Basic (see Figure 9.9), you can see that it now requests a specific username and password. If your source requires simple authentication, this would be where you put the credentials.

FIGURE 9.9: Editing basic username and password credentials

The other authentication method that is far more secure is OAuth2. If your data source supports OAuth2, then when you select that option, the username and password will go away. However, once you click the Sign In button, it will pop up an OAuth login window and attempt to connect. (OAuth2 is a security protocol that is used across many of the services you use every day. If you're really curious, you can learn more about it at `https://oauth.net`.)

If your data sources are files that you can store on OneDrive, then when you set the authentication method, you'll use OAuth2 to connect. Then, every time you update the file, Power BI will connect to your OneDrive and will authenticate with your saved credentials.

If you're interested in how to use OneDrive as a data source, you'll find that it's not a data source type listed in Power BI Desktop. You simply need to provide the file path to where it's located in OneDrive and it will store as a *web* source, just like my previous example with the GDP dataset. You can find detailed instructions about how to use OneDrive as a connection for Power BI at `https://learn.microsoft.com/en-us/power-bi/connect-data/desktop-use-onedrive-business-links`.

Power BI Data Gateway

It's quite possible that your data source, however, resides on private networks hosted by your organization. In the IT world we call that *on premises*. That means the servers where the files and databases are stored are not publicly accessible by applications in the cloud like the Power BI Service. But that's not a showstopper. If your files or databases are located on premises, then what you need to explore is the Power BI Data Gateway. The Data Gateway is a free software application provided by Microsoft (see `https://powerbi.microsoft.com/en-us/gateway`) to enable access to your on-premises data (see Figure 9.10).

There are two types of gateways: standard and personal. The personal gateway is typically installed on a personal computer that is always up and running and has access to the Internet. This is used for limited scenarios and is not advisable for ongoing business scenarios. As Microsoft puts it, it's good for when "you're the only person who creates reports, and you don't need to share any data sources with others." (`https://learn.microsoft.com/en-us/power-bi/connect-data/service-gateway-onprem`).

The standard gateway is the right solution for accessing data sources on premises when you need to share your reports with others (as we'll talk about in just a little bit). I wrote this book with a specific audience in mind—business users who aren't in IT. That doesn't mean folks in IT can't read and benefit from the book! Installing the Power BI Data Gateway is not difficult, nor does it require much maintenance. However, it is typically something someone in IT will manage. The reason for that is because it is important to consider what data is being shared externally and by whom and how often. Furthermore, your IT department will need to consider firewall requirements. That all being said, it's a safe, secure, and simple application to set up and maintain. If you're looking for more information on how to set it up and configure it, you can find more information at `https://learn.microsoft.com/en-us/data-integration/gateway/service-gateway-app`.

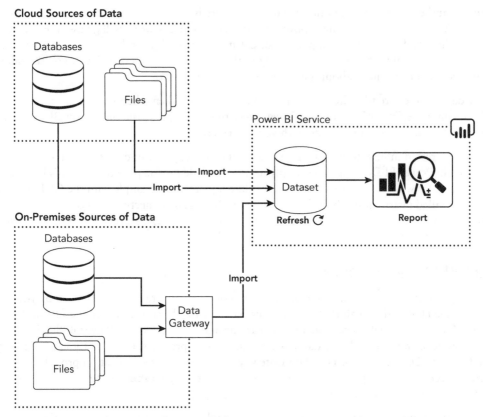

FIGURE 9.10: On-premises data comes through Data Gateway into the cloud into your dataset.

Once you've installed a gateway, you'll be able to configure the dataset's Gateway Connection setting (see Figure 9.11). There you can select the Use An On-Premises Or VNet Data Gateway option. When you select that, it will list the gateways that are visible.

Scheduling Refresh

You may be saying, "But it would be really nice if I didn't have to go click that Refresh button in the Power BI Service!" I have good news for you! You can schedule to refresh datasets so that they execute automatically on a predetermined basis. Even if you're using the Data Gateway application, the scheduled refresh will operate and reach out to your organization and reimport the data.

To access the schedule, go to the Dataset Settings (where we set the credentials) and go to Scheduled Refresh (see Figure 9.12). Toggle the On/Off button. Then pick the frequency you want the refresh to happen. If you pick Daily, you can configure up to eight different times throughout the day if you have a Power BI Pro subscription. With Premium or Premium per User, you can have 48. That's how simple it is!

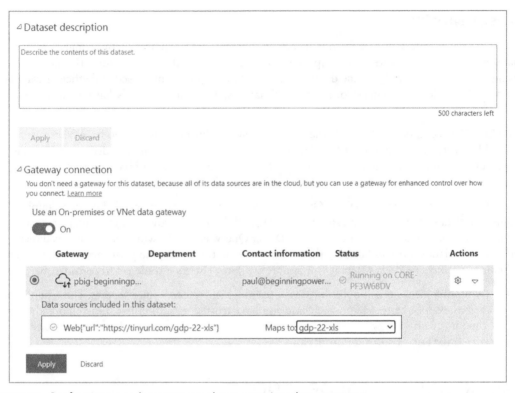

FIGURE 9.11: Configuring your dataset to use the on-premises data gateway

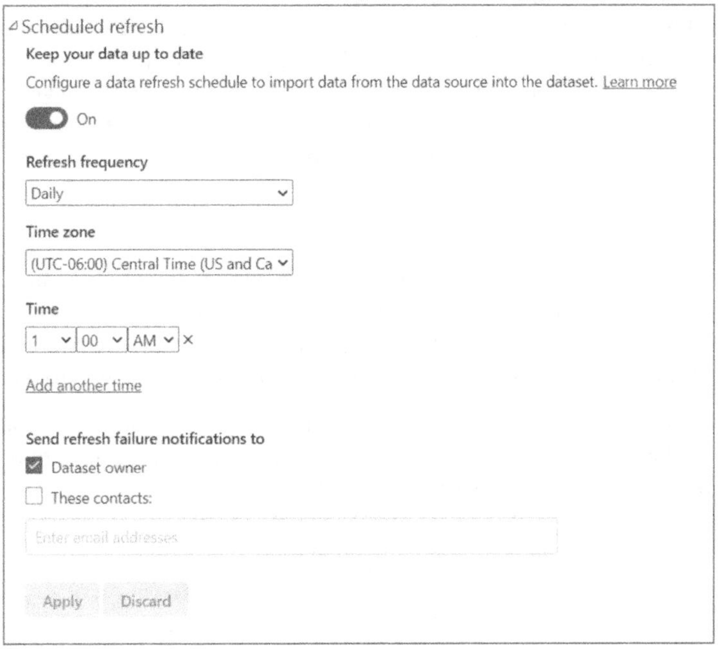

FIGURE 9.12: Setting up the schedule to refresh your data

Dataset Modes

So far, we have dealt with data for our reports in two ways: importing data and connecting to a dataset. These two ways are called Import and Live Connect. In the Import mode, the data you are using is literally *imported* into the dataset and stored in a highly compressed and efficient way. This mode is the mode I recommend for nearly all situations, if you don't already have a dataset available to connect to.

The Live Connect mode is the mode that I recommend for business users who have been given access to build reports by utilizing published datasets. These datasets are often provided by an IT Analytics department within an organization. When you build your reports using Live Connect, you are ensured of getting the most-up-to-date data available in the dataset.

The other connection mode is Direct Query. Direct Query is sometimes needed if, for example, the volume of data is very large and cannot be aggregated (billions of rows, for example) or if you want your users to have real-time reporting. With Direct Query, Power BI will execute queries directly against your data source and display the results. Note: in this mode, the performance of your reports will almost always be slower than if you import the data. There's a trade-off to consider there.

Ideally your organization will publish datasets upon which you can build reports. These published datasets may even be certified, in which case you have trusted data to utilize. Learn more about dataset modes at `https://learn.microsoft.com/en-us/power-bi/connect-data/service-dataset-modes-understand`.

SHARING AND COLLABORATING

Everything we have created up to this point we published to our own personal workspace. You might recall in Chapter 3 when we talked about frequented hotpots in Power BI that there are two kinds of workspaces: My Workspace and workspaces. My Workspace is handy for your own personal work and for getting things ready before sharing with others. However, once you have your first super-duper awesome report ready to share, you can't keep it in My Workspace because that workspace is reserved just for you. This is where the *regular* workspaces come in.

Workspaces

As we learned in Chapter 3, workspaces are how you organize content and secure content. In workspaces, you should keep only related content for the same audience for each workspace. For example, it will make your life easier in the long run if you create a Sales workspace and Finance workspace for those two business areas instead of piling all your reports into a single workspace.

You can find the Workspaces area by clicking the Workspaces button on the bottom-left side of your Power BI screen in the Power BI Service. In my example in Figure 9.13, I have two workspaces in addition to My Workspace: GDP Exercises and IMDB.

FIGURE 9.13: Finding the Workspaces area in the Power BI Service

Creating Workspaces

Creating a workspace is not complicated, but depending on the policies in place at your organization, you may not be able to do this. Let's try to create a workspace together.

In the Workspaces list, click the New Workspace button to open the Create A Workspace window and enter a name for your new workspace (see Figure 9.14). Optionally, you can upload a custom image to display alongside the workspace name and can provide a description of the workspace. Then click Save.

If you don't have permissions to create a workspace, you'll receive an error saying, "App Workspace creation is disabled." In this situation, you'll have to request permission from your organization's IT department that manages Power BI.

Publishing

After you've created your first workspace, go back to Power BI Desktop and open an existing report you've created before. Then click the Publish button. When you click Publish, you will be given a list of available workspaces where you can publish reports. In the list you will now see the new workspace you created (see Figure 9.15).

Selecting the new workspace you just created will publish the report to a place where others can see your new report *if they have the right permissions*. So, let's talk about that.

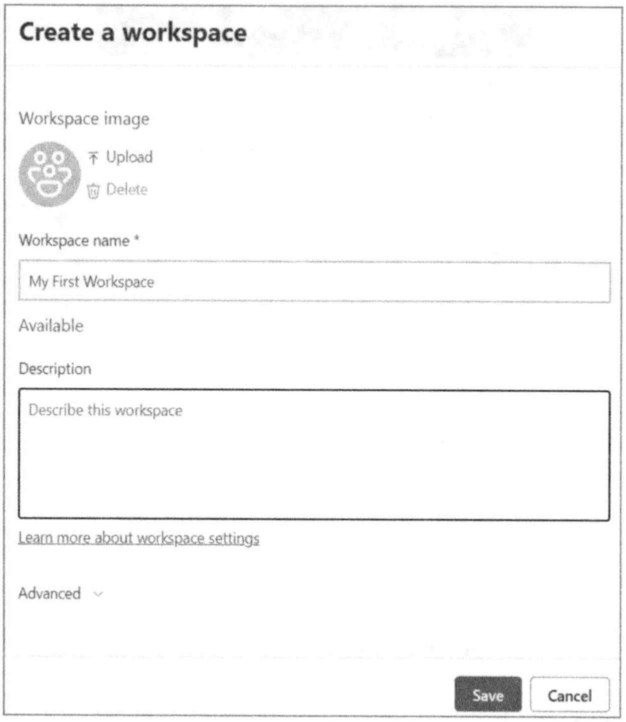

FIGURE 9.14: Entering the details for a new workspace

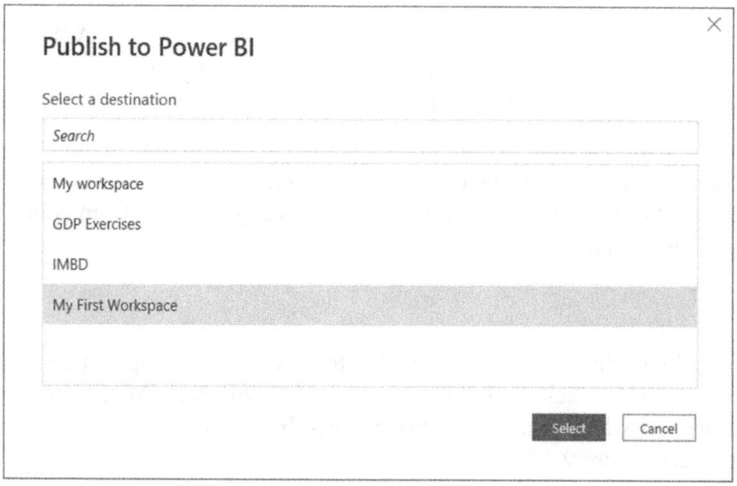

FIGURE 9.15: Picking a workspace in which to publish a report

Security and Permission Levels

It should go without saying (but I'll say it anyway) that individuals must have at a minimum, some paid Power BI subscription such as Pro, Premium per User, or Premium. Simply because you published your report to a workspace does not mean that report consumers can use your report if they do not have a subscription.

But beyond having a subscription, individuals must have the appropriate access rights within your workspace. There are many different aspects you can learn about workspace security, but for our purposes I want you to just focus on two important aspects: making use of security groups and permission levels. Another way of putting this is: one is about who can access your workspace and the other is about what they can do. And yet another way you might have heard of it is: access rights and privileges. Let's talk quickly about access rights.

Making Use of Security Groups

You *can* add individual users as participants in your workspace, one by one, but that's a bad idea. It's possible, but it'll come back to bite you later. Trust me on this. The better way to handle membership is to use security groups that list the members of each group. If you are part of a small organization, you may be able to just reach out to someone you know who can create an Active Directory security group (see `https://learn.microsoft.com/en-us/windows-server/identity/ad-ds/manage/understand-security-groups`). But in larger organizations there is often a defined process and maybe even an application for requesting these kinds of groups.

Security groups are managed by an application in Microsoft's Azure cloud service called Azure Active Directory (AAD). An individual within your organization who manages AAD can create groups for you. When they create a group for you, it should have some kind of consistent naming convention that at least indicates the audience and the role that audience will play in your workspace. In my example in Figure 9.16, the AAD administrator is creating a group for the IMDB audience that will be Viewers only, which we'll discuss soon. (More information for learning about AAD groups can be found at `https://learn.microsoft.com/en-us/azure/active-directory/fundamentals/concept-learn-about-groups`.)

After the group is created, members must be added to the group. In my case, I have added two individuals: my work Power BI subscription and Zach's Power BI subscription (see Figure 9.17).

A security group like this will list the specific users you want to have access to your workspace, but *the group itself does not specify what the users can do*. It is just a container. The second thing we need to think about is how to indicate that this group has permission to do this or that.

Workspace Roles

Now that I have an AAD security group created, I want to go to the management of my workspace I created and tell it to use that group. As you may have noticed in other areas of Power BI, there are 100 different ways to get to the same place. The same is true for Workspace Access settings.

One way to get to the Workspace Access settings is to click the ellipsis next to a workspace name (see Figure 9.18).

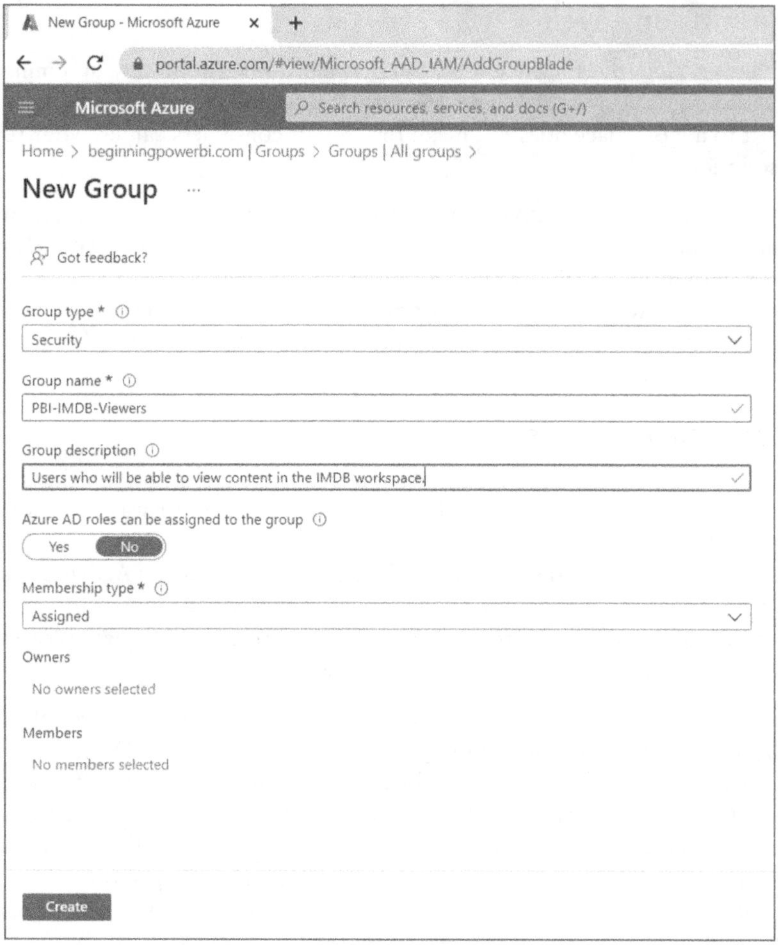

FIGURE 9.16: Creating a new security group in Azure Active Directory

FIGURE 9.17: Members listed in a security group

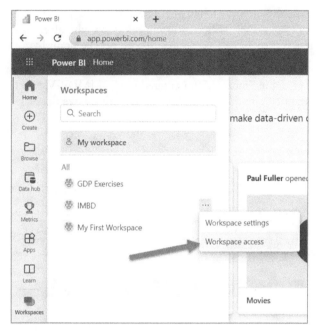

FIGURE 9.18: Menu link to the Workspace Access area

The other way to get there is while viewing the contents of your workspace, you can click directly on the Access button (see Figure 9.19).

FIGURE 9.19: Button to navigate to the Workspace Access area

In the Access window that appears, you can enter individual email addresses of people in your organization, but as I said earlier, that's not a good idea. It really will come back to haunt you later if you do. The main reason why you want to use security groups is because of the maintenance night-mare that will occur for you when your organization starts to be blown away at how amazing your new reporting capabilities are. Everyone and their brother and sister will want to build their own reports and make sure that only so-and-so can see it. But you'll be tempted to think, "Maybe it's OK if I, just this once, add Suzie's email to the list." And next thing you know, you're in a quandary because you want to take that new job offer, and when you leave your position, the next person who is left supporting your reports is left with a mess not knowing who all these different people are in the workspaces! "OK, enough preaching, Paul." I'm sure you get the point by now.

Instead of entering an email address here, you can enter the name of the group you had requested to be created. That's what I did in Figure 9.20: I entered my PBI-IMDB-Viewers group. As you type the name of the group in the field, it will display AAD groups that have that same text.

FIGURE 9.20: Adding the security group to the Workspace Access area

But below the name is another very important field. In Figure 9.20, it just says Member. That Member is a workspace *role*, a permission level you are granting. It is saying this individual or, ideally, group has *this* particular permission level. There are four levels of permissions for group memberships. I'll work from the bottom up (see Table 9.1).

TABLE 9.1: Power BI Workspace Roles

ROLE	DESCRIPTION
Admin	Has Contributor permissions plus: Can update or delete the workspace and add other admins
Member	Has Contributor permissions plus: Can add members to workspace
Contributor	Has Viewer permissions plus: Can create, edit, and delete content; publish content; copy reports; and schedule refreshes
Viewer	Can view and interact with items in the workspace

To expand a little on Table 9.1, *Viewer* means you simply have permission to view content in the workspace such as Reports or Dashboards. *Contributor* means you have Viewer permission *plus* permission to create new content such as reports or dashboards. This means you can work together with other people on your team to manage the same workspace content. *Member* means you have Contributor permission *plus* you can add other Members to the workspace. *Admin* means that you have Member permissions but can also add other Admins. Admins can update or delete the workspace. Other than that, everything else that can be done in a workspace can be done by a group or individual in the Member role. (To learn more about the host of actions that are possible in the different roles, check out this site: `https://learn.microsoft.com/en-us/power-bi/collaborate-share/service-roles-new-workspaces`.)

Now let me throw you a curve ball: I personally don't think you should ever give out Viewer roles to anyone. It's just my opinion, but I think I could make a pretty good case for it. I think that if a person *truly needs* access to a workspace, then they're needing to do something in the workspace more than just view reports. They want to create stuff too! But you may say, "What about just my users who really don't have the time or need to build stuff? They just want to use my reports. Shouldn't they be put into the Viewer role?" Well, before this Microsoft feature we'll discuss briefly, I would've said yes. But the reality is, there's a better place to direct this type of report consumer: to Power BI Apps.

Power BI Apps

Power BI Apps are a way to present a view of just the content you want, to the audience you want to target. Imagine you have three reports in the same workspace that you want to pull together into a single area. And imagine that you want to include web pages from the Internet. A Power BI App allows you to do that. It's very much like creating a package of Power BI content you want to share with specific groups. Let's walk through how to do that!

One of the key things to remember about Power BI Apps is that you get *one per workspace*. You cannot (at least at this time) have an app with a couple of reports from your workspace and then another app with reports from the *same* workspace. Conversely, apps cannot contain reports from different workspaces. There is a one-to-one relationship between an app and workspace. As Microsoft releases new Power BI enhancements monthly, there is always the chance that this may change in the future.

In my environment, I have a workspace called GDP Exercises. If I navigate to that workspace, you'll notice that I have a Create App button in the upper-right corner of the screen (see Figure 9.21).

When I click Create App, it takes me to a screen to begin defining an App (see Figure 9.22).

The first thing to do is give the app a name *and a description*. Descriptions for Power BI Apps are not optional. What is optional, though, is that you can change the app theme color and apply an image as the logo to display in the App icon. After you click the Next: Add Content button, the content editor will open. Click the Add Content button, as shown in Figure 9.23.

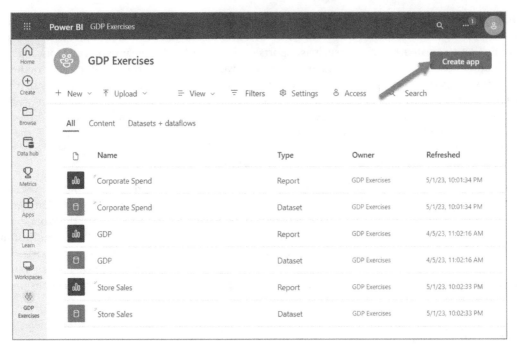

FIGURE 9.21: Location of the Create App button

When the Add Content window appears (see Figure 9.24), you will be presented with a list of content from the workspace from which you can choose to add to the app. You can add Power BI dashboards, reports, and even Excel files, if you have uploaded an Excel file to the workspace.

After I selected the reports that I want to include in my app, they are listed on the left. The app content can be organized into sections in the menu. To add a new menu section, I can click Add Content ⇨ Add A New Section.

Adding a new section will create the section with the default name, New Section. I am going to immediately rename it **Taxes & Industry,** by clicking the ellipsis (. . .) and then clicking Rename.

After adding the new section, I'd like to link in a couple of web pages that my users will find helpful. (Note: As I'm demonstrating how to build apps, I realize that the content I'm gathering here doesn't really go together: Corporate Spend analysis doesn't usually go along with GDP analysis. But for learning's sake, I'm just demonstrating how you can package content into an app.)

Besides just gathering reports and dashboards into an app, you can also add links to content on the Web or even your own intranet. To do so, select Add Content ⇨ Add Link. This will prompt you to provide information about the link, as shown in Figure 9.25.

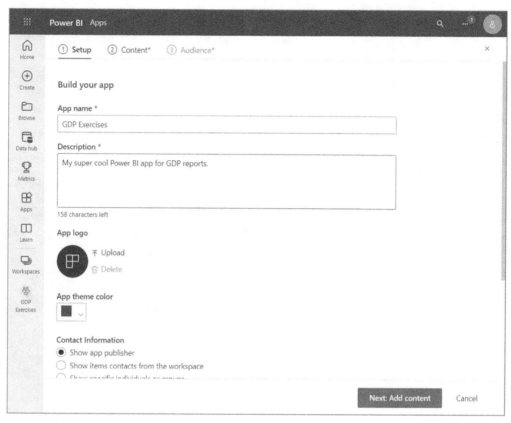

FIGURE 9.22: Defining a Power BI App

In my example, I gave the link the name **Property Taxes** and then entered the URL (`https://tinyurl.com/proptaxesbystate`) of the web content I want to include into the Link property.

The Open In property has a drop-down with various options. The New Tab option causes the URL to be opened in a new browser tab. The Current Tab option causes the app to navigate to the URL in the current browser tab. The Content Area option allows the web page to be loaded into the app content area as if it is inherently part of your app. While that's cool, not all Internet or intranet content can be loaded into the content area. For example, it might occur to you to try to put the URL of a Power BI Report from another workspace in the link. That trick won't work! But you *can* specify the URL of a Power BI Report from another workspace to open in another or the same browser tab. The effect of that is to just help your users navigate to the workspace where the report resides.

In my example, I also added another link (`https://tinyurl.com/industryfacts`) and named it **Industry Facts**. But this time instead of loading it into the Content area, I set it to open in a new tab.

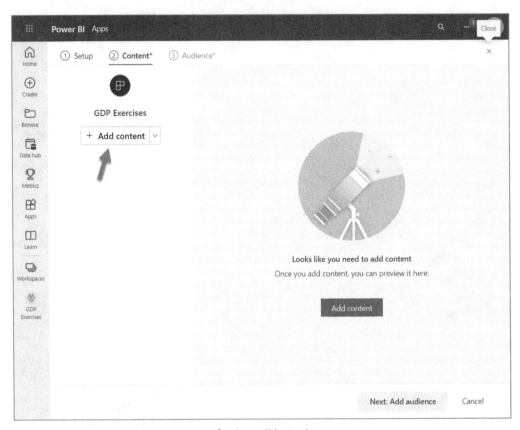

FIGURE 9.23: The Add Content button to specify what will be in the app

After you finish configuring your app content, you can click the Next: Add Audience button.

In the Audience section, you specify who the users of your app will be. Just like for the workspace security, I do not recommend adding specific usernames. Instead, I recommend using security groups here as well. In Figure 9.26, I am adding the PBI-IMBD-Viewers security group to my app. This means that if an individual is listed in the PBI-IMBD-Viewers security group, then they will be able to find, connect, and use the new GDP Exercises app I'm building.

What's also very useful is that you can create different audiences for your single app. By clicking on the New Audience button (see Figure 9.27), you'll be able to configure *who* the audience is and *what* they can see in the app.

FIGURE 9.24: Selecting content for the app

What may not be obvious is *how* you configure what each audience can see or not see. The visibility icon for each piece of report content is the key. As you hover over each item in the app, you'll see the familiar Power BI visibility icon. By clicking or unclicking that icon, you can control what parts are visible for each audience you are configuring for your app (see Figure 9.28).

After you've configured the audiences for an app, you can publish it by clicking Publish app. Once the Power BI Service finishes publishing your app, you'll receive a success message that contains a button Go To App.

In the example in Figure 9.29, I arrived at my newly published app. If you click the Property Taxes item under the Taxes & Industry section in my app, notice that on the right side of the content area a page loads that contains a map of the United States. Power BI did not create this map as it was content that already existed on the web page at `https://tinyurl.com/proptaxesbystate`. I used it here to demonstrate how simple it is to embed web content into your app that would help supplement the content.

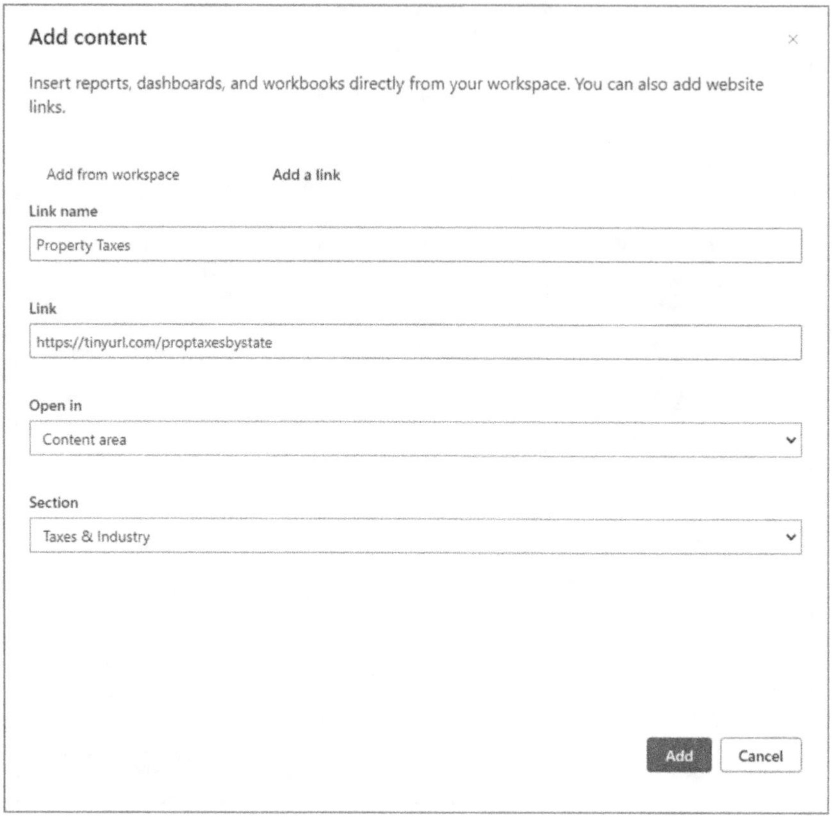

Add content
Insert reports, dashboards, and workbooks directly from your workspace. You can also add website links.
Add from workspace
Add a link
Link name
Property Taxes
Link
https://tinyurl.com/proptaxesbystate
Open in
Content area
Section
Taxes & Industry
Add
Cancel

FIGURE 9.25: Describing a link to add to the app

Edit Audience
GDP Exercises
Grant access to
Entire organization
Learn more
Specific users or groups
PBI
PBI-WorkspaceCreators
PBI-IMDB-Viewers
Workspace users
Publish app
Cancel

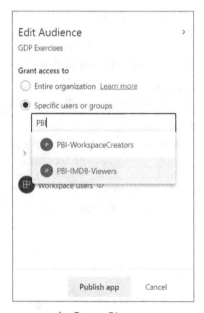

FIGURE 9.26: Specifying security group to use the Power BI app

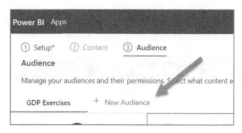

FIGURE 9.27: The New Audience button

FIGURE 9.28: Hiding or unhiding content for an audience

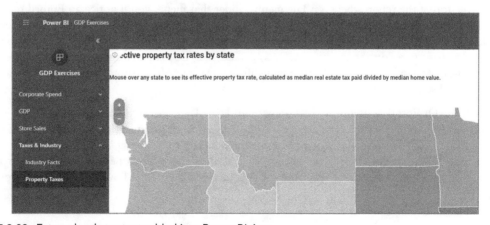

FIGURE 9.29: External web content added into Power BI App

To find any apps you have published or that others have published and you have access to, click the Apps button on the left side of the screen, as shown in Figure 9.30.

FIGURE 9.30: Apps link in the Power BI Service

Sharing

You can share content from your Power BI reports in a handful of ways. In my example in Figure 9.31, I am looking at the IT Spend Trend report page within the Corporate Spend report now displayed within my GDP Exercises app.

Along the top of the report, there is a File menu. Under that menu, you'll notice an Embed report section that offers you three options for embedding your report within other things. The SharePoint Online option provides you with a URL to embed your report within a SharePoint report web part: `https://learn.microsoft.com/en-us/power-bi/collaborate-share/service-embed-report-spo`. Using this feature will still require your SharePoint users to also have a paid Power BI subscription.

The Website Or Portal option provides you with an HTML snippet that you can include within an IFrame control on a web page. The Developer Playground is for organizations that are paying for Power BI Embedded as a service. Power BI Embedded has its own pricing structure different from the Power BI subscription levels discussed in this book. It allows web developers to include Power BI content in their websites without requiring the users to have a separate Power BI paid subscription.

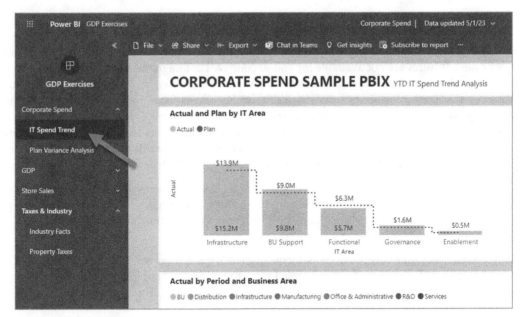

FIGURE 9.31: Finding the IT Spend Trend report page in the app

Under the Share menu you have two options: Copy Link and Manage Access. The first one simply gives you a link to the report itself that you can provide to others through email, chat, and so on. However, the individual you share the link with will need both a paid Power BI subscription and membership in the workspace to at least view the report. Manage Access takes you back to the Access area where we managed permissions. While you're at the Access area, you might notice the Direct Access section. The Direct Access section shows how specific reports or dashboards have been shared to specific people or groups. This is narrower than giving someone access at the workspace level. If a person isn't a member of a workspace but is given permission at the report level, they will be able to see *just that shared content* within the workspace. However, please note that giving direct access to reports is not good practice. The best practice to provide view-level only access to report consumers is to configure an audience within an app.

The Export menu has a PowerPoint section, which allows you either to share an image of the report you're interacting with or to actually embed a live report within a PowerPoint slide. This feature requires you to have enabled the Power BI add-in within PowerPoint. But once the add-in is enabled, you can use the URL that the Embed Live Data menu item provides to embed your report within your slides (`https://learn.microsoft.com/en-us/power-bi/collaborate-share/service-power-bi-powerpoint-add-in-install`).

> **NOTE** *For Power BI embedding in PowerPoint to work, you have to be logged into M365 (formerly known as Office 365) the same way you logged into Power BI (this is known as logging into the "same tenant").*

SUMMARY

As usual, we've covered a lot of ground in this chapter. It's quite possible that in your organization many of these features are not available for you to control. That might be frustrating but understand there are good reasons for IT organizations to lock some things down because of bad actors or to ensure well-governed environments that don't devolve into chaos. That might sound dramatic, but in my years of consulting, I have seen many situations that are quite messy because there was a lack of governance. If you find yourself hitting roadblocks in your organization with some of these features, I encourage you to reach out to the IT group that manages your Power BI estate and seek to understand. You may be surprised because either they may not realize it's locked down *or* they might be glad to give you permission to that area!

If you're working through this chapter and everything you saw is available to you in your organization, then you might want to consider discussing with your IT department the need to introduce governance over these incredible and useful features!

So, what's left? Well, in terms of Power BI learning, there's much more you can learn out there! This is just the beginning of a journey. The final topic I want to give you a brief introduction to is DAX. We've played a little bit with it, but let's take that skillset just a step further before we wrap up this book!

10

Introducing DAX

Though we covered this definition earlier, Data Analysis Expressions (DAX) is a formula language that is used for creating calculated columns, measures, and custom tables. It is a collection of functions, operators, and constants that can be used in a formula or expression to calculate and return one or more values. You can use DAX to solve a number of calculations and data analysis problems, which can help you create new information from data that is already in your model.

In this chapter, you will be introduced to the basics of DAX. We will whet your appetite by covering a handful of DAX functions. Even though it will be minimal, it will teach you the important foundational principles.

To do this, we are going to work with a star schema–modeled Azure SQL database that contains sales data from a standard Microsoft demo database, AdventureWorks. In the next section, I'll quickly walk you through the setup of the Power BI Desktop file. However, if you'd rather just jump to the meat of this chapter, then skip the "Setup" section and find the c10base.pbix file from the book resources file.

SETUP

The following steps show how to set up the Power BI Desktop file, and we've discussed all these concepts earlier in the book. Walking through these steps yourself will be an excellent test of applying what you've learned so far. However, if you get stuck, you can find the c10base.pbix file and start with that. So, let's get going!

1. Open a new Power BI Desktop session.
2. Open the Get Data window and select SQL Server Database.

3. When prompted, enter **bpbi.database.windows.net** for the server name and **BPBI** for the database.

4. If you've already connected once to this database to import a DimDate table in Chapter 6, then the credentials are likely saved for you. However, if you're prompted to enter credentials, select Basic authentication, and enter the following:

    ```
    User Name: bpbiuser
    Password:  Turn D@t@ Into Information 5o You Can Gain Ins1ght!
    ```

5. After you've authenticated, select all of the tables visible to you (except DW.DimDate), and click the Load button instead of Transform.

6. When you import all of those tables, they will all be named *DW* _____. You can rename each of them by right-clicking each table name in the Data pane and selecting Rename. Remove the DW portion from each name.

7. In the Model view (where you see how the tables are related to each other), you'll see that Power BI tried to automatically figure out the relationships for you. It does pretty well, but it doesn't know what to do with the Calendar and ShipDate tables. That's because the key names don't match up to columns in any of the other tables. Delete the relationship between Calendar and ShipDate.

8. Define a relationship between the Sales fact table and Calendar from OrderDateKey in Sales to DateKey in Calendar.

9. There are several date key values in the Sales fact, but for our purposes, we are going to just use OrderDateKey and ShipDatekey. Define the relationship between ShipDateKey in Sales to DateKey in ShipDate.

10. Hide all the columns that end in ___*key*.

11. In the Sales fact, select the SalesOrderLineNumber column, open the Properties' Advanced section, and set the default Summarize By to None. Do the same thing for TransType and RowNumber.

12. Go to the Data view and select the Calendar table.

13. Mark the Calendar table as a Date table.

14. Set the DayNameOfWeek column to sort by DayNumberOfWeek.

15. Set the MonthName column to sort by MonthNumberOfYear.

16. Finally, repeat steps 13, 14, and 15 for the ShipDate table.

You should now have a Power BI report file that has a data model with a well-defined star schema, as shown in Figure 10.1.

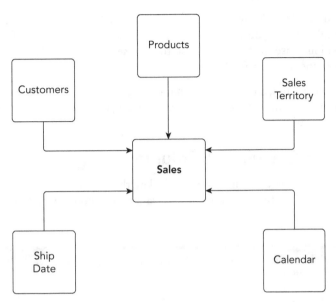

FIGURE 10.1: Sales star schema data model

CALCULATED COLUMNS

The first kind of formula we are going to consider is called a *calculated column*. DAX allows you to augment the data that you bring in from different data sources by adding columns to your tables based on formulas you create. These formulas can utilize data that is in the row you're working in, within the table you're working in, or even from other tables that are related to the table you're working in.

There are a couple reasons why you might want to do this. First, you might have only a few columns of data for a source, but given those columns, you might be able to infer information such as a product margin when you have the sales amount and product cost available in the row. Second, sometimes it is faster to have some of the calculating work done beforehand when you're refreshing your data than trying to do it dynamically in a "live" formula in your report.

When the information needed to be calculated is *not* dependent on a changeable context but would be true regardless of how your data is filtered in your report, then it would likely be ideal to add the calculation directly to your table. It may not be a good idea, however, to add a calculated column to your dataset if the calculation is very complex and/or has to be performed on millions of rows *and* if there is not a high likelihood that the column will be used that often.

It's hard to say definitively whether you should or shouldn't use these because it depends on several considerations. Knowing this one fact will help you decide whether you should add a calculated column or not: for each row in a table, the calculated column is computed, and then upon refreshing the dataset, the result is stored statically in each row. The only time that result is updated is if the formula is redefined or a Data Refresh operation is performed. It should be used carefully because for each row for each calculation, you will increase storage size (since the result of the calculation is stored), and you will increase the time to refresh the dataset (since the calculation is performed on every row every time the data is refreshed).

So, let's get started on creating a calculated column using DAX. You may be surprised to find out that you already have done this. In a previous chapter, I walked you through it and said, "Trust me, we'll cover it later." Here we are!

How to Create a Calculated Column

We'll begin by creating a new column that will calculate the margin on our product sales. Begin by opening the Data view, select the Sales table in the Data pane, and then click New Column (see Figure 10.2).

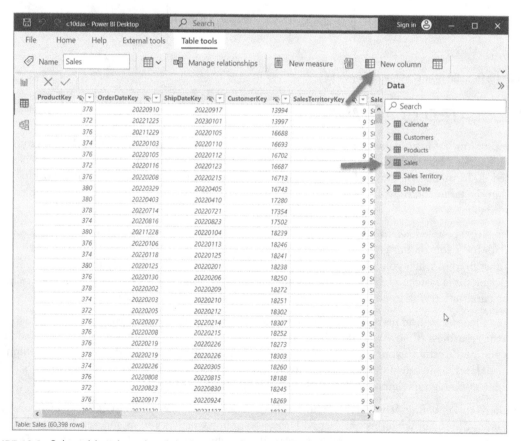

FIGURE 10.2: Sales table selected and the location of the New Column button

When you do this, a formula editor appears above the data, as shown in Figure 10.3. This editor is similar to Excel when adding formulas. The X button on the far left cancels the creation of the DAX formula you started. The checkmark button saves your work as does simply hitting the Enter key after entering the formula. The drop-down arrow on the far right opens the formula editor in a larger window. This is helpful because eventually your formulas will take up more than one line of text. DAX formulas can be formatted with multiple lines by holding the Shift key and pressing Enter.

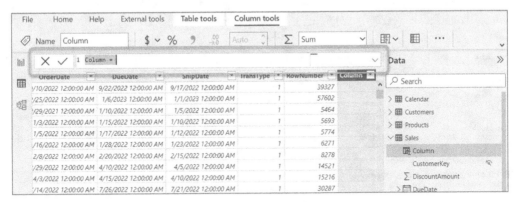

FIGURE 10.3: DAX formula editor window

> **TIP Using DAXFormatter.com** *To make your DAX formulas easy to read and consistently formatted, you can use* https://daxformatter.com *to paste your formula, apply formatting, and then copy the well-formatted formula back into the Power BI formula editor.*

The format of a DAX formula is always like this:

```
ColumnNameOrMeasureName = Some code here
```

Even if your formula has multiple lines, that first line will always start with what you want your column or measure (as we'll learn soon) to be called, followed by an equal sign, and then your code.

In the DAX formula editor, type the following code and hit Enter or click the checkmark button to save your formula:

```
Margin = 'Sales'[SalesAmount] - 'Sales'[TotalProductCost]
```

Notice that we referred to each column by prefixing it with the name of the table where the column is located. Technically, you don't have to specify the column name, but it is highly recommended for readability by others or for when you come back the next morning to look at your work and wonder what in the world you have created!

After you have saved your formula, you'll see in the fields under Sales in the Data pane that you have a new column called Margin (see Figure 10.4). In the ribbon at the top, you'll also see properties for that new column. You can quickly rename your column there as well as change the data type of the column. In addition, you can control how the data is formatted such as specifying the number of decimal places.

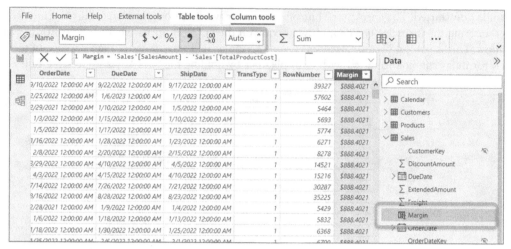

FIGURE 10.4: Formatting a DAX measure

Now what you have created is a new column that will always be recalculated every time you refresh the dataset. This Margin column does not get created on your data source from where you retrieved the data. It is added to your table, and every time you refresh the data imported, it will recalculate those values on every single row one time and save them so that they are easily accessible.

Now let's add another column that tells us our margin as a percentage of the sale. Another way to add a new column is by right-clicking the table name and selecting New Column.

Enter the following formula for your new Margin % column:

```
Margin % = DIVIDE ( 'Sales'[Margin], 'Sales'[SalesAmount] )
```

After you saved this formula, you might notice that everything shows up as a decimal value (see Figure 10.5). You can make sure that it always is formatted as a percentage by clicking the Percent formatting button in the ribbon above.

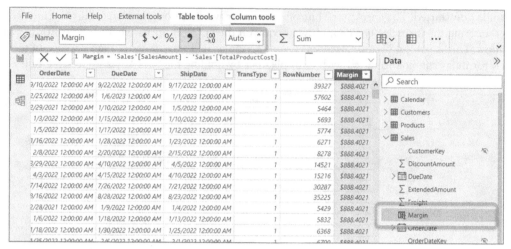

FIGURE 10.5: Location of the Percent formatting button

For your new Margin % column, select the column and then change the default aggregation to Average (see Figure 10.6). This is important because if you want to use your Margin % value in a visual, it will try to sum up your Margin % values, which would not make sense. However, an Average margin percentage will make sense.

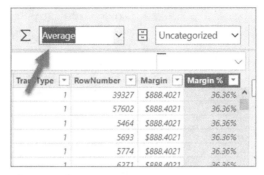

FIGURE 10.6: Selecting Average for the default aggregation

This formula we created could have been written like this:

```
Margin % = 'Sales'[Margin] / 'Sales'[SalesAmount]
```

That would have worked most of the time. But we used a function called DIVIDE for a reason. The DIVIDE function allows us to divide numbers and not get an error in case our denominator is zero or empty. There may be times when a zero-dollar sale is recorded. Or sometimes there may be a problem in the data you imported, and the value was empty. If we weren't prepared for a zero denominator, we would get an error in our table calculation. You've probably seen a similar infamous error in Excel: #DIV/0. The DIVIDE function is a way to prevent that from happening and to quickly create a formula that is shorter than using an IF condition to check the denominator.

Now we have added a new column that also refers to a column we created on the fly. That's pretty powerful. That's where the magic of DAX takes you beyond Excel. Imagine trying to do that in Excel. You wouldn't be able to refer to your Margin formula in other cells—you'd have to redo it every time. Your code would look something like this:

```
Margin Pct = ( 'Sales'[SalesAmount] - 'Sales'[TotalProductCost] )
/ IF ( 'Sales'[SalesAmount] = 0, 0, 'Sales'[SalesAmount] )
```

Why do all that when you can reuse your formulas and use nice shorthand like the DIVIDE function? (By the way, the IF statement syntax in DAX is the same syntax as the Excel IF. You'll find that the basic elements of the Excel formula language are here in DAX.)

Now, just for fun, let's use our new calculated columns in a Matrix visual. Go to the Report view and add a matrix to the canvas. In the Rows property, add the Category column from the Products table. In the Columns property, add the CalendarYear column from the Calendar table. And in the Values property, add our Margin % column from the Sales table. You should have something like Figure 10.7.

What you just did there is some pretty awesome stuff! In a matter of minutes, given just raw sales data, particularly the sales amount and a product cost, product description, and a Calendar table, you were able to identify what the average margin is across all of the sales data and break that down by year and by product category. And sure, you could do that with Excel in a pivot table, but could you do that with two pivot tables side-by-side and have them interact with each other as you highlight data from one pivot table? I don't think so! Now let's dig into the next kind of DAX formula: measures.

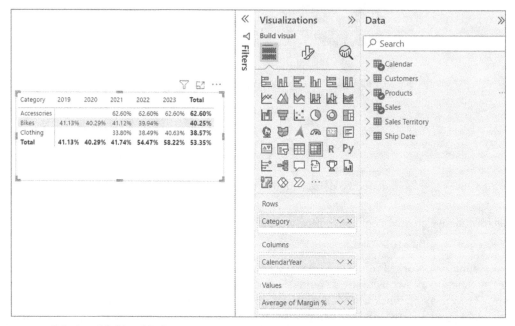

FIGURE 10.7: Calculated fields added onto a Matrix visual

DAX MEASURES

Calculated columns are useful, but they operate row by row across every row in a table where you have a calculated column. However, other situations might require a more dynamic method. For example, consider a situation where you want the total sales of all rows in your table. In addition, you want to slice and dice those sales by other things, such as total sales by year, by employee, or by product. And as you slice and dice, remember that is filtering the data in your table. When you slice and dice like that, you want that total sales to work automatically by only adding up sales that are not filtered out at that point. To accomplish these tasks, you would use a *DAX measure*. You can think of a DAX measure like a portable Excel formula that you can use in different ways on your reports.

Creating a DAX measure is similar to how we created a calculated column. You can right-click a table name in the Data pane and select New Measure. Or you can click the New Measure button on the ribbon across the top on any of the views (Report, Data, or Model), as shown in Figure 10.8.

FIGURE 10.8: The New Measure button on the Home ribbon

When you create a new measure, you will see a formula bar appear just like we had for calculated columns. Measures will have a different icon in the Data pane than calculated columns.

The calculated columns will have a table icon with a sigma in the lower-right corner. The measure will have a calculator icon (see Figure 10.9).

FIGURE 10.9: Identifying calculated columns versus DAX measures in the Data pane

The key difference between a calculated column and a measure is that measures perform their calculations at the time that the user is working with them in a visual, and a calculated columns is calculated *and stored* when the dataset is refreshed.

Up to this point, with a couple of exceptions in some of the exercises, we have worked with *implicit* measures. Implicit measures are not ones where you write any code. They are automatically available if you have a numeric data type for a column. You know that a column has an implicit measure if it has a sigma icon next to it in the Data pane. But what we are learning about in this chapter are *explicit* measures where we *explicitly write DAX code*.

Let's create a DAX measure on the Sales table called Total Sales. This will be the simplest measure we could write, and it will likely do exactly what you expected it to: it will add up all the sales values. Click the New Measure button and enter the following code:

```
Total Sales = SUM ( 'Sales'[SalesAmount] )
```

Select the new Total Sales measure you created on the Sales table and change the formatting so that it displays no decimal values (as shown in Figure 10.10).

FIGURE 10.10: Controlling the number of decimal places displayed when using the DAX measure

Let's make a copy of the Matrix visual we were working on and paste it below. Then remove the Average of Margin % from the Values property and drag your Total Sales measure to that Values property. Those values that will show up are going to be kind of large, so let's figure out how to abbreviate those amounts into units.

1. Go to the Format properties for your new Matrix visual.

2. Scroll down to the Specific Column section.

3. Make sure the Apply Settings To property of Series is set to Total Sales.

4. Under the Display Units section, select Thousands.

This will cause the Total Sales values to show up in the matrix as abbreviated amounts in the thousands. By doing this in the example shown in Figure 10.11, the columns from the first matrix align with the columns in the second matrix.

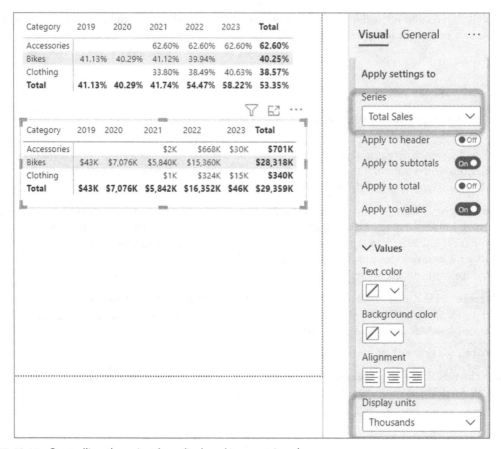

FIGURE 10.11: Controlling the unit values displayed in a matrix column

This Total Sales measure really doesn't seem all that impressive, especially because it is doing the same thing the implicit measure on the SalesAmount column would do. However, most experts say that the best practice is to avoid implicit measures to ensure better scalability and adaptability to changing requirements. In other words, create a measure for every calculation you need to so that you can have more fine-grained control.

Now let's create a new measure called Profit. This measure will actually summarize the calculated column value we created.

```
Profit = SUM ( 'Sales'[Margin] )
```

Measures can refer to other measures. Let's do that and create a measure that shows profit as a percent of total sales. After you create this measure, specify the formatting as a percent.

```
Profit % = DIVIDE ( [Profit] , [Total Sales] )
```

Notice that when I refer to measures in my DAX formulas, I don't specify the table name in front of the measure name. You can, but you don't have to. I like to not specify the table name when referring to measures because it helps me know that I'm working with a measure when I look at it later. Measures have to be uniquely named in your report. You cannot have two measures named Profit %.

Now let's go nuts! Add a new Line And Clustered Column Chart visual to your report. Stretch the visual across the top half of your report and move your Matrix visuals below it. Then add the CalendarYear to the X-axis, your Total Sales measure to the Column y-axis, and your Profit % measure to the Line y-axis; finally, add Category (from the Product table) to the Small Multiples property (see Figure 10.12).

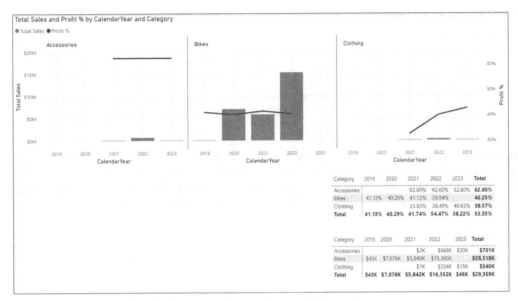

FIGURE 10.12: Using the Small Multiples property on a Clustered Column chart

The Small Multiples property forces the visual to display a separate chart for each value in the category. In my example in Figure 10.12, I went to the Format properties of the visual and set the Small Multiples Layout property to have one row and three columns.

In our visual, we have two axes on each chart. One y-axis shows the Total Sales measure values, and the other y-axis shows the Profit % values across the top of the other y-axis. Here we can see that although the Total Sales for bikes is very high and the Total Sales for Accessories are very low, our best profits come from the sales of accessories. Accessories has a Profit % of above 60 percent.

In summary, measures are calculated *on demand*. That means Power BI calculates the correct value *only* when the user requests it. It performs the calculation based on what data can be "seen" relative to filters and slicers. Measures do not add to the overall disk space of the Power BI `.pbix` file.

So far, in creating our DAX measures, we've used the following two DAX functions: DIVIDE and SUM. Now, let's introduce you to two more DAX functions.

COUNTROWS and DISTINCTCOUNT

The COUNTROWS function counts the number of *visible* rows in a particular table. By *visible*, I mean that if you are using slicers and filters to hide data, COUNTROWS will count only the subset of rows that are not filtered out. Those rows not filtered out of a table are considered *visible* (even if you can't see them yourself on the screen).

The DISTINCTCOUNT function will count the number of *unique* values in a particular column within the *visible* rows of a table.

Let's create some measures using these functions, and then we'll put them into a Table visual to see them in action.

Create the following measures:

```
1. Transactions = COUNTROWS ( Sales )
2. Days Selling = DISTINCTCOUNT ( 'Sales'[OrderDateKey] )
3. Avg Sales per Transaction = DIVIDE ( [Total Sales] , [Transactions] )
4. Avg Sales per Day = DIVIDE ( [Total Sales] , [Days Selling] )
```

Add a slicer to the lower-left corner of your report and add the CalendarYear value. In the remaining space on your report, add one more Matrix visual. To the Rows property, add the MonthName column. In the Values property, add the Avg Sales per Transaction, Days Selling, Transactions, and Avg Sales per Day measures. Your report should now look something like Figure 10.13.

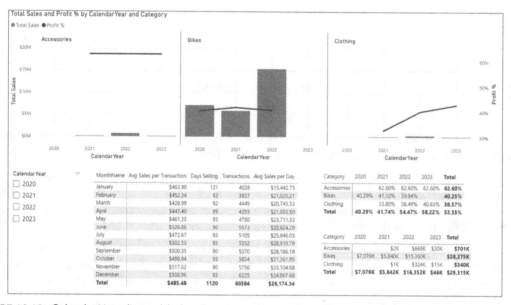

FIGURE 10.13: Calendar Year slicer added to the report along with another Matrix visual

Let's talk about what these two *counting* DAX functions are doing.

First, we built the Transactions measure. That measure counts the number of *visible* rows in the Sales table. In our new visual, it shows that there are 3,857 sales in the month of February. You can see what I mean by *visible* if you select the year 2021 in your Year slicer. When you do that, the number of transactions in February dropped to 260. You see the first number (3,857) is the count of all rows in the Sales table across all the years of data available. However, when we used our slicer to pick just the year 2021, Power BI then filtered the Sales table down to just sales in the year 2021: that is, only 2021 sales rows are *visible*. So, 260 is the number of sales in February of 2021.

Second, the Days Selling measure uses the DISTINCTCOUNT function. If you think about it for a second, you'll realize that to calculate the number of days on which sales occurred, we cannot simply count the number of rows in the Sales table. This is because the Sales table ideally has more than one row on January 15, 2021, for Sales. There should be several rows with an Order Date value of January 15, 2021. What we want to do is count the number of unique values of the Order Date. This will tell us how many days sales did occur. So, if there were only five sales in the Sales table and they all occurred on January 15, 2021, the DISTINCTCOUNT function should return a value of 1.

Before you selected 2021 in the Year slicer, the matrix displayed 83 in the Days Selling column for the month of February. This is not simply a count of the number of days in each month. If that were the case, the DaysSelling column should have said 85 since there are 28 days in February, except in 2020 when there were 29. However, if you select the year 2020 in the slicer instead of 2021, you'll see that the DaysSelling column will only show 27 for the month of February, which means there were two dead days with no sales.

When you look at the new Matrix visual with subtotals across the rows and at the bottom of the columns, you need to ask, where do those totals numbers come from? For most people, it would seem that the numbers on a total line summarize or average the numbers above. However, that is simply not the case.

While it may not seem intuitive, it's important to think about the process at which the DAX engine arrives at those numbers. Otherwise, when you start to build complexity into your measures, it'll be hard to figure out why things are the way they are.

The first key principles to understand about how measures work are these: Always think about that underlying source, not the table on the screen. *The value in one cell (or position on a visual) never impacts the value in another cell (or position on a visual).*

> Measures are calculated based on how contexts affect the underlying tables in a dataset. They are not calculated in reference to other calculations on a visual.

There are two important contexts to understand when learning DAX. One is rather simple and not something we'll go into here, but it is called *row context*. Row context is the surrounding context of a column value situated within a specific row in a table. A calculated column is an example of working within row context. The calculation is performed based on what it sees within *that row*.

FILTER CONTEXT

The other context is called *filter context*. These filters may be filters created by the report user by using the Filters pane, by using slicers, or by filtering capabilities in some kind of visuals. But there are often other filters. Within a Table or Matrix visual, for example, the coordinates on the grid are filters in themselves. For example, in the matrix we created, the Rows property has the Month Name column added. This actually functions as a filter in itself. Specifically, on the first row in our matrix, the Values across will be filtered by the value of January. The second row, February. And on to December. However, on the Total row, the Month Name value *has been removed*. This means that the measures in the Total row will be calculated without the filtering of a month name.

All of these filters combine to create the filter context. And all of that filter context is applied *before the DAX measure is actually calculated*.

The three charts in Figure 10.14 demonstrate how filter context affects DAX measures so you can see how they interact together. All three visuals in that image use the same DAX measure: Total Sales.

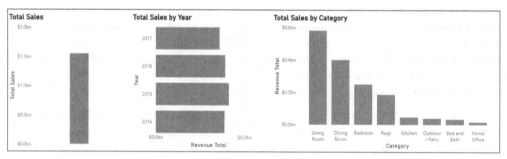

FIGURE 10.14: Three charts demonstrating filter context

Think for a minute about how these are different and how they are the same.

Though each visual uses the same DAX measure and, therefore, the same DAX formula, the visuals produce different results. For instance, the first visual shows the Total Sales measure for the entire dataset. In this dataset, Total Sales is 1.35 million USD. In the second visual, Total Sales is broken down by year. For instance, in 2014, Total Sales is 0.23 million USD. In the third visual, Total Sales is broken down by product ID. In the first visual, no filters are applied. In the second visual, the y-axis contains the Year value, which means that the year is filtering each bar in the graph. The third visual has a filter context of a product ID.

Interactions between visuals will also change how the DAX measure is calculated. For instance, if we were to select the second visual and then select 2015, the results appear as shown in Figure 10.15.

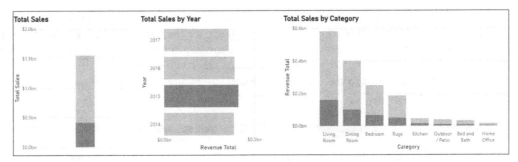

FIGURE 10.15: Filter context working in conjunction with highlighting

Selecting 2015 in the second visual changed the filter context for the DAX measure. It modified the first visual to equal the sales for 2015: 0.66 million USD. It also broke down the total sales by product ID, but only shows the results for 2015. Those calculations quickly changed in memory and displayed the results in a highly interactive manner to the user.

The definition of the DAX measure has not changed; it's still the original measure: Total Sales = SUM(SalesAmount). But, it is dynamically calculated based on how filter contexts affect the underlying tables. This is different from how calculated columns perform because filter context will not change the results of the DAX formula since each calculation on a calculated column is performed at refresh time without any filtering.

Now, let's go back to our table of measures we added to the lower left corner of our report (see Figure 10.16). Add the Total Sales measure to the values of the matrix. *How is the total for Avg Sales per Day calculated?* The natural thought is that it is the average of the values in the rows above. That's what many people would think. However, this is why you always need to consider filter context and how it affects the DAX measure being calculated in that exact spot. Understanding this principle will make you very successful going forward in learning DAX. Remember that each calculation on the screen knows nothing about the other calculations that have happened on that visual but knows only what has been filtered *at that location on the visual.*

MonthName	Avg Sales per Transaction	Days Selling	Transactions	Avg Sales per Day	Total Sales
January	$463.90	121	4028	$15,442.75	$1,868,573
February	$452.34	83	3857	$21,020.21	$1,744,678
March	$428.99	92	4449	$20,745.53	$1,908,589
April	$447.40	89	4355	$21,892.50	$1,948,432
May	$461.33	93	4780	$23,711.32	$2,205,152
June	$526.86	90	5573	$32,624.20	$2,936,178
July	$472.67	93	5105	$25,946.03	$2,412,981
August	$502.53	93	5352	$28,919.79	$2,689,541
September	$500.35	90	5070	$28,186.18	$2,536,757
October	$499.94	93	5834	$31,361.95	$2,916,661
November	$517.62	90	5756	$33,104.68	$2,979,421
December	$508.96	93	6225	$34,067.68	$3,168,294
Total	**$485.48**	**1120**	**60384**	**$26,174.34**	**$29,315,256**

FIGURE 10.16: Total average sales per day calculated across the whole year

Let me explain what I mean. I'm going to export the contents of this matrix into a CSV file so that I can analyze it in Excel. To quickly copy the contents, click the ellipsis in the upper right of the visual, and you will see the Export Data menu option. Using that will prompt you to save the content as a CSV file somewhere on your computer. From there, open the new file in Excel. Figure 10.17 shows the Power BI matrix right next to the CSV data in Excel (see Figure 10.17) so we can double-check its results.

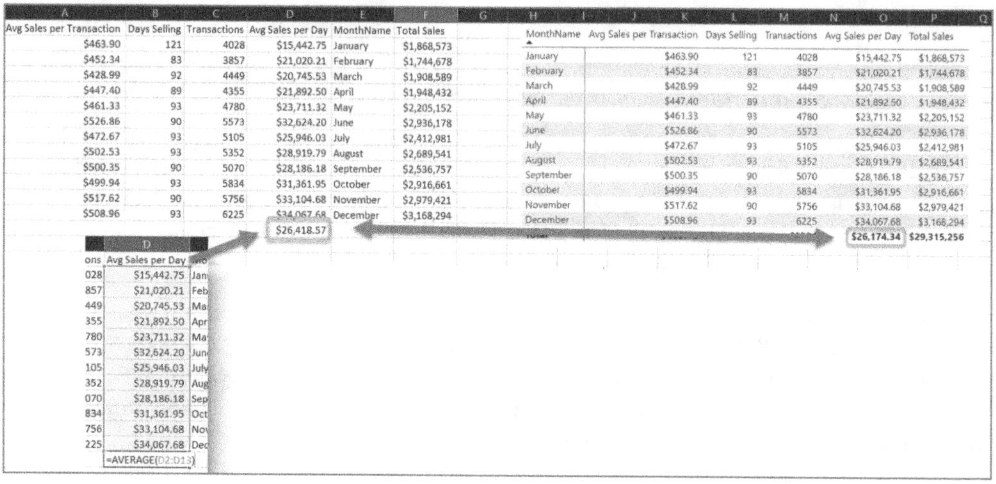

FIGURE 10.17: Excel averaging values in the cells above versus Power BI averaging values across all sales data in the year

When adding an Excel AVERAGE function to average the values above the total, I arrived at a completely different number than what Power BI did. I show you this to underscore the point I'm trying to make that the DAX measures on the matrix know nothing about the calculated values in other places on the same matrix.

Recall that our Avg Sales per Day measure is calculated like this:

```
Avg Sales per Day = DIVIDE ( [Total Sales] , [Days Selling] )
```

This means the Total Sales measure is calculated, then the Days Selling measure is calculated, and finally the two results are divided. But remember that each measure is calculated in relation to the filter context. So, given the location of our total row, what is different about the filter context there versus on the rows above? (This is where I as a trainer wait for the long uncomfortable silence!)

The difference is that on the rows above, the Avg Sales per Day measure (and within it, the Total Sales and Days Selling measures) are seeing rows from the Sales table only *for a given month*. In other words, the filter context is Sales rows filtered by the month of January, for example. So, given the month of January, the Total Sales measure is calculated as the sum of SalesAmount across only rows where the OrderDate occurred in January. And if we had no year values selected on our slicer, it would be January of 2020, 2021, 2022, and 2023.

However, on the total row of the matrix, the filter context is different! It does not see just one particular month of sales. It sees *all* the rows in the Sales table. So, the Days Selling measure calculates as 1,120 because that's how many rows are *visible* in the Sales table. And the Total Sales measure calculates as $29,315,257 because that's the sum of SalesAmount across all rows of the Sales table. And if you divide $29,315,257 by 1,120, you will get $26,174.34, which is exactly what is displayed on the Power BI Matrix total row!

Let's introduce you to one more DAX function, one that will change your whole analytical world. I'm hesitant to even introduce you to it because I can only skim the surface of the power of this function. Frankly, misuse or misunderstanding of how this function works has produced much consulting revenue for the team I work on! But, against my better judgment, I'll introduce it here and then leave you in better hands.

CALCULATE FUNCTION

Have you ever used the SUMIFS (or its older brother, SUMIF) function in Excel? SUMIFS in Excel adds up the values of cells based on a condition that can look at a whole set of data. This CALCULATE function does that and so much more.

The CALCULATE function in DAX is one of the most important functions that a data analyst can learn. The function name does not adequately describe what it is intended to do.

This function is your method of creating a DAX measure that will override certain portions of the filter context to express the correct result. For instance, to create a measure that always calculates the total sales for 2020, regardless of which year you're looking at (or what month is on the grid), create a measure that looks like the following sample:

```
Total Sales 2020 =
CALCULATE ( SUM ( 'Sales'[SalesAmount] ), 'Calendar'[CalendarYear] ) = 2020 )
```

Add that measure to your Sales table and then let's put it onto a Table visual along with the Calendar Year value and Total Sales measure to see what this is going to do (see Figure 10.18).

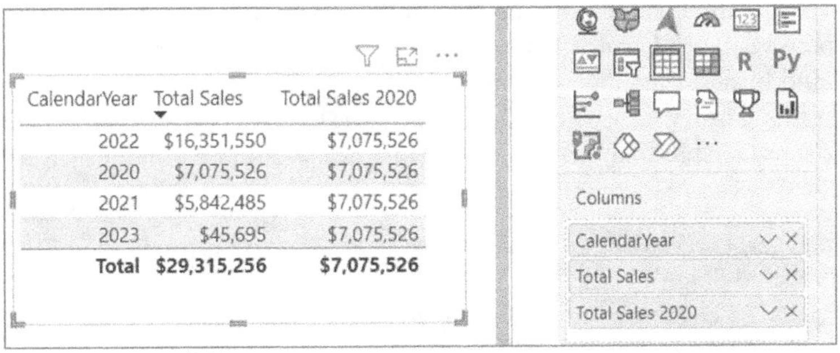

FIGURE 10.18: Total Sales 2020 measure added to the Table visual

Every row in the Total Sales 2020 column has the same value. That's exactly what we're looking for. But how does that work given what we just learned about filter context?

First, the syntax for the CALCULATE function is as follows:

```
CALCULATE(<measure expression>, <filter 1>, <filter 2>, ...)
```

Understand that when Power BI processes this measure using the CALCULATE function, the filters you specify in the CALCULATE function will *override* the Filter Context. For example, in the measure we have created here, we have overridden the Year value that is coming through from the grid coordinates (Total Sales for each *year* displayed). We overrode that Year value by specifying a filter that would reduce our Calendar table to only rows where the CalendarYear value is 2020, because the relationship in our data model flows from the one to the many (from the Calendar table to the Sales table). When we filter the Calendar table just momentarily in our measure to 2020, all of the rows in the Sales table will feel the effect of that by also being filtered to only Sales that happened in 2020. Then our Total Sales measure will be calculated based on *that* view of the data. The sum of all the SalesAmount for 2020 then is returned every time, but without affecting the filter context for everything else. Kind of mind-blowing, huh?

As you can imagine, this can be extrapolated into all kinds of possibilities. For example, with the new measure (Total Sales 2020) you could create another measure that compares Total Sales against Totals Sales 2020 to identify growth or decline since 2020.

```
Growth Since 2020 =
DIVIDE ( ([Total Sales] - [Total Sales 2020] ) , [Total Sales 2020] )
```

The possibilities that can happen now, given the ability to completely control the filter context, are unlimited to you!

CONCLUSION

I realize that you may have tracked with me all the way through this book up to this moment and then thought, "You lost me, Paul." That's the way I felt when I first tried to learn how to use the CALCULATE function. I just didn't get it. I've tried to explain simply, but understand that there is much going on here. To fully understand how the CALCULATE function works, I would like to introduce you to Marco Russo and Alberto Ferrari. Marco and Alberto are authors, trainers, and public speakers on all things DAX and business intelligence. They maintain several websites and tools that can help you go further down this journey of learning DAX (www.sqlbi.com/about). But I think the next step you should take in understanding the CALCULATE function would be to read their article here: www.sqlbi.com/articles/introducing-calculate-in-dax.

After you've read that, I recommend two more books to help you grow in your DAX journey. First, Rob Collie and Avichal Singh's book, *Power Pivot and Power BI: The Excel User's Guide to DAX, Power Query, Power BI & Power Pivot in Excel 2010–2016*. It's very dated at this point, but its simplicity in teaching DAX is very helpful. Second, Marco and Alberto's reference guide that is essentially the bible for DAX programming, *The Definitive Guide to DAX, 2nd Edition*.

Apply the principles in this book and then learn from them how to go further with DAX. When you've done that, you'll be able to take over the world. At least you'll feel like it!

11

Conclusion

We've come a long way in your journey of learning Power BI. As you might have gathered already, there is much more that lies ahead for you. But my hope is that you have gleaned a solid foundation for turning your data into analytical insights. To wrap things up here and set you on the next phase of the journey, I want to answer these two questions: where does my organization begin, and where do I go from here?

WHERE DOES MY ORGANIZATION BEGIN?

There are at least three kinds of people reading this book. There are those who work in an organization that has not started using Power BI (or really anything beyond Excel) and they know it will do something big for them. There are probably some readers who are in a role within their organization who read this book to understand what Power BI could do for their organization, not necessarily to build out reports for themselves. Then there are those who work in an organization that uses Power BI significantly, and these readers want to get started on the right foot.

All three of these types of people must think about *how* Power BI will be delivered to the end users (the report consumers) in their organization and *who* will be creating Power BI content, among many other questions. These questions revolve around what is called *delivery strategy*.

Delivery Strategy

When implementing Power BI (or restarting a Power BI implementation), it's important to understand the different delivery strategies available. Figuring out which strategy best fits your organization can help answer questions like what licensing you need and how your data needs to be organized.[1]

---

[1] I owe much of this section to my peers at Core BTS who have published and maintained it over the last couple years in this blog post: https://corebts.com/blog/power-bi-governance-guide. (Thanks, Marcus Radue, Bob Charapata, and Jason Devlin!).

Within the information technology (IT) industry, there is a notion of *self-service* business intelligence. Think about the difference between a full-service gas station and a self-serve gas station. In times past, at a full-service gas station, you pulled your vehicle up to the pump, and they would take care of making sure your fuel was topped off, your windshield cleaned, and your oil checked. They provided not just the pumps and gas but also the people to service you. You would pay and tip them and then drive off. At a self-serve station, they provide the pumps and fuel, but it's up to you to fill up the tank. This analogy can be applied to the notion of self-service business intelligence as it relates to delivery strategy options.

Your options include business-led self-service, IT-managed self-service, and corporate BI. Any organization may fall on a spectrum between these three general delivery strategies illustrated in Figure 11.1.

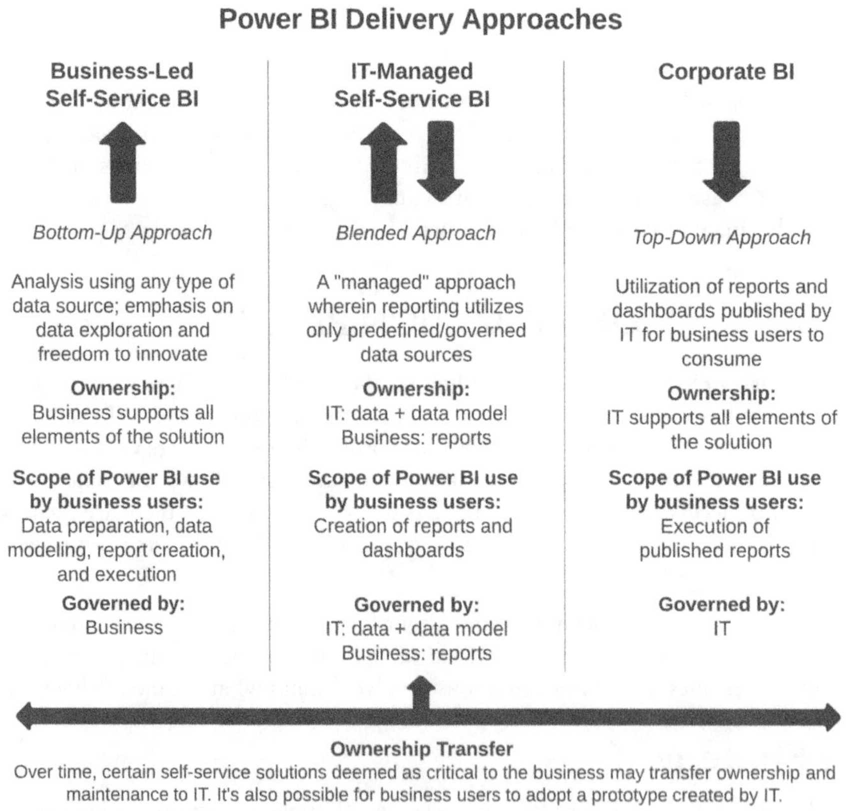

Power BI Delivery Approaches

Business-Led Self-Service BI	IT-Managed Self-Service BI	Corporate BI
⬆	⬆⬇	⬇
Bottom-Up Approach	*Blended Approach*	*Top-Down Approach*
Analysis using any type of data source; emphasis on data exploration and freedom to innovate	A "managed" approach wherein reporting utilizes only predefined/governed data sources	Utilization of reports and dashboards published by IT for business users to consume
Ownership: Business supports all elements of the solution	**Ownership:** IT: data + data model Business: reports	**Ownership:** IT supports all elements of the solution
Scope of Power BI use by business users: Data preparation, data modeling, report creation, and execution	**Scope of Power BI use by business users:** Creation of reports and dashboards	**Scope of Power BI use by business users:** Execution of published reports
Governed by: Business	**Governed by:** IT: data + data model Business: reports	**Governed by:** IT

⬅━━━━━━━━━━⬆━━━━━━━━━━➡

Ownership Transfer
Over time, certain self-service solutions deemed as critical to the business may transfer ownership and maintenance to IT. It's also possible for business users to adopt a prototype created by IT.

FIGURE 11.1: Power BI delivery approaches in an enterprise

Business-Led Self-Service

Business-led self-service is a bottom-up approach, meaning that the business units in your organization are completely self-sufficient with analytics. They take ownership of the data preparation, integration, data modeling, report creation, and execution. As shown in the chart, BI ownership and governance are completely managed by the separate business units in this delivery strategy.

It is rare to see a completely business-led self-service BI model in an organization. Business-led self-service BI models require a mature analytics environment because business units are required to source data themselves. In this situation, each business unit would need skillsets such as business analysts, data modeling, and even integration skills to transform the data into a format that can be used for reporting and analytics.

A completely business-led self-service BI model requires a lot of resources. This delivery strategy is often used at very large companies because they can have those skillsets in each business area. That's why IT-managed self-service BI delivery is much more common.

IT-Managed Self-Service

In my experience, IT-managed self-service is the most common approach. It's a hybrid between business-led self-service strategies and the corporate BI strategy.

In this strategy, the IT department (or your BI department within IT) is responsible for data preparation, integration, and making the data available to the business so they can report on it. The different business units are responsible for the creation of those reports and dashboards in a tool like Power BI. In short, the data ownership is on the IT side, while report governance and management ownership belong to the business side (or to each of the business units).

We discussed data preparation and data modeling in Chapters 5 and 6. Those topics are really large, and we just introduced them to you. But you might be able to see now that if you rely on IT to manage data preparation (and integration) and modeling, then that will reduce how much those skillsets are needed in your business units. The business mostly needs analysts who can learn the Power BI Desktop application and become proficient at making reports and visualizations from datasets made available to them from IT. These analysts can work with the business (end users) to understand what insights they want to gain.

Corporate BI

Corporate BI is more of a top-down approach and the opposite of business-led self-service. This would be like the full-service gas station. In a corporate BI delivery strategy, all your BI reporting and data is managed by the IT department. They own all elements of reporting and data management, including data preparation, integration, and availability. They also own the creation and publication of reports and dashboards, as well as sharing them with appropriate groups. The corporate BI delivery strategy isn't as common and has some limitations regarding flexibility in providing business units with the data and reports they need in a timely fashion. Essentially, in this model, this book would be mostly pointless for a person in the business side.

Which Delivery Strategy Is Right for My Organization?

It's important to know which strategy you're going to pick when implementing and deploying Power BI in your organization. If you're not in a position of influence in this area, it's still important to understand which strategy has been chosen for your organization because there may be constraints upon which things you can use that you've learned from this book. Understand that there are good reasons for each approach.

How can you determine which of the three strategies (or what mix of strategies) works best? It's crucial to be realistic with the resources you have. If your organization has a very small IT team or limited data preparation experience, it will limit your delivery strategy options. You need to consider the data culture within your organization and how willing different departments are to provide the analytical skills required to support a self-service IT approach. Finally, you need to evaluate your data architecture and determine if it is scalable enough to support a self-service IT approach.

But let's say you just want to know what the next steps in your Power BI education are. Let's get you equipped!

WHERE DO I GO FROM HERE?

There are so many resources online for learning Power BI. Because of that, I am humbled that you would choose to use an old-fashioned way of learning—thank you, reader, for purchasing and working through this book! I hope it was valuable to you. Here is a short list of recommendations and advice.

Top Gurus

Lean on people who are respected across the industry. While there are more than I can list here, here are the top gurus that I go to for help with Power BI:

- ➤ Marco Russo and Alberto Ferrari: `https://sqlbi.com`
- ➤ Melissa Coates: `www.coatesdatastrategies.com` (her writings on *delivery strategy* and implementation guidance are particularly helpful): `www.coatesdatastrategies.com/blog/new-power-bi-implementation-planning-guidance`
- ➤ Adam Saxton and Patrick Leblanc: `www.youtube.com/@GuyInACube`
- ➤ Reza Rad: `https://radacad.com`
- ➤ Chris Webb: `https://blog.crossjoin.co.uk`

Advice

I have been using Power BI since it was first released several years ago. In the beginning, I learned how to use it by simply trying it. I was able to progress quickly because of the simplicity of its design. But I ran into walls that I would not have had I not taken the time to understand how it was supposed to be used. By taking the time to go through this book, you will not run into those same walls. You have begun your Power BI journey well!

I want to leave you with some advice that I have tried to adhere to diligently myself. My hope is that by heeding these points, you'll soar in your ability to turn data into insights!

- ➤ Grow in your report development skills. Don't settle for good enough. I spent a good deal of space earlier in this book talking about creating your content in a way that works with the human mind. People like Stephen Few continue to study and produce helpful resources that when followed will make your reports not just appear beautiful but will be *truly* useful in leading toward insight.

➤ Don't get sloppy with your data modeling. It's so tempting to join a fact table to another fact table. It's tempting to start *snowflaking* (creating dimension tables off of other dimension tables off other dimensions). Don't do it! Even with all the advances in features for Power BI that have come and are still coming, the basic principle of organizing your data into a star schema that keeps the facts in the facts and the attributes in the dimensions still need to be applied.

➤ Grow in your DAX programming skills. We barely skimmed the surface in the previous chapter. I have seen that many people grasp the basic ideas of DAX and then get very sloppy in their use of it. Then when their reports come to a crawl they're frustrated. This is why it is critical to dig deeper into DAX and learn how it works because when you do, you will find that your most difficult formula challenges can be addressed.

➤ Meet others. Find out who in your organization is also using Power BI and ask them what they've learned lately and what challenges they're trying to solve. Consider starting a group within your organization that promotes best practices and provides a forum for advancing Power BI development. But don't stop inside your organization! Attend conferences like the Power Platform conference or the Power BI Summit. Also consider participating in local user groups: `https://dynamicscommunities.com/community/groups/power-platform`.

➤ Stay on top of Power BI releases. Microsoft releases new updates to Power BI *every month*. You can learn more about what is released each month by checking out its blog (`https://powerbi.microsoft.com/en-us/blog`) or by watching the videos Microsoft produces (`www.youtube.com/@MicrosoftPowerBI`).

➤ Read and learn about Microsoft Fabric. During the week I was writing this conclusion, Microsoft announced its new analytics platform called Fabric. Like a fabric, it will weave together data and analytics tools at an organization from end to end, including Power BI (`https://learn.microsoft.com/en-us/fabric/get-started/microsoft-fabric-overview`).

INDEX

Q

R